One Man's Family

by
Dona L. Cuttler

HERITAGE BOOKS
2012

HERITAGE BOOKS
AN IMPRINT OF HERITAGE BOOKS, INC.

Books, CDs, and more—Worldwide

For our listing of thousands of titles see our website at
www.HeritageBooks.com

Published 2012 by
HERITAGE BOOKS, INC.
Publishing Division
100 Railroad Ave. #104
Westminster, Maryland 21157

Copyright © 2001 Dona Lou Cuttler

Original artwork by
Louise Ehlers

All rights reserved. No part of this book may be reproduced or transmitted in any form or by any means, electronic or mechanical, including photocopying, recording or by any information storage and retrieval system without written permission from the author, except for the inclusion of brief quotations in a review.

International Standard Book Numbers
Paperbound: 978-0-7884-1882-2
Clothbound: 978-0-7884-9498-7

*Dedicated to
My Grandfather
Lester William Hebbard
July 21, 1914
to
September 12, 2000
A gentle person who
was a powerful teacher*

Acknowledgments

Many individuals have contributed information to this book. Others have helped me by providing church records, cemetery records, family histories and a place to stay while researching. Thank you Margaret E. Myers, Ethel L. Hebbard, Peggy Ann Hebbard Wolford, Mary Beth Thompson McDonough, Eloise Haney Woodfield, Mary Lou Beall Ballew, Jane Evans Best, Kitty Linthicum, Larry Cecil, Anice Lee Cecil Dancy, Louise Hebbard Ehlers, Bill McElfresh, Ann McElfresh Bolt, Betty Gilbertson, Edith Mahone Herndon, Bernardine Gladhill Beall, Lynn Glassbrook, Dorothy J. Elgin, Ann Cecil Morrison, and posthumously Sara Jane Allen Myerle, Frances Wolfe, Margaret Wolfe Aldridge C. Douglas Cecil and Lester Hebbard.

4612 49th Street, Garrott Wolfe Home

Table of Contents

Cecil	1
Roelke	31
Wolfe	56
Linthicum	69
McElfresh	79
Hyatt	88
Davis	91
Henckel	93
Mattingly	97
Beall	104
Mahone	108
Hebbard	112
Blood	120
Bradford	123
Bibliography	125
Index	126

Foreword

All of the family lines in this book are the author's mother's family. The reference to one man in the title is a reference to how all the lines relate to George Mortimer "Mort" Cecil, who married Sarah Jane Roelke and had thirteen children. He lived between Hyattstown and Comus in upper Montgomery County, Maryland. This book was originally complied for a family reunion in 1996 at the Comus Inn. It was updated for publication and the information is continually being revised. Each chapter contains allied families which can be traced from marriages within the author's family lines. Thousands of vintage photographs have been collected during the process, and a few were included to represent some of the families. John Linthicum Wolfe started the process, his daughter, Ethel Wolfe Hebbard continued the project, assisted by her daughter, Peggy Hebbard Wolford, and then by her granddaughter, Dona L. Cuttler.

Credits for Photographs and Illustrations

Cecil Farm	Louise Ehlers	cover
Garrott Wolfe Home	Louise Ehlers	Ackn.
Sugarloaf Mountain Chapel	Louise Ehlers	12
Cecil Home	Louise Ehlers	18
Mort Cecil Family	collection of D. Cuttler	28
Cecil brothers	collection of D. Cuttler	28
Fisher family	collection of D. Cuttler	29
Roelke/Cecils	collection of D. Cuttler	29
S. Roelke, B. Roelke	collection of D. Cuttler	30
John C. H. Roelkey family	courtesy of Margaret Myers	30
Oedelsheim Church	Louise Ehlers	55
Smokehouse	Louise Ehlers	66
Garrott Wolfe family	collection of D. Cuttler	67
John Wolfe family	collection of D. Cuttler	67
Joel Wolfe home	Louise Ehlers	68
John Wolfe home	Louise Ehlers	68
John Wolfe's mail wagon	Louise Ehlers	78
Charles M. McElfresh family	courtesy of Betty Gilbertson	87
Hyattstown Grist Mill	Louise Ehlers	90
Davis House	Louise Ehlers	95
Monrovia Store	D. Cuttler	96
Davis House	D. Cuttler	96
Mattingly familey	collection of D. Cuttler	102
Mattingly reunion	collection of D. Cuttler	102
Thomas Mattingly	collection of D. Cuttler	103
Comus Road	Louise Ehlers	106
Owen & Lee Beall	collection of D. Cuttler	107
Elaine Mahone	collection of D. Cuttler	110
Mahone sisters	collection of D. Cuttler	111
Hebbard brothers	collection of D. Cuttler	118
Hebbard/Wolfe family	collection of D. Cuttler	118
Hebbard/Blood reunion	collection of D. Cuttler	119
Les Hebbard family	collection of D. Cuttler	119
Wolfe barn	Louise Ehlers	125

Cecil

William Cecil moved to Prince George's County, Maryland, along with his brother Joshua, an attorney and vestryman. One of Joshua's son's, Sabert, owned land near Sligo Seventh-day Adventist Church. The family burial grounds were located at what is now the corner of Greenwood and Prospect Avenues.

William Cecil was a tenant farmer for Mareen Duvall on one of his plantations, off 424 near Route 50. He and his wife had three children.

    I. John Cecil   12-24-1690
♦   II. Philip Cecil   3-28-1692
    III. Susannah Cecil   1-??-1696

His wife's dying request was that he give the children to Mareen Duvall, to ensure their future. She died c. January 1697 and the court document was signed on March 19, 1697 when Susannah was three months old.

When the Cecil boys reached 18 they received a small amount of money and they struck out on their own. Susannah, raised as a Duvall, married a local planter. John Cecil went to Virginia. II. **Philip Cecil** married Elizabeth Gittings and they had two daughters born on a farm near Bladensburg in Prince George's County, before Philip purchased "Land Above" from Thomas Gettings [Gittings] for three thousand pounds of tobacco and located his family between Deep Branch and Cattail Marsh Branch on land that is now in Frederick County. His children were:

    A. Susannah   3-15-1715
    B. Mary   7-2-1716
    C. John   c. 1719
    D. **Philip, Jr.**   c. 1721 - 1803
    E. Joshua   c. 1724
    F. Elizabeth   c. 1727 m. Thomas Whitten
♦   G. **William**   c. 1730 m. Elizabeth c. 1750

D. **Philip Cecil, Jr.** was christened in West Branch Hundred, Prince George's County, Maryland and married Elizabeth Thomas. They had ten children in what is now Montgomery County, Maryland.

    i. Ann   c. 1761 m. Basil Warfield 2-16-1803
    ii. Elizabeth   c. 1762 m. Jesse Smallwood
    iii. **Zephaniah** c. 1763
    v. Verlinda   c. 1764
    v. Jane   c. 1768 m. Benjamin Belt 2-26-1803
    vi. Eleanor   c. 1769 m. John Smith Suite 1784
    vii. **Samuel**   c. 1773 - 1824 m. Elizabeth Belt and had two children before her death:

iii. **Zephaniah Cecil** married first Catherine Jones in 1788. She died in 1806 and he married her sister Rachel Jones on November 27, 1809 in Montgomery County, Maryland. The first nine children were Catherine's, Rachel's are the last two:

    (1) Sarah   c. 1789
    (2) Elizabeth   c. 1790
    (3) Samuel   c. 1792
    (4) Richard   c. 1794
    (5) Eleanor   c. 1796
    (6) Philip A.   3-15-1798 - 11-26-1861
    (7) Thomas   c. 1800
    (8) **William**   8-9-1803 - 3-15-1883
    (9) Catherine   1805 m. Samuel Perry 2-21-1824 in Mont. Co., Md.
    (10) Martha
    (11) Joseph

Samuel Cecil (1792) married Rebecca V. and had at least:
    (a) Richard Thomas
    (b) Sarah Catherine

(8) **William Cissel** (1803) married Rachel Sarah Williams on December 30, 1829. She was the daughter of Humphrey Williams and Sarah Beall* Williams and was born August 12, 1812 and died June 8 1861.~ William and his brother Philip purchased the farm of Alexander Whitaker called 'Mount Pleasant' near Poolesville, Montgomery County, Maryland, approximately 1820. They were buried on the farm, but on September 1, 1896 the stones were moved to Monocacy Cemetery in Beallsville, Montgomery County, Maryland. They had thirteen children:

    (a) Philip A.   2-6-1831 to 3-6-1858
    (b) Elizabeth   2-6-1833 to 12-8-1835 ~
    (c) David Thomas 7-20-1825 to 12-13-1919 was born near Poolesville and died in Washington, D. C. He married Sarah Sinclair Young on July 13, 1859 in Poolesville. She was a daughter of Samuel and Sophia Craven Young. She was born at Killmain (a neighboring farm) on July 9, 1839 and died October 9, 1917 in Washington, D. C. They had six children:

      1. Ada Glen   6-1-1860 to 5-7-1882
      2. Samuel Corneliu 5-8-1862 m. Martha Louise Lemon b. 1-10-1869
      3. William Arthur   10-16-1864 to 12-31-1864
      4. Martha Eugenia 5-31-1867 to 6-24-1868

*Sarah Beall Williams above, was a daughter of Richard Beall and Rebecca Adamson Beall. Richard was a son of Ninian Beall and Catherine Duke Beall.

5. Eugene Ernest 3-17-1871 to 4-23-1928 m. Charlotte Elizabeth Braley 1-2-1872 to 6-6-1939 brd. Monocacy Cem
6. Edward McCauley 8-19-1872 to 2-12-1876

(d) Mariel Rebecca 5-17-1837 to 3-15-1927 m. Benjamin Collison Gott, son of Richard and Sarah Collinson Gott. He was born 5-28-1814 and died 4-23-1885 in Boyds, Montgomery Co., Md. They are buried in Monocacy Cemetery. They had eleven children:
1. George R. Gott 1855 m. Mary R. Brewer 11-25-1878
2. Mary E. Gott 1856
3. Ann E. Gott 1858 to 10-10-1885 buried in Monocacy Cemetery
4. William F. Gott 1859
5. James Perry Gott 2-17-1861 to 2-11-1937 m. Annie Laurie Covington (2-16-1864 - 11-30-1896) in 1886. They had four children, and after her death he married Lillian Pearl (12-25-1877 - 4 -23-1940) in 1902. They had four children. They are buried in Monocacy Cemetery.
  a. Lulu Beall Gott 6-25-1889 - 3-11-1968 m. Oliver Belt White (9-22-1888) on 2-26-1913 in Barnesville, Md.
  b. James Perry Gott, Jr. 9-1891
  c. Mabel Covington Gott 6-1895 m. Franklin LeVern Troost on 6-6-1923
  d. Lucille Warren Gott 8-2-1887 - 10-12-1968 m. Ernest Chiswell Allnutt (1-21-1884 to 1-13-1928) son of Edwin and Hester Chiswell Allnutt on 1-17-1916 and had:
    (1). Ernest Chiswell Allnutt, Jr. 2-15-1918
    (2.) James Gott Allnutt 10-20-1921 to 10-20-1921 brd. Monocacy
  e. Dorothy Virginia 1-10-1903 - 1-14-1968 m. Bernard Trundle Brosius (12-23-1893 to 2-2-1955) on 1-22-1924 brd. St. Mary's, Barnesville
  f. Rachel 1905
  g. Richard V. 5-18-1907 to 7-27-1978 m. Marguerite Hayden (6-4-1903 to 4-1-1985) brd. Monocacy Cemetery
  h. infant 1910

6. Ann E. 1863
7. Benjamin Collison 4-20-1866 to 9-12-1946 in Annapolis, Md m. Elizabeth L. Allnutt (9-18-1867 to 2-23-1969). They are buried in Monocacy Cemetery. They had two children:
  a. Benjamin Collison III 4-14-1903 to 8-2-1904 brd. Monocacy Cemetery
8. Nathan Elwood 7-13-1868 to 10-11-1917 in Boyds, Md. m. Chloe Ann Warfield (9-15-1873 to 1-5-1964) a daughter of John and Rachel Dorsey Warfield on 4-8-1897. They are buried

in Monocacy Cemetery. They had four children:
   a. Eleanor M.   11-1893
   b. Muriel Virginia   2-15-1898 m. Dowell Jenning Howard 1-31-1920
      son of Henry and Mary Jones Howard. They had
      (1). Dowell Jennings Howard, Jr. 4-2-1924
      (2). Marianna Virginia Howard
   c. Elizabeth L.   9-1899
   d. Louise Warfield   3-10-1903 m. William Asbury Bowman
          11-20-1924
9. Elizabeth Beall 2-26-1871 to 11-21-1970 in DC, brd. in Monocacy Cem.
10. Anne Warfield 9-15-1873
11. Lillian Pearl 12-25-1877

(e) Martha Ann   3-1839 to 6-1-1924 m. Henry Claude Young, Jr.
      (11-10-1871), son of Henry and Margaret Chiswell Young.
      He was born 8-18-1829 and died 7-27-1918
      in Poolesville, Md. They are buried in
      Monocacy Cemetery. They had three children:
   1. Mary E.   10-26-1872 to 9-2-1873
   2. Ardella Rebecca 9-1873 to 12-16-1964
   3. Henry Cissel 9-16-1879 to 12-26-1969 m. Louise Jones (d. 1-12-1968)
      They are buried in Monocacy Cemetery with their daughter
     a. Henrietta Louise 9-30-1914
(f) Sarah I.   c. 1841 m. Andrew Jackson Jones 12-5-1859
      had Rebecca Jones 5-26-1861 to 8-6-1862
(g) William C.   c. 1843
(h) Mary E.   c. 1845
(j) Eugene E.   1847   to 4-23-1928 brd. Monocacy Cem.
(k) Elizabeth Belle 6-14-1849 to 12-19-1892 m. Arthur Young
      4-18-1870 in Poolesville, son of Samuel and
      Sophia Craven Young. He was born 8-18-1847
      and died 12-21-1928. They had six children:
   1. Drusilla   3-24-1872 to 5-12-1886
   2. William Cissel 11-27-1874 m. Lucy Flager
   3. Arthur Ludwick 10-9-1877 m. Peggy Ann Duffield
   4. Eugene Sinclair 10-24-1879 m. Helen Backus and had four children:
     a. Arthur Lewis Young   3-8-1907
     b. Margaret Lewis Young   3-2-1910
     c. Mildord Eugene Young   10-3-1913
     d. Mildred Irene Young   11-13-1915
   5. Elmer Hill   12-26-1883
   6. David Thomas Cissel 4-11-1890 born in Poolesville,
Montgomery Co., Md.

       m. Margaret Verah Bell and had at least:
 a. Helen Gwendolin Young 10-20-1915
 (l) Richard Humphrey 6-14-1849 to 12-6-1911 m. Julia Griffith on 10-28-1874, duaghter of Thomas and Sarah Chiswell Griffith, born 9-4-1853 died 12-11-1924 They are buried in Monocacy Cemetery. They had eleven children in Darnestown, Montgomery County, Maryland:
  1. William Howard 6-5-1876 to 4-5-1900
  2. Richard Thomas 1879
  3. Humphrey 1881
  4. George Newton 4-3-1883 to 4-19-1888 (foster child)
  5. Sarah Newton 12-18-1884 to 12-22-1946 m. John Thomas Williams (1-21-1884 to 5-20-1972) son of Arthur and Annie Dawson Williams. They are buried in Monocacy Cemetery and had:
   a. Julia Elizabeth Williams 12-5-1907 to 12-31-1934 brd. Monocacy
   b. Eleanor Newton Williams
  6. Elmo 8-13-1886 to 8-16-1886 brd. in Monocacy Cem.
  7. Mary Eleanor 10-4-1887 to 4-4-1926 m. Julian Boyd Waters (1878) on 3-25-1908. They had five children:
   a. Julia G. Waters
   b. Ella Virginia Waters
   c. Lorraine J. Waters
   d. Mary Poultney Waters
   e. Julian Boyd Waters, Jr.
  8. Eugene Walter 3-16-1890 to 3-17-1931 m. Cecil Tschiffley, daughter of Frederick Tschiffley and had:
   a. Richard Humphrey Cissel 1918
   b. Ruth Irene Cissel 7-30-1926 m. Walter Johnson, Jr. (10-14-1920 to 11-17-1973) brd. Mountain View Cemetery
   c. Eugene Wilbur Cissel 1924 to 3-10-1983
   d. Lawrence M. Cissel
  9. Albert Jones 11-23-1892
  10. William Griffith 12-18-1884 to 6-20-1930 m. Pauline Claire Jones (8-1-1898 to 5-5-1978) daughter of John and Edna Manakee Jones. They are buried in Monocacy Cemetery and had:
   a. Lisa Lorraine Cissel
  11. Charles Leroy 1-9-1897 to 8-8-1922 brd. in Monocacy Cem.

(m) Wilburfisk 1850
(n) Samuel   1854 had a son Samuel c. 1872

Samuel Cecil (1773) of Philip Cecil, Jr., married first Elizabeth Belt and had two children before her death. He then married her sister, Isabel Belt, on February 28, 1806. Samuel's children were:
- (1) Samuel 1803-1863 m. Margaret D. Beall (1808-1878) on 1-20-1825, 9 children:
  - A. Benjamin G. 1830
  - B. Sarah E. 1833-1913 m. Joseph Samuel Childs 1830-1904
     - i. William H. 1859
  - C. George Washington 1834-1904
  - D. Charles A. 1838
  - E. Thomas Beall 1839
  - F. William H. H. 1844 m. Emma Bradley had two children:
     - i. Charles H. 1876-1878 brd. Congressional Cemetery
     - ii. Marie 1892-1902 brd. Congressional Cemetery
  - G. Samuel N. 1847-1898 m. Mary A. Hearne in 1874
  - H. Elizabeth 1848 m. John Waters
  - I. Edward G. 1850-1907 m. Helen D. Wilson on 10-27-1881
     buried at Grace Protestant Episcopal Cemetery, SS, Md.
- (2) Susie 1805
- (3) Osborn 1807
- (4) Zephaniah 1808-1859 m. Mary Ann in 1832. They had three children:
  - A. Ann E. 1833
  - B. Benjamin C. 1838
  - C. Frederick C. 1840
- (5) Benjamin G. 1811 m. Mary Ann Childs (1836) in 1852. They had four children:
  - A. Samuel 1853
  - B. William W. 1865 m. Cora Bell Cissel (1867) 6-9-1891
  - C. Milton 1866
  - D. Byron V. 1869 m. Mary Ada Cissel (1869) 6-18-1897
- (6) Philip 1814 m. Sarah Carr (1805) on May 19, 1838. They had five children:
  - A. George W. c. 1835
  - B. Samuel T. c. 1837
  - C. Wilbur F. c. 1838
  - D. Mary L. c. 1841
  - E. Isabell R. c. 1843
- (7) James 1816 m. Rebecca (1819) in 1844 and had seven children:
  - A. Clinton M. c. 1845
  - B. Benjamin A. c. 1847
  - C. Mary Isabelle c. 1849
  - D. Henry c. 1850
  - E. Carol c. 1852
  - F. Sallie c. 1856
  - G. Rebecca c. 1859
- (8) Sarah 1817

(9) Richard Cissel 1819 -1882 m. Margaret E. Walters (1824) and had eleven
children:
- A. James M.   c. 1844
- B. Elizabeth W.   c. 1846
- C. Samuel W. F.   c. 1848
- D. William B.   2-1850
- E. Theodore V.   1854
- F. George Osborne B.   1857 - 9-1910 m. Catherine E. Stubbs (1874 - 1910) and had two children:
  - i. Hardy Stubbs Cissel 1893 - 1-1914
  - ii. Edward Carroll Cissel 1896 - 10-7-1918
- G. Ella   c. 1860
- H. Richard Ernest   c. 1864
- I. Cora Belle   c. 1867 m. William W. L. Cecil above
- J. Mary Ada   1869 m. Byron V. Cecil above
- K. John P.   1870

(10) Margaret 1820
- viii. Zachariah   c. 1776
- ix. John   c. 1777
- x. Rebecca   c. 1779

G. **William Cecil** (1730-1807), son of Philip Cecil, Sr., was the constable of Sugar Loaf Hundred in 1750 and he was one of the Presidential Electors in 1796. William married Elizabeth c. 1751 and had ten children, many of whom left this area and moved to Randolph County, North Carolina. Of those who chose to remain in the area Benjamin was the "favored son" and received most of the land holdings of his father William. Archibald did receive a share of the land grant and probably lived close to what is now Old Hundred Road at Slate Quarry Road. William Cecil's children, except for Mary, were born at "Wildcat Springs" East of Hyattstown.

1. Mary   1752-1816 m. William Ball, moved to NC
2. George   1754 m. Elizabeth Linton
3. Thomas   1757 moved to Randolph Co., NC
4. **William**   1759 bought 40 acres "Plummer's Delight" from father 6-15-1805
5. Elizabeth   1760 m. James Toole 6-8-1782
6. Philip   1762 m. Rachel, a.Philip Jr. 3-15-1798 to 11-26-1861
   b. William 8-9-1803 to 3-15-1883
7. Benjamin   1763 m. Ann Fisher, bought "Wildcat Springs," "Widow's Purchase" and "Chance" from father 7-2-1805
8. John   1765 m. Mary Linton, buys part of "Chance": 80 acres from father, 78 1/2 from Archibald 7-19-1805
9. Susannah   1766 m. William Kirk 6-26-1888

♦ 10. **Archibald** 1767

4. **William Cecil** married Rachel S. (9-26-1812 to 6-6-1861). They lived in Beallsville, Md. They and their children were buried in Monocacy Cemetery, Beallsville.
- A. Philip A.   2-6-1831 to 3-6-1858
- B. Elizabeth E.   2-6-1833 to 12-8-1835
- C. Martha A.   1840
- D. Mary E.   1844
- E. Richard H.   1848
- F. Elizabeth B.   1848
- G. Eugene E.   1847
- H. Samuel   1854

"Wildcatt Springs" was granted to William Cecil from His Lordships Land Office on August 10, 1753. This land is east of Hyattstown near what is now Little Bennett Park. The house is standing inside a chain link fence, off Prescott Road. On July 25, 1767 he sold 489 acres to Brice Beall and Thomas Worthington of Anne Arundel County, Maryland.

10. **Archibald Cecil** (1767-1820) married Priscilla Willson of John Willson. The Willson farm was purchased from William Cecil, and was on part of the original land grant. Their house stood near the present-day Otho Upton Cecil house. Priscilla's brother William Willson witnessed the estate signing of Archibald's will. Priscilla was the mother of six of Archibald's seven children.

♦   A. **Samuel**   1788
-   B. Priscilla   1791 m. Henry Fitzgerald Jan. 10, 1827
-   C. Bessie   1793 m. Samuel Carr Feb. 14, 1832
-   D. Ann Selah   1795 m. James Andrews
-   E. Benjamin   1797 m. Charlotte Phelps Feb 10, 1836
-   F. Mary   1800 m. Ezra Ward

After Priscilla died, Archibald married Sarah Robinson on December 13, 1804. She was the mother of:
- G. William M.   6-17-1806 Frederick Co., Maryland

Archibald left land records and filed a will. They are interesting, in that they are mostly parts of the original land grant, resurveyed and renamed.

10-25-1795 Archibald Cecell of Montgomery Co. buys from Richard Cash for 150 pounds, tract called "Paschaham." [along Peachtree Road] 8-22-1801. Archibald Cecil and John Cecil sell tract called "Squirrel Trap," 8 1/2 acres. 4-27-1805 William Cecil sells to Archibald tract called "Chance," 78 1/2 acres. 12-7-1815 Archibald Cecil sells to John Winemullen tract called "Squirrel Trap." 12-5-1820 Archibald sells to Wilfred Delahay tract called "Paschaham," 1 acre. 11-9-1835 Sarah, widow of Archibald sells to Samuel Cecil a parcel of "Chance" on tract of "Paschaham."

The administrator of Archibald's will was his son Samuel Cecil. The inventory lists his estate as $360.62. November 14, 1822 a statement of the estate lists $269.01 left to his widow, Sarah, and to John Rhodes, Mary Cecil, and George Rhodes. His funeral expenses were $8.00.

A. **Samuel Cecil** (1788-1864), son of Archibald Cecil, married Honora Rhoades on February 3, 1807. Her father, John, was the son of Nicholas Rhodes, Sr. Elisha, John and Nicholas, Jr. served in "Lee's Legion" as privates in the company of Captain Smith. They enlisted in 1776. Of Samuel's nine children, Honora was the mother of five.

    (1) **Otho Upton**   5-7-1808-1873 m. Charlotte Howard (1808)
    (2) **HammonDatha**   1810
    (3) Charlotte   1812 m. Benjamin Johnson
♦   (4) **Wilson Hammond** 9-19-1820
    (5) Rhoda Ellen   1822 m. Samuel Hobbs c. 1851

After Honora died, Samuel Cecil married Annie Rice on October 27, 1832. She was the widow of George House of Jefferson, Maryland. The children from her first marriage were:

    A. Peregrine Thomas R.   11-?-1818 to 8-?-1839 d. OH
    B. Martha E.   12-8-1819 to 11-9-1906 m. Benjamin Johnson
        (1) Elizabeth "Annie"1833,
           (2) Mary E. 1838 (m. James Holland, brd Mtn. Chapel)
        (3) Martha M. 1840
        (4) Jacob Israel 1842 (m. Beulah McDonough, Comus)
        (5) Marscilla 1848
        (6) Eliza C. 8-8-1856 to 9-16-1863.
    C. George E.   10-19-1820 to 2-23-1904 m. Ann Burnside
    D. Rebecca Annie   9-10-1821-1835
    E. William Richard   5-4-1823 m. Ann Norris

(6) Ann and Samuel Cecil had four children:
(7) Catherine V. 1834 m. Charles H. Baker March 20, 1850
(8) **Levin R.**   1836 m1 Emily Holland 1841 m2 Mary G. Thompson
(9) William John   184?
(10) Amanda A. 1845-1934 m. George E. Baker brd. Mtn. Chapel, Comus.

Samuel's land records show: 8-15-1826 purchased part of "Labrynth," part of "None Left," part of "Wilson's Lot," part of "Rhoades Best," and land in Hyattstown from Mary Rhoades Holland. 9-23-1834 the road from Greenfield Mills to Clarksburg was laid out, (this is now Comus Road). It went through the land of Samuel Cecil, Peter Hawkins, et al. 1-13-1836 Samuel Cecil sells to Ann S. Cecil and James Andrews part of "Paschaham" $1.00. 11-9-1836 Samuel Cecil buys

"Labrynth" and "Self-Defence" for $50.00 from Perry Price. 10-30-1837 Road to Barnesville was cut through and damages were paid to Eli Wolfe and William Wilson, Samuel Cecil, Samuel Hobbs, John Willson, among others. This is now Old Hundred Road. 11-27-1838 Samuel Cecil sells "Labrynth" to Eli Wolfe. 11-1-1851 Samuel Cecil sells to Benjamin Johnson "Self-Defence" and the rest of "Labrynth" for $450.00. Part of this property is still in tact today and is run by the Dyker family. The last time it was listed for sale $650,000.00! It is on Linthicum Road, on the right hand side.

Samuel's will was administered by Isaac Davis on September 5, 1864. G. E. Saunder's was the undertaker, and the funeral costs were $35.00. The Isaac Davis farm is near Labrynth on Thurston Road it was formerly the farm of Roger Johnson and extended to Comus Road (which was not yet cut through), SugarLoaf Road and Old Hundred Road (hence it's name from the back hundred of Johnson's land). The addition to the main house was built by William T. Hilton and Isaac Davis was the Justice of the Peace for Hyattstown at this time. His sister Mary Davis was the grandmother of Garrott Davis Wolfe. (see Wolfe Chapter)

```
       Inventory            489.37
       Personal Property    151.40
       Interest              21.05
       received from debtors
       George E. House      213.90
       Otho Upton Cecil     179.00
Total                     1,054.72
       Total Payments       112.57
       Bond                   7.40
       to widow             264.76
       to each child         75.64
```

(8) Levin R. Cecil's children's families are listed below.
    a. Mary Agnes   1-12-1862 to 1-28-1914 m. Benjamin F. Norwood
    b. Ida Leonida   1868 m. Jeremiah Norwood 1886
        i. Charles M.   1889
        ii. Mary Lilian   1892
        iii. Mamie E.   1900
        iv. Katherine S.   1905
        v. Cecile   1907
    c. Wilbur E. 1871-1949 m. Ann Elizabeth Sears (8-3-1869 to 3-19-1947) on 12-23-1896. She was a daughter of William Thomas Sears and Sarah Jane Nichols Sears.
        i. Edward Ralph   1898 m. Helen Martrell
        ii. Mamie Adelaide   11-27-1899 m. Charles H. Carver
                had twins 6-20-1929 Dorothy J. & Josephine D.
        iii. Talmadge Noble   1901 m. Vernice Irene Geesey 1924,

  I. Talmadge Jr. 1925 m. Frances Hudson
  II. William Emory 11-22-1928 m. Kathleen Andrews
    had William Jr. 5-26-1951
    Kathy Lynn 10-12-1960
  III. Ruby Irene 1930 m. Richard Crist
  iv. Ira Herbert 7-29-1905 to 6-9-1906 brd. Mt. Pleasant
        M. E. Cemetery, Dickerson, Md.
  v. James Lester 9-17-1908 to 10-8-1981
    m. Viola Hilderbridle had Barbara Jean m. John Parker
  vi. Wilbur Thomas 1-4-1912 to 3-15-1985
        m. Edith Fogle (3-18-1914 to 3-18-1995)
        on 6-5-1930
    Wilbur Thomas, Jr. 2-5-1930
    Walter Harry 6-22-1931
    Evonne Virginia 3-7-1933
    Richard Allen 12-25-1935
    Kenneth Reno 11-26-1938
d. Sadie Alma   1876
e. James Leroy 7-6-1877 to 3-7-1957

  G. **William M. Cecil,** son of Archibald Cecil, was born in Frederick County 6-17-1806 and married Lydia Feaster of Feagaville on 8-24-1825. They resided near Buckeystown in "The Manor." They are buried at Mt. Zion. Lydia was the daughter of Henry Feaster and Druscilla Johnson. She was christened at Christ Reformed in Middletown and her sponsors were Daniel Beiser and his wife. They had nine children.
  1. Samuel T. 3-10-1826 m Margaret Keefer October, 1857
    a. Charles Clayton m Lona Cummings Weller
    b. Lauretta V. 1858-1943 m Christian D. Ogle
    c. Ida A. 1860, brd, Mt. Olivet
    d. John T.1868-1946 m. Nettie Cockrell
  2. Margaret A. 2-4-1828 brd "Stranger's Row" Mt. Olivet
    a. Thomas Jefferson Cecil
  3. William Martin 2-6-1830 to 12-29-1916 m. Mary Jane Hewitt 1858
    a. Emma Cecilia 1859-1921 m. George McCormick
    b. William Franklin 1862
    c. Florence Genet 1865
    d. George Wesley 1868
    e. Elsie Idella   1873
    f. Oda Etta Alice 1877 m Marshall C.V. Smith
      i. Freeda Evelyn 1899 m Charles C. Doll,
        I. Martha Jean 1926 m J. D. Weddle

        II. Charles C. Jr. 1927 m. Margaret Jane Blumenaur
    ii. Merhl Smith   1902-1955
4. Greenberry   1834-1837
5. Archibald Hammond   3-24-1838 to 10-24-1918 brd Mt. Olivet
6. Jonas   12-22-1840-12 to 17-1866m Ann F. Stewart
        brd Mt. Olivet, Frederick
7. Susan R.   5-7-1844 to 2-16-1924 m. Fred Thompson
8. George W.   3-22-1847 to 4-7-1929 brd Mt. Olivet
9. John R.   1850

Lydia Feaster's sister Catherina Feaster was christened at Christ Reformed on 6-28-1801, and was sponsored by Eliss Mahn. She married Richard Thompson and they had:

1. Mary Ann   1819 m HammonDatha Cecil
2. William N.   1829 m. Julia A. b 1832
3. David H.   m. Sarah J. Hawkins 12-17-1858
4. Jerome L.   1834 m Mary Ann Waters 12-27-1862
5. Charlotte D.   5-20-1836 to 7-4-1919 m.
    Horace L. Murphy and had 13 children

Sugarloaf Mountain Chapel

Otho Upton Cecil
Son of Samuel Cecil

Otho Upton Cecil 5-7-1808-1873 married Charlotte Howard in 1832. They had four children.
1. Sarah Elizabeth 1833 m. Thomas A. Salser
2. John William 1837 m. Mary Hobbs 9-15-1874
3. Emily 1840 m. Hirsch had George P. and Charles W. Hirsch
4. Otho Frank 1842 m. Ida Smith
   - A. Annie 4-27-1881 to 9-16-1881 brd Mtn. Chapel, Comus
   - B. Catherine 4-27-1881 to 9-16-1881 brd Mtn Chapel, Comus
   - C. Walter 4-21-1883 to 3-25-1957 m. Rhoda Holland Burdette 12-17-1902 and had five children:
     - (1) Ida Virginia 1906
     - (2) Walter Smith 7-6-1908 50 5-28-2000 m. Carrie Viola Cordell
     - (3) Elizabeth
     - (4) Ruth
     - (5) Catherine m. Kelly
5. George W. 1845

4-23-1839 Otho Upton Cecil buys part of "Labrynth"
4-30-1839 Otho Upton Cecil sells part of "Labrynth" to James Hobbs.

Otho Upton Cecil's farm was located on Old Hundred Road across from the current "Sugarloaf Nursery", but slightly closer to Hyattstown on the East side of the road, north of Wilson Hammond's cabin. It included 66 acres, and is identified on the map of Montgomery County 1878 by G. M. Hopkins. His "town house" was deeded to his wife "Lottie" and shows on the map of Hyattstown as the "Lottie Cecil" house. He also left his wife a horse named Charley and the buggy and harness.

HammonDatha Cecil
Son of Samuel Cecil

HammonDatha Cecil (c. 1810) married Mary Ann Thompson (1820) on October 23, 1837. She was a daughter of Richard Thompson and Catherina Feaster Thompson mentioned above. They had five children before he was bitten by the gold bug. He joined the "Forty Niners" and went by train to Columbus, Ohio where he hired a wagon. He stopped in Nevada and found a small vein of gold, but with no water or way to mine it, he continued on to California. He sent money back to the family, but was not heard from again after 1855. When he left, his wife and children went to live with three different households. The oldest two went to live with their paternal grandfather, the middle child went to her Uncle's (Wilson Hammond) and the maternal grandparents took in Mary Ann and the two youngest children.
1. Samuel Thompson 1838 to 11-27-1905 brd Wesley Methodist, Urbana, Frederick Co., Md.

                  m Anna M. Nicholson 1864
   A. Charles   1865
   B. Anna Mary   2-1-1866 to 4-18-1906 m. James Titus Bennett
                  on 3-24-1885 and had nine children:
                    (1) Charles Fulton   8-26-1885
                    (2) Bessie Mae   12-19-1886 to 1927 brd. Clksbg
                    (3) Thomas   1888 to 1890 brd. Clarksburg
                    (4) James Herbert   11-5-1889 to 3-1914 brd. "
                    (5) William M.   8-20-1891 to 1955 brd. "
                    (6) Lula Maranda   5-7-1895 to 7-7-1960
                          m. Horace Melvin Thompson on 12-11-1920
                          (a) Mary Elizabeth 1-31-1927
                              m. Louis Arnold McDonough
                              I. Joyce Elizabeth 8-21-1946
                              II. Jacqueline Elaine 8-31-1950
                              III. Randy William 11-30-1945
                          (b) Barbara Ann 12-28-1932
                              m. Ellis Lee Roberson
                              I. Ellis Wayne 10-8-1950
                              II. James Warrend 10-8-1952
                              III. Larry Ray 12-19-1955
                              IV. Kevin Ellsworth 7-14-1957 to 7-16-1947
                              V. Gwenda Mae 12-18-1958
                    (7) Clifton Monroe   10-20-1896
                    (8) Russell C.   9-4-1900
                    (9) Mabel E.   5-28-1905
   C. Morgan   1869 m. Margaret Earl Molesworth
   D. Munroe   1869 to 1870
2. Frances Amanda   1841 m. Thomas W. Crawford (12-4-1836
                  to 2-11-1896) on 11-25-1858 and had two:
   A. Ellen Victoria   1859 m. Zacheus C. Thompson
   B. Virginia   1864
3. Christopher Columbus 5-25-1842 to 3-28-1901
                  m. Mary E. Crawford (5-9-1846 to 6-9-1915)
                  in 1866 and had nine children:
   A. Florence Lee   1867-1941 m. Robert E. L. Kanode (1869-1922)
                  on 2-11-1885 and had six children
   B. Clara Edith   1868 m. William B. Dorsey on 10-9-1888
   C. Jennie S.   1870-1960 m. Charles Wm. Kidd (1865-1934)
                  on 12-6-1888 and had two children
   D. Arabella   1872 m. C. M. Dryer
   E. James Newton 7-21-1877 to 1-2-1934 brd. Forest Oaks
   F. Emma   1879 m. R. Renneberger

        G. Edward W.   3-24-1882 to 8-4-1914 brd. Forest Oaks
        H. Nettie B.   1885 m. Charles A. Fulks
        I. Minnie Ethel   9-3-1887 m. F. E. Huseman 1907

4. Mary Jane   9-1843 to 2-17-1925 m. Francis P. Knott (3-1838 to 4-30-1906) on 6-15-1862 had five children:

    A. Francis Alexander 1864 m. Louise Albine Merz and had three children:
       (1) Mary A. 1901
       (2) Joseph Stanislaus 6-13-1904
       (3) Cecelia A. 1909
    B. Sarah Adeline Bennett (adopted daughter) 1-28-1870 to 7-2-1956 m. Charles Mortimer Ward (2-21-1857 to 6-10-1926) and had ten children.
    C. Frances E.   2-15-1872 to 11-7-1933 m. John W. Tabler (2-6-1844 to 1-16-1919) and had five children
       (1) John Francis
       (2) Rachel E.
       (3) Robert Lee
       (4) Harriet Irene m. George K. Brandenburg
       (5) Mary Margaret
    D. Arthur   1877
    E. Harry   1879

5. William Henry   1848 m. Mary E. 3-14-1846 to 3-14-1894

Wilson Hammond Cecil
son of Samuel Cecil

5. **Wilson Hammond Cecil** (9-19-1820 to 5-8-1907) married Mary Ellen Smith of Hyattstown on January 11, 1843 in Frederick County, Maryland. He purchased the part of "Labrynth" called "Wilson's Discovery" on the west side of Old Hundred Road. Their first home was built about a quarter of a mile closer to Hyattstown than the home that stands today. It was destroyed by fire, but the location is identifiable each spring when the cluster of daffodils bloom. Their second home was a two-story log cabin and is now the office for the "Sugarloaf Nursery" on Old Hundred Road. They had five children.

♦   A. **George Mortimer**   10-10-1843
     B. **Luther E.**   9-9-1846
     C. Emory   1850 died before 1860
     D. Clara V.   8-6-1854 to 3-10-1876 m. George P. Hirsch 1876
     E. **Everett**   6-16-1860 to 1-1-1921
                              m. Julia Mae Thompson 7-3-1880

Cecil Homeplace, Comus, Maryland
George Mortimer Cecil
son of Wilson Hammond Cecil

George Mortimer Cecil attended "Mountain" school, and his grandson has the copy book that he used in 1855. It shows practical math problems, handwriting practice, and other interesting notes. On April 8, 1867 George "Mort" Cecil married Sarah Jane Roelke (see Roelke chapter) at the Calvary Methodist Parsonage in Frederick. Asbury Hobbs and Otho Franklin Cecil were the witnesses. Her wedding dress was dark green with gold cording.

◆
    1. **Lillian Gertrude** 1-18-1868 (see Wolfe chapter)
    2. **William Wilson**   12-11-1869
    3. **Cora Estelle** 12-20-1871
    4. Ira Victor   5-7-1874 d. 6-27-1875 pneumonia brd. Mtn Chapel
    5. **Annie Mary** 11-2-1876
    6. **Charles Mortimer** 1-4-1878
    7. **George Remington** 11-19-1879
    8. **Alice Smith** 7-26-1881
    9. **Ellen**   8-19-1883
    10. **Daisy**   5-2-1886
    11. **George Minor** 9-6-1889

12. **Arthur DeWitt** 8-6-1891
13. **Lawrence Lee** 1-10-1893
Up the hill behind the first home, Mort had a cabin, about a mile up from Old Hundred Road. Sometime around 1900 he had a large house built. It was built by local builder William T. Hilton. Upon reaching the age of 21, Mort presented each of his children with an Elgin watch. The girls had pin-on watches, the boys had pocket watches.

1. **Lillian Gertrude Cecil** (1-18-1868 to 8-19-1945) was born in the log house. See Wolfe Chapter for her lineage.

2. **William Cecil** (12-11-1869 to 11-27-1935) was born in the log cabin across from the Cecil house. He married Margaret Elizabeth Kinna on November 11, 1893. David Kinna's (1-21-1756 to 6-9-1835 brd Simmon's) grandson was William Kinna (12-26-1811 to 2-1-1887). He married Sarah E. (3-1811 to 4-12-1891). They had David 1838, Margaret 1841, Nathan 1843, Mary E. 1845, and John W. 1850 Nathan (4-17-1891 to 12-19-1921) married Jane Rebecca Pickens (8-3-1849 to 3-25-1919). They had seven children:

    A. Luella   9-1872-1964 m. Joseph H. Price (1868-1943)
    B. Edith Belle   1874-1961 m. John L. Anderson (1873-1961)
    C. Margaret Elizabeth   3-8-1875 to 9-4-1969
    D. Samson   5-15-1877 to 8-26-1907
    E. May Lillie   5-28-1879 m. Ernest B. Ballenger (2-25-1872 to 7-9-1941)
    F. Etta Mary   3-1884-1957 m. Ernest W. Mullican (1884-1935)
    G. Rena Victoria 8-29-1886 to 1-12-1965 m. Willie W. Price (2-19-1876 to 8-12-1956 had Nina Kinna 12-22-1918 to 2-15-1919
    and Dean Kinna Price

Willie Cecil and Maggie K. Cecil had three daughters:
    A. Ethel Jane   5-10-1894 to 1986 m. R. Clifton Darby
    B. Marian Annie 10-31-1895-1981 m. Edward Miles
        of Samuel Miles and Carrie McDonough
        (1) Elizabeth Thomas 10-11-1921 m. William Edwin "Pete" Burdette in Clarksburg 8-21-1941 and had:
            (a) Judith Ann 6-23-1942 m. Carroll Shry 1-22-1965
            (b) William Maurice 6-23-1942 b&d
            (c) James William   9-29-1946
        (2) Edward Cecil   4-29-1918-1953

    C. Edith Marguerite 9-7-1897 m. Earl Howard Stup (9-11-1893 to 3-31-1965) of Charles Howard Stup (1866-1937) and Annie Elizabeth Stockman (1869-1954); on December 21, 1916
        (1) Earl Howard Jr. died age 7

(2) Grayson Hammond 8-7-1920
m Eliza Ann Jakeway 9-6-1947
(3) Robert William m. Lorraine Moberly

3. **Cora Estelle Cecil** (12-20-1871 to 9-3-1959) was the first of the children to be born in the house that Mort built across from the log cabin. She was called "Prissy" by the family. She had a twinkle in her eye and a sense of humor. She was quick, spry and cat-like. She graduated from Shenandoah College after attending school at Comus. She taught at Clarksburg Academy until she married Hanson Groomes Cashell on January 16, 1901. They lived in Redland, Maryland on a large farm. He was the Registrar of Wills for Montgomery County. His two sisters, Henrietta and Emily, also lived with them. They had four children.

    A. Nellie Thomas 12-25-1901 a nurse at Union Memorial Hospital, Balto.
        Dupont Corp., Delaware, and Gilman School, Balto.
    B. Edna Mortimer 9-25-1903 to 11-30-1903
    C. Mary Lee   3-11-1905 to 9-29-1993 Sec'y Federal Home Loan Bank,
        and legal secretary
    D. Thomas Franklin 8-8-1912
        m. Bertie Caruthers (12-13-1913 to 12-5-1990)
        on May 25, 1943. He was the budget and financial officer for the Federal Power Commission & General Accounting Office, Washington, DC.

They had two children.
    (1) Douglas 10-3-1943 who has Kelly Brooke Cashell 8-4-77
    (2) Lois   5-10-1947 lawyer for the Federal Energy Regulatory Commission.

Cecil Home On Old Hundred Road
Prior to 1900

George Cashell was born in Ireland in 1748. He married Mary Wade in 1773 and died in 1808 in Maryland. George and Mary had three children.
   A. **George**   9-3-1776 to 8-20-1862
       m. Elizabeth Butt (1789-1866) June 17, 1804
   B. James   1777 m Jane
   C. Mary Wade   m William Wheatley

George and Elizabeth Cashell had ten children.
   (1) George Washington 7-4-1807 to 12-7-1875 m1 Octavia Yewell
          m2 Mary Ann Yewell
   (2) **Hazel Butt** 1808-1886 m1 Caroline Groomes, m2 Harriet Jones
   (3) Richard Hamilton 6-2-1811 to 6-28-1886 m1 Angeline Yewell
          m2 Margaret C. Havanner
   (4) Samuel Swearingen 4-26-1813 to 1885
      m. Christiannia Groomes
   (5) James Washington 9-9-1814 to 2-1-1841
      m. Mary Elizabeth Groomes
   (6) Andrew Jackson 4-11-1817 to 10-31-1887
      m. Margaret V. Nicholson
   (7) Thomas Franklin 12-26-1818 to 11-11-1889
      m. Esther Jefferson
   (8) Elizabeth Henrietta 4-20-1820 to 1893
      m. Hanson Groomes
   (9) Emily Maria   1-25-1824 to 11-1-1891 m Jacob Miller
   (10) Malvinia   3-27-1829 to 7-19-1833

(2) Hazel Butt Cashell and Caroline Groomes had four children.
   (a) James Groomes 1839
   (b) **Thomas Franklin** 6-6-1840 to 12-20-1907
      m. Emily Elizabeth Groomes
   (c) Amanda   m. William Metzgar
   (d) William Lycurgus 11-27-1843 to 5-17-1915
      m. Ellen Rebecca Groomes

(b) Thomas Franklin Cashell and Emily Elizabeth Groomes (7-24-1846 to 10-15-1911) were first cousins. They had five children.
     i. **Hanson Groomes** 1876-1942 m Cora Estelle Cecil (see above)
     ii. James Lycurgus & Thomas Walter twins, died
     iii. Henrietta Lee   1885-1970
     iv. Emily Thomas   1889-1959

5. **Annie Mary Cecil** (11-2-1876). One time her papa was trying to identify who had put a scratch on the organ. Annie volunteered, "It couldn't have been me, I don't have any tintag to scratch it with." She had a reputation for getting what she wanted. She married first John Tilden Burch on April 20, 1898. He died 3-28-1928. They had three children in Boyds:
    A. Russell Lee 3-7-1899 to 11-29-1956 m. Margaret Bailey ~
    B. Edgar Lewis 2-15-1903 to 10-19-1964 m. Martha Ellen Clarke
       (6-16-1904 to 2-1996)
       (1) Patricia Louise 3-31-1930 m1 Charles Barden Walter, Sr.
          (a) Charlene Louise 8-12-1957
          (b) Charles, Jr. 1-23-1960
      Patricia L. Burch m2 Joseph Raup
      (2) Marcia Mae 7-18-1939 m. Thomas R. Kurtz III
          (a) Suzanne 11-8-1965
          (b) Thomas R. IV 4-9-1968
    C. John Tilden 1-5-1909-1987 m1 Ruth m2 Jeanette Shoemaker
       (1915-1978) brd. Potomac Methodist
Annie Cecil Burch then remarried to a man by the last name of Riley. She had a cottage at North Beach, Maryland.

    John Tilden Burch, Sr., was a son of John L. Burch and Alice R. Basford Burch. John L. Burch was a son of Francis E. and Henrietta Burch, buried in Monocacy Cemetery, Beallsville, Montgomery County, Maryland.

    6. **Charles Mortimer Cecil** (1-4-1878 to 3-20-1948) married Luella Helvin (11-29-1884 to 4-5-1947) on 2-27-1906. He ran a grocery store at 4 1/2 Street SW in Washington, DC. They had four children.
    A. Helen Louise 12-18-1906 - 1918
    B. Mildred Irene 10-8-1908 to 11-13-1992 m. William R. Embrey had
       (1) Elaine Mildred 10-13-1945 m. Steve Emanuel
       (2) Donald Roy 6-10-1948 m. Sandra Lee
    C. Charles Mortimer, Jr. 3-12-1910 to 5-13-1981 m. Lera Woodruff had
       (1) Frank William 9-1-1936 m. Jean Hellwig
       (2) Charlotte Ann 4-2-1942 m. Kenneth Sizemore
    D. Dorothy Mae 2-17-1925 to 5-11-2001 m. Benjamin Sisson
          (8-27-1924 to 10-19-1999)
       (1) Charles Rodney 5-11-1951 m. Caron E. Raley
       (2) John Roland 3-6-1953 m. Becky S. Leach

    7. **George Remington Cecil** "Remmy" aka "Tim" (11-19-1879 to 7-24-1952) married Viola Simmons on October 21, 1908 in Frederick. They had two daughters.
       A. Alice Evelyn 11-9-1909 to 1971 m Ralph Sinyard
       B. Dorothy May 10-29-1914 m Malcolm Wagner (5-3-1909) on

10-7-1939

Remmy probably met Viola when she was visiting her grandparents on their farm "Labrynth". They belonged to the Sugarloaf Mountain Chapel, so they may have met there. After they were married, they lived first in the Cecil home across from the two-story log house. Their first child, Evelyn was born there. Remmy then got a job with the United Railway in Baltimore and they moved in with Viola's parents in Govans, Maryland. Dorothy was born there. She recalls praying for her father to not get shocked as he worked underground. Later, they lived on Edmonson Road, in Baltimore. Remmy died at 220 Newcomb Street SE, Washington, DC.

The Simmons were from the Thurston area. Samuel T. Simmons married Helen Savilla and they had at least two children.

Robert Gassaway 11-17-1864 to 6-14-1944. He married Ida May Martin (1-26-1866 to 12-5-1931). She died at 5506 Ivanhoe Street, Baltimore. He was born on the farm near Comus and died at 1949 You Place, Washington, DC and is buried at Western Cemetery, Baltimore. Robert was a wire chief for Western Union. His sister Jessie ran the farm on Linthicum Road and died 5-2-1947. His brother, John Lee was an inventor and pioneer in the aviation industry; he died in Bladensburg. Robert and Ida May had four children.

    A. Robert Gassaway Jr. 4-26-1893 to 11-3-1928
        m. Louise Buckingham on April 22, 1914.
        (1) Harry Louis 7-15-1916
        (2) Robert III
    B. Harry Samuel 8-5-1897 married Sarah Jane Pippen October 11, 1917. They had five children.
        (1) Harry S. Jr. 9-18-1918 to 6-29-1951
        (2) Vaughan Pippen 11-19-1922
            m. Marguerite Massino (4-22-1916 to 2-2-1990)
            (a) Jefferson V.
            (b) Malynda Sarah
        (2) Ellen May 8-6-1929 m1 T. Keyes had Linda,
            m2 E. Paddison had Kimberly and Karen.
        (3) Nancy Jane 8-6-1929 to 11-15-1987
            m. Thurlow Leister had David
        (4) Peggy Ann 6-22-1933 m. Melvin Buttion had Glenn
    C. Viola May 7-11-1889 m. G. R. Cecil (above).
    D. Grace Lee (12-4-1899 to 9-25-1977)
        m1 Fred Doulong
        had Jean (m. Padgett) Grace Lee Simmons m2 Clifford Beach

8. **Alice Smith Cecil** (7-26-1881 to 10-31-1971) was engaged to a man named Gerhard, who was killed during World War I. Alice played the organ for the Sugarloaf Mountain Chapel and worked as a practical nurse. Later, she was a live-in

companion to Mrs. Louise Glancy, who lived at 1661 Crescent Place, NW. Mrs. Glancy's son was an executive for the Hudson Motor Company, and she had a Packard, driven by Gary, the chauffeur. Her cook was Ethel. Alice later worked for the Geiman's in Westminster. She was excellent at frying chicken and loved for the girls to brush her long hair. Later, Alice lived with her two sisters in the Falkland Apartments in Silver Spring.

9. **Ellen (Ellie) Cecil** (8-19-1883 to 4-20-1981) Ellie was a die hard Washington Senators fan who kept house for a widower, Dr. George St. Maur Maxwell, (2-18-1868 to 2-2-1933) who had four children. They were later married on May 29, 1929. His children from a former marriage to May Bryson Taylor were:
    A. Jay Arthur   4-5-1911 to 6-1961
    B. Robert Austin "Babe"   7-3-1913 to 8-1993
    C. George St. Maur Maxwell Jr. 8-20-1917 m. Helen Warner on 1-9-1946
    D. Wilor Marie   8-24-1919 m. Ozzie Bluege of the Senators
                            on 10-20 1940
      (1) Carol Elaine 2-18-1942
      (2) Wilor Marie 8-2-1943
      (3) Lynn Louise 5-18-1951

10. **Daisy Cecil** (5-2-1886 to 6-16-1972). Daisy was a school teacher in Barnesville. She boarded with her Uncle Luther Cecil during the week, and came home on the weekends. In 1922 she went to work for the Veteran's Administration. At that time, she moved to her sister's home on 49th Street.

11. **George Minor Cecil** (9-6-1889 to 5-15-1961). Minor married late in life. Grace Jones was divorced and had a daughter Maxine. Minor was the best man at John Wolfe's wedding in 1913. He worked in Baltimore.

12. **Arthur DeWitt Cecil** (8-6-1891 to 10-15-1968). Arthur married Isabel Collins and moved to New York City. They had one son. Art Jr. was born 1-15-1919 and married Gladys Elaine Barton on May 30, 1942 Arthur was a good tennis player and golfer. He died in Tucson, AZ. Gladys (12-17-1919) and Art had two sons.
    A. Arthur DeWitt III 6-20-1944 m Donna-Lee Frank
                       (6-9-1942) on August 9, 1962
        (1) Leslie Ann   7-31-1963
             m. Kenneth Leslie Masters (9-17-1964) on June 15, 1985
                (a)Kenneth Leslie Jr. 6-5-1986 Fayetteville, NC
                (b) Kelsey Leighann 1-31-1990 Clarksville, TN
        (2) Donna Lee   3-28-1968
    B. James Barton   4-22-1947

William Collins married Isabella Ingalls and they had four children in

Langley, Virginia: Franklin, Katherine, Emma Rosalind and James Buchanan Collins. James married Grace Cotton of England and they had three children, Grace died in child birth with the third child.

    Jeanette 9-16-1889
    Isabel   9-28-1891 to 3-21-1945 m. Arthur DeWitt Cecil (above)

    13. **Lawrence Lee Cecil** (1-10-1893 to 9-12-1953). Lawrence won an oratorical contest while attending Comus School and received a lovely medal, which he proudly wore it on his watch chain. He competed in spelling bees against the students from the Hyattstown school, where he met Anice Murphy. Anice and Lawrence used to go sleigh riding down Long Hill. He worked on the Cecil farm and one of the traditional yearly events was related by his son, Larry.

Father's would take their sons around the boundaries of the property on the Sunday before the planting season was to begin. Sometimes, even the preacher would come by to bless the fields and crops. The son was often given a whipping at the boundary, or dunked in the stream (if that was a boundary). This was to "teach" the boy to always remember the edges of the land. Mort did this with Lawrence. Their marker was a pile of stones, and Mort gave Lawrence a whipping there. Lawrence took Larry there and told him about it, but did not whip him.

Lawrence married Anice Julia Murphy at the Hyattstown Methodist Episcopal Church on June 16, 1917. Frank Jaggers performed the ceremony, and the reception was held at the home of Charlie and Gertrude Murphy (the bride's parents). Mercer and Happy Wolfe attended the wedding, as did Richie Benson, who was six years old at the time. She says that the clothes had been made by hand and were beautiful. She helped pick wild flowers for the wedding and took home a banana from the reception for her sick mother. This was the first banana either of them had seen.

Lawrence was also proud to be a Mason and he worked for the Democratic Party. Lawrence and Anice are buried in the Hyattstown Community Cemetery. They had four children.

    A. **Anice Lee**   9-17-1919 m. Allen J. Dancy
    B. **Lawrence Lee Jr.** 3-5-1922 m Margaret Marie Fischbach (3-19-1929)
        on January 3, 1953
    C. **Charles Douglas** 9-5-1929 to 5-2-2001 m. Norma Jean Selkirk
        (5-5-1934) on August 25, 1956
    D. **Alice Louise**   4-24-1932 to 12-23-1977
        m. Laurence Leonard Frost II
        son of Laurence Leonard Frost and Agnes Greenwood Frost

    A. Anice Lee Cecil married Allen J. Dancy on June 22, 1945 and they adopted Allen Lee (9-23-1956) and Linda Cecil (1-13-1958), who married Bruce Dean Robinette (7-1957) on November 13, 1994 in Cape Coral, Florida.

    B. Larry Cecil and Peggy had five children.
    (1) Lawrence Lee III 10-31-1953 Norfolk, VA

  m. Debra Sue Bruce, 8 31-1980
   (a) Simon David 12-21-1982 Ft. Collins, CO
   (b) Noah Murphy 6-28-1984 Ft. Collins, CO
   (c) Wilson Lawrence 3-27-1987 Ft. Collins, CO
 2. Chris Alan 7-21-1955 Riverside, NJ m. Mary Schwed, 11-30-1995
   (a) Matthew Benjamin 11-30-1997
   (b) Catherine Leah 11-19-2000
 3. Holly Beth 6-29-1958 to 11-22-1960
 4. Peter Dean 1-7-1960 m. Susan Clapp, January 26, 1991
   (a) Daniel Peter, 4-4-1995.
   (b) Ruth Samantha 1-6-1998
 5. Robin Lois 4-12-1962 Orange, NJ m Rodney D. Vaughn, 7-24-1982
   (a) Heather Noelle 1-25-1983 Loveland, CO.
   (b) Aaron Micah 4-26-1984 Ft. Collins, CO
   Robin then married Michael Eade (12-20-1960) on 6-24-2000

 C. Charles Douglas Cecil and Jean have three children.
  (1) Charles Douglas Jr. 6-19-1957
   m1 Stella O'Rioridan 1987-1990.
   m2 Sheri Shifter (7-24-1972)
  (2) David Patrick 8-8-1959 m1 Lucinda Bostic (12-11-1960 to
   1-1997) on February 1, 1980
   m2 Mary Beth 9-17-1998
   (a) Sarah Eden 8-10-1983 New Castle, VA
   (b) Adam David 8-9-1985 New Castle, VA
  (3) Susan Jean 12-20-1961 m Larry David Melvin (12-12-1960)
   on April 21, 1990

 D. Louise Cecil and Larry Frost had one son and adopted a daughter.
  (1) Laurence Leonard III 4-7-1957
  (2) Amy Louise 10-27-1965 m1 Rick Stubbs
   m2 James Elmo Nance
   (a) Christopher Stubbs (8-13-1985)
   (b) James Elmo Nance Jr. (12-2-1989).
 After Louise died, Larry Frost (2-18-1925, North Platte, NE) re-married: Elizabeth Fleming on October 28, 1978.

Luther E. Cecil
son of Wilson Hammond Cecil

 2. **Luther E. Cecil** (9-9-1846 to 5-18-1919) married Mary C. Hawkins (5-3-1849 to 10-16-1918) and settled in Barnesville. They had five children and lived next to the post office and store.
  A. Medora H. 1870 m. Maurice W. Watkins 11-22-1887 (12-15-1867 to

3-31-1940) Bethesda Methodist, Browningsville
B. Oscar Thomas 5-20-1871 to 12-30-1922 m. Selma E. Gibson
(8-5-1884 to 1-22-1966) on 10-15-1912.
She was a daughter of Robert Frank Gibson and Florence Maude Thompson.
   (1) Oscar Thomas, Jr. 8-24-1913 to 6-20-1977
      m. Mary Ione Mac Williams (1-16-1916 to 9-30-1989) on 9-2-1934. They had three children:
      (a) Ann Barbara 1-9-1936 m. Earl Joseph Morrison
      (b) Thomas William 12-5-1945 m. Elisabeth Diekman
      (c) William Gerard 10-14-1949 m. Mary Jo Moore
   (2) Selma Regina 2-11-1916 to 7-15-1995 m. Edward Henderson Johnson (12-8-1913) on 2-14-1939. They had 4 children:
      (a) Patricia 10-8-1940 m. John Schaefer
      (b) Margaret 7-23-1943 to 8-1981 m. Frank Novak
      (c) Edward Cecil 8-13-1949 m. Linda Louise Hicks
      (d) Kathryn 12-5-1950 m. Robert Tranter
   (3) Reginald W. 9-26-1922 to 12-30-1990 m. Elsie Richardson

C. Murrell L.   1877 m. Margaret Lydanne Murrell died in Philadelphia
D. Reginald W.   1874-1930 m. Lenora Andrews
E. Clara L.   9-1876 to 8-20-1958
      brd. at Monacacy, Beallsville. "Callie" was a teacher
F. Luther M.   1889 ~

Everett Hammond Cecil
son of Wilson Hammond Cecil

5. **Everett Hammond Cecil** (6-16-1860 to 1-1-1921) married Julia Mae Thompson (6-28-1864 to 11-25-1937) on 7-3-1880. She was the daughter of David H. Thompson and Sarah J. Hawkins Thompson. They had fourteen children. Five are buried at the Methodist Community Cemetery, Hyattstown.

A. Harry   5-26-1881 to 4-23-1906
B. Nellie   9-10-1882 to 11-14-1941 was blind & single
C. Georgia Mae   2-26-1883 m. James Edw. Johnson (1885) on 6-2-1905
   (1) Mary Elizabeth 6-22-1913
   (2) James Edward, Jr.
   (3) Julia
D. Myrtle   11-1887 m. C. U. Landrum
E. Wilson Hammond   9-1889 m. Blanche Soper (1890) daughter of Wm. W. Soper and Elizabeth J. King
F. Everett Linden   5-2-1891 to 1-11-1947 single
G. Mary Ellen   10-1892 to 1948 m. Levi Price (1881-1935) 1915
   (1) Levi "Mutt"

(2) Robert
H. Laura Elisabeth   3-17-1895 to 11-1962 m1 Roland Walker
                                              1886-1934
                      m2 J. Herbert Becraft 1-28-1896 to 2-7-1967
        (1) Charles Roland 2-16-1919 to 3-14-1989 m. Doris Talbert
        (2) Mary Louise 11-10-1920 m. Thomas E. Robertson
        (3) Elisabeth Cecil 9-20-1927 to 10-14-1932
I. Maurice Norman   10-31-1896 to 2-7-1929 single
J. Millard L.   10-13-1900-6-18-1949
K. Melvin Eugene   1901 Single
L. RogerMarshall   4-5-1903 m. Thelma Baker, Western Ave. DC
M. Elmer E.   1-28-1907 to 3-11-1942

Murphy is a Gaelic name meaning "Sea Warrior." It was originally O'Morchoe. Charles Richard Murphy's father came from Ireland, and had two sons, the other being John, who moved to Ohio. Charles Richard Murphy (1799 to 8-14-1879) married Julia A. Richardson (3-11-1804 to 4-28-1853) and they had nine children.
        A. Charles "Richard" 9-9-1828 m. Eliza Rebecca Mannakee
                             (3-21-1832 to 9-12-1832)
        B. Randolph Richardson 1830 Methodist Minister (Hyattstown 1880-1882)
        C. **George Washington** 4-19-1833 to 4-11-1915 m. Julia Ann Shriner
        D. Annie E.   10-1836 m. William R. Windsor
        E. Mary Lucinda   1838 to 8-5-1910 m1 Robert Lumley July 22, 1882
                                              m2 John H. Gibson, 1900
        F. Helen   1840 to 7-14-1865 m. Jacob B. Richards d. 7-11-1892
        G. Frances Windsor   1842 to 6-15-1907
        H. Florence (Woottie) 1846 to 6-1-1899

Charles Richard Murphy married again, after Julia's death, her sister, Mary E. Richardson (1815 to 1-19-1893) on December 12, 1854. The two wives and many of the children are buried at Clarksburg Methodist Church, as is Charles Murphy. They had five children.
        I. John Spencer
        J. Vernon
        K. Sherwood
        L. Daisy
        M. Lily

C. **George Washington** "Wash" **Murphy** and Julia Ann Shriner (11-23-1841 to 5-4-1907) were married on February 21, 1861 and had eight children.
        (1) Charles Basil 3-13-1862 to 6-16-1925 m Ara Gertrude Thompson
                (11-29-1871 to 4-14-1946) on September 27, 1893.
                        (a) Elsie 12-23-1890 to 8-18-1894 brd. Hyattstown Methodist

(b) Anice Julia 10-2-1893 to 1985 m. Lawrence Lee Cecil
Anice attended the school at Stronghold and Towson Normal School and then taught at Froggy Hollow School in Kingsley. She married Lawrence Cecil, and lived at the Cecil Farm in Comus. See child 13 of George Mortimer Cecil.
    (c) Elizabeth Rosalee 8-11-1895 m. Louis A. Elliott
    (d) Violet Louise 12-6-1897 to 1966
       m. Samuel Richard Russell in 1925
       i. Thomas Richard 11-6-1926 m. Nora Carter, had
       ii. Sharon Susan 8-10-1950 m1 Brian Hart, m2 Joseph Lafferty had Bret 1-8-1973, Lane 9-9-1976 & Joseph 1-7-1980
       iii. Patricia G. 6-20-1928 to 1975
       iv. Betty Lou 4-13-1934 m. Nolan Burgess 1957, had Scott 9-16-1958 and Leigh 8-24-1963
    (e) Charles Russell "Pat" 5-5-1905 to 1972 m. Pauline Bryant
(2) Helen Burton Murphy 2-21-1866 m. Jacob Burton Richards
    (a) Carl 4-1893
    (b) William Clark 6-1896
    (c) Hazel 3-1897 m. Earl Payne (d Mary Ann m. Webster Windsor)
(3) John M. 3-4-1868 m. Margaret Turnball
    (a) George
    (b) Cornelius
    (c) Margaret
(4) Louis W. 9-9-1869 to 2-24-1919 m. Mary Gertrude Holland (1-24-1874 to 2-1-1920) on November 22, 1892
    (a) Lucinda Holland 5-25-1894
    (b) Harry L. 1-1895 m. Lizzie J.
    (c) Marian Louise 1904
    (d) James Vance 1-23-1906
    (e) Robert L. 12-1909
(5) Minnie Moore 4-21-1870 to 1950 m. William H. Dutrow on November 23, 1892
(6) George Lewis 1871-1962 single brd Hyattstown Community Cemetery
(7) Elizabeth Burnside 1883 m1 Jonathan Richard Benson (1858) on December 21, 1897
    (a) William Paul 9-11-1901 to 3-25-1967
       m. Evelyn Dorothy Carlisle (3-20-1907)
    (b) Richie 9-30-1908 m John Andrews
       i. Elizabeth 1945.
Elizabeth m2 John Beall (12-24-1856 to 8-26-1917) in 1912
    (c) Bob 1913 m. Jean Skaden
Elizabeth m3 Ernest Franklin Harris (1874) in 1919
(8) Eugene Shriner 2-21-1877 to 5-2-1955 m. Marian Clark Wood

(12-893 to 10-16-1933)
(a) George Wood 8-25-1921
(b) Julia Marie 7-25-1928

George Mortimer Cecil Family

Brothers George "Mort", Luther and Everett Cecil

Mame Roelke Fisher, Roger and Moses Fisher

The Roelke and Cecil Families

Sarah Jane Roelke & Mort Cecil **Bettie Roelke**

John Christian Henrich Roelke Family

ROELKE

Oedelsheim is on the river Weser, in Hannoverische-Munden, Hesse-Kassel, Germany. It is near Hofgeismar and Uslar, North of Frankfurt. It is one of five small villages that together make up Oberweser. The streets are still narrow and although some modernization has taken place, the village looks much the same now, as it did when the family of Roelke's immigrated to Frederick, Maryland. The Rolicke family is recorded in the church record books as far back as 1643.

Johann Heinrich Rolicke, (10-03-1700 to 10-11-1756) of Oedelsheim, Germany, married Anna Rosina Breide in March of 1724. They had **Johann Georg Gerhard Rolcke**, (12-25-1730 to 9-26-1758). Georg married Anna Christina Jordan (1733 to 2-3-1798) on November 24, 1757. Their son **Johann Conrad Rolke**, (8-6-1758 to 3-20-1820) was only a month old when his father died (9-26-1758). Johann Conrad married Elisabeth Niemeyer on January 15, 1782. Margarethe was the daughter of Johann Jost Niemeyer and Marie Elisabeth Dalfuss. She was born 3-20-1763 in Weissehutte and died 5-16-1837, in Oedelsheim. Johann Conrad Rolke died 3-20-1820. They had ten children:

♦ 1. **Johannes** 10-6-1782
2. Anna Christina 10-17-1785
3. Georg Christoph 12-10-1789 to 6-2-1847
4. **Johann Christian Heinrich** 2-9-1793
5. Marie Elisabeth 8-18-1796
6. **Heinrich Freidrich Wilhelm** 2-20-1802 to 5-23-1853
7. **Heinrich Friedrich Ludwig** 1-20-1804 married Maria Elizabeth
8. Maria Justina 5-29-1806
9. George Wilhelm 5-14-1809 to 3-20-1843 buried in Oedelsheim, Germany

Johannes Roelke
son of Johann Conrad Rolcke
1782-1855

Johannes was born in Oedelsheim, Germany on October 6, 1782 and died in Frederick, Frederick County, Maryland on February 1, 1855. He married Dorothee Justine Westermann (2-17-1791 to 11-20-1859) on October 31, 1811 in Oedelsheim. Dorothee's (pronounced Dorothea) parents were Johann Georg Westermann (11-21-1746 to 3-8-1831) and Maria Christina Wienecke (3-6-1751 to 5-10-1826). They were married on January 18, 1785 in Oedelsheim. Johann Georg was the child of Heinrich Ernst Westermann and Anna Maria Timmer. The eight children of Johannes and Dorthee were born in Odelsheim and all were baptized by Johann Phillip Theobald before coming to Maryland. After Easter 1832 the family sailed to Baltimore arriving on Whitsundtide, the 8th Sunday after Easter. Oral tradition states that they walked to Frederick and worked as carpenters, cabinet makers and other trades. The church where they worshipped is now the site of Trinity Chapel and is located in Frederick on East Church Street across from the present Evangelical

Reformed Church. Built in 1766, the building was demolished in 1880, except for the tower and steeple. Johannes (known as John) applied for citizenship on January 2, 1834 and was naturalized on July 13, 1837. Henry Nixdorff was the witness. Johannes wrote to his brother Johann Christian Heinrich in Germany after he received citizenship and had his family come to Frederick. Johannes and Dorothee were buried in the German Reformed Cemetery behind what is now Trinity Chapel.

    A. Christine Fridericke   2-17-1812 to 4-10-1888
    B. Georg Friedrich Augustus   10-6-1813 to 2-16-1870
    C. Wilhelmina Christiane Charlotte 2-11-1816 to 2-2-1887
                                                    married David Meisinger
    D. Christine Sophie Wilhelmine   3-23-1818 to 1-7-1892
♦   E. **Christian Friedrich Wilhelm**   2-20-1820 to 10-14-1900
    F. Marie Elise Mathilda   4-12-1822 to 2-5-1889
    G. Heinrich Ludwig Peter   5-10-1824 to 5-28-1892
    H. Heinrich Wilhelm Hermann   5-2-1828 to 4-14-1916

After getting settled in the Frederick area, Johannes' brother Johann Christian Heinrich brought his family to Frederick. The family of Johann Christian Heinrich follows this section on page 42. In 1848 the cornerstone was laid for the main building of the Evangelical Reformed Church, directly across East Church Street from Trinity Chapel. The Pastor, Daniel Zacharias, was there from 1835-1873. To accommodate the German members who were traditional and those who were integrating into American society, he offered two services. One was in German, and the other in English. This is the building in which Christian Friedrich Wilhelm "William" Roelke was the choir director.

Christine Fridericke Roelke
daughter of Johannes Roelke
1812-1888

    A. Christine (pronounced Christina) was born in Oedelsheim, Germany on February 17, 1812 and married John Henry Koester (12-7-1795 to 2-28-1864) of Hesse-Kassel, Germany. They were married on June 16, 1833 by Rev. D. F. Schaeffer in Frederick. John Henry Koester was naturalized on July 13, 1837. They had six children. John Henry was a shoemaker turned baker. Christine died April 10, 1888 in Frederick, Maryland. They are buried in Mt. Olivet Cemetery, Frederick, Md.

       (1) Sophia m. William H. Whaley on 11-13-1859 in Frederick, Maryland
           (a) Charles Koester 1860-1860 brd Reformed Cemetery,
Frederick, Maryland

       (2) Lewis [aka Louis] 9-23-1837 to 8-10-1919 m. Alice H. Faubel
           (8-3-1840 to 8-4-1925)
           She was the daughter of David F. and
           Mary Ann Kleinard Faubel.

They are buried in Mt. Olivet Cemetery.
(3) William A. 1839 to 7-2-1863 a stone cutter, killed in Civil War
(4) Martha married Thomas Grayson Haller on 12-10-1861
(5) Mary K. 3-9-1845 to 1-14-1882 buried in Mt. Olivet Cemetery
(6) Anna C. 6-12-1852 to 8-2-1854 buried in Mt. Olivet Cemetery

Georg Friedrich Augustus
son of Johannes Roelke
1813-1870

B. Georg Friedrich Augustus Roelke was born in Oedelsheim, Germany on October 6, 1813 and was baptized on October 17, 1813. He married Mary Ann Turner on May 17, 1836 in the Reformed Church in Frederick and was naturalized on 7-20-1837. Mary Ann (2-1-1819 to 1-8-1894) was the daughter of Isaac and Elizabeth Brashear Turner. They are buried in Mt. Olivet Cemetery. They had four children.

(1) Frederick Augustus 1837 to 7-21-1854 m. Amelia Whitley
(d. 5-27-1900). He is buried in the Reformed
Cemetery, Frederick, Maryland.
(2) George Frederick William 7-5-1838 to 1-17-1905 m. Mary "Mollie"
Catherine Getzendanner (6-24-1848 to 2-22-1921)
on 11-5-1868 in Frederick, Maryland. She was the
daughter of John and Margaret Walker Getzendanner.
They are buried in Mt. Olivet Cemetery, Frederick, Maryland.
  (a) Eleanor Ann 9-?-1869
  (b) Eli Getzendanner 1874-1952
  (c) Richard Johnston 11-7-1872 to 4-22-1957
  (d) William 8-11-1874 to 8-24-1874 buried in Mt. Olivet Cemetery
  (e) George Wentz 9-12-1877 to 3-14-1931
  (f) Robert Emmett 1-23-1879 to 3-5-1930
  (g) Margaret Walker 11-12-1880 Christened 12-24-1880
  Evangelical Reformed Church, Frederick
  (h) Monroe Franklin 5-10-1884 to 3-5-1930
(3) Edward
(4) Samuel

Christine Sophie Wilhelmine Roelke
daughter of Johannes Roelke
1818-1892

D. Christina Sophia Wilhelmina Roelke was born on March 23, 1818 in Oedelsheim, Germany and married Costantin "Charles" Lange on December 8, 1835. Her second husband was John Simon Burucker. They were married on March 14, 1842. John Berger, a baker, was her third husband, married in 1860. She is buried in Mt. Olivet Cemetery. There were two children by her second husband.

A. George Augustus 8-13-1849 to 2-5-1864
B. Oscar M. 2-2-1852 to 8-6-1911 married Grace S. G.
(9-3-1864 to 6-9-1901)

Christian Friedrich Wilhelm Roelke
son of Johannes Roelke
1820-1900

E. Christian Freidrich Wilhelm Roelke was born February 20, 1820 in Oedelsheim, Germany and was known as William. He was naturalized on 2-22-1841. He married Sarah Ann Sier (pronounced Sear) who was born October 20, 1817 and died on September 9, 1902. They were married on February 6, 1844 in the Reformed Church in Frederick. William was a cabinet maker and tobacconist. He directed the church choir at the Evangelical Reformed Church in Frederick. They had nine children.

The following notices were taken from "The News" Frederick, Maryland, Wednesday, September 10, 1902. Mrs. Sarah A. Roelke, widow of the late C. F. William Roelke, died last night at 10:20 o'clock at the residence of Mr. Moses Fisher, South Market Street, of heart trouble, aged 85 years. She leaves the following children: Mrs. G. M. Cecil, of Comus; Mrs. William Funk, of Green Valley; Mrs. Lewis Kolb, of Linganore; Mr. John W. Roelke of Baltimore; Mrs. Moses Fisher, and Mrs. Frank Chew of this city. The funeral will take place tomorrow at 3 o'clock. Interment to be made at Mt. Olivet cemetery.

Friday, September 12, 1902. The funeral of the late Mrs. Sarah A. Roelke took place from her home, South Market Street yesterday at 3 o'clock. The pall bearers were all sons-in-law of the deceased Messrs.: G. M. Cecil; William Funk; Moses Fisher; and Frank Chew. The interment was made at Mt. Olivet cemetery. C. C. Carty was the funeral director. These children will be discussed in the next section.

    (1) John Sier   2-1-1844 to 11-5-1845 buried in Reformed Cemetery
♦   (2) Sarah Jane   12-21-1846 to 1-9-1926 married George Mortimer Cecil
    (3) **Ann Eliza**   2-12-1849 to 2-12-1940
    (4) John William   11-6-1850 to 2-14-1925
    (5) **Mary Ellen** "Mame"   2-25-1852 to 11-19-1939
    (6) Christina   8-30-1855 to 5-3-1912m. B. F. Chew
    (7) Christian Charles   8-30-1855 to 10-03-1855
    (8) Clara Bethsheba   7-10-1858 to 9-?-1858
    (9) **Bettie**   10-14-1859 to 4-18-1941

Marie Elise Mathilda
daughter of Johann Conrad Roelke
1822-1887

F. Marie Elise Mathilda Roelke was born April 12, 1822 and was baptized 4-21-1822 in Oedelsheim, Germany. She married David H. Haller (3-21-1816 to

10-15-1887) on March 31, 1840 in Frederick, Maryland. She died on February 5, 1887. They are buried at Mt. Olivet Cemetery.
    (1) Mary Ellen 12-29-1840 to 3-7-1921
    (2) Elizabeth K. 1845 to 3-1-1860 married William H. Ziegler
        (a) Clara Grant
    (3) Anna M. 1858 to 4-1-1860
    (4) George A. October 1860
    (5) Infant d. 4-15-1867
    (6) George W. 1868-1945 married Nettie M.
        (a) Grover C. 1893-1959
        (b) George W. Jr. 1899-1958

Heinrich Ludwig Peter Roelke
son of Johannes Roelke
1824-1892

G. Heinrich Ludwig Peter Roelke was born on May 10, 1824 and was baptized 5-23-1824 in Oedelsheim, Germany. In records he is listed as C. L. Peter Roelkey. He married Mary Ellen Anderson (10-20-1828 to 12-24-1917) on February 28, 1850. She was the daughter of Robert and Mary Ann Anderson. Peter died May 28, 1892. He and his wife, Mary Ellen, are buried in Mt. Olivet Cemetery. They had nine children.
    (1) Anna Mary 12-22-1850 to 10-4-1889 m. Jacob Michael Shawbaker
        November 27, 1873 in Frederick County, Maryland.
        He was the son of George Shawbaker.
        (a) Emma Elizabeth m. Vernon Webster Nicodemus
          i. Mary Louise 5-6-1899 to 9-22-1949 married Merhl Hench Ramsburg
            a. Merhl Hench, Jr.
            b. Ruth Elizabeth
            c. Sarah Ann
          ii. Allen Webster 9-2-1900 to 2-10-1973 married Mary E. Mercer
          iii. Emma Lucille 9-6-1905 married Albert Earl Mentzer
          iv. Ruth Elizabeth 9-1-1917 married David Stauffer Dorman
            (7-13-1918) on March 22, 1941
            a. Michael David
            b. Steven Lee 7-5-1949
            c. Mary Ellen 6-2-1960
    (b) Nettie Worman
    (c) George Peter Roelkey
    (d) Anna Maria 12-26-1883 to 10-9-1890
    (e) Jessie June 8-26-1885 to 8-25-1976
    (f) Jacob Garfield 1-1-1888 to 9-30-1976 m. Ethel Irene Fogle
            (1890 to 7-7-1956)
    (2) Emma Frances 8-20-1852 m. Jacob Michael Shawbaker in 1890

(a) Infant
(3) David Henry Sr. 9-18-1854 to 1-19-1919 m. Martha Alice Renn
 (2-8-1855 to 1-28-1919) on March 10, 1880.
 (a) Sarah Maude 12-30-1880 to 7-3-1961 m. Willis Edward Derr
  (3-8-1876 to 11-13-1940) 1-30-1901.
  She is buried in Mountain View, Emmitsburg, Frederick Co., Md
  i. Dorothy Maude 7-8-1902 married Emory Earl Remsburg
   (1-7-1899 to 10-24-1886) 6-2-1921
   a. Dorothy Virginia 6-26-1922 m. Donald Monroe Schwartz
   b. Kathleen 9-11-1923 to 5-23-1924
   c. Emory Earl, Jr. 1-22-1926 m. Mary Elizabeth Toms
   d. Willis Derr 5-21-1927 m. Nettie Kolb
    (7-12-1927 to 12-25-1955) and then
    Edith Blumanauer (11-25-1927) on December 12, 1958
   e. Paul Douglas 9-14-1934 m. Emogene Main (9-14-1934)
   f. Robert Thomas 2-22-1930 m. Lois James (10-19-1932)
    on August 10, 1952
   g. Marianna 9-14-1931 m. Carlton Shea
   h. Rachel Lucille 9-5-1937 m. Charles Thomas Ford
  ii. Richard Willis 5-12-1904
  iii. Ruth Helen 9-8-1910 m. Charles Thomas King
   a. Sarah Ann Kathryn 5-26-1941 m. Ralph Jones Adkins
   b. Helen Jo Ann 4-24-1947
  iv. David Edward 8-12-1913 m. Leone Duvall (9-7-1911)
   a. Ann Duvall 12-5-1939 m. Lawrence White (12-23-1926)
    (i.) Deborah Lynn 3-11-1961
    (ii.) Craig Elliott
    (iii.) Pamela Michele
   b. Sue Elizabeth 1-13-1943 m. Robert Hulbert Bowyer
    (3-12-1940) on 11-23-1961
    (i.) Cheryl Ann 7-19-1962
    (ii.) Christopher Eugene
   c. David Edward, Jr. 2-25-1944
  v. Francis Henry 5-19-1917 m. Ida Barnes (9-9-1908)
   a. Frances Elizabeth 6-11-1944
 (b) Mary Alice 6-24-1882 to 11-10-1947 m. Robert Wesley Doty
  (8-23-1876 to 7-30-1942)
  They are buried at Mt. Olivet Cemetery, Frederick, Maryland
  i. Louise Roelkey 5-13-1906
 (c) Ida Ruth 3-30-1984 to 9-27-1951 m. Edgar Young Shafer
  (3-28-1881 to 7-11-1966) on 3-17-1913 in Frederick County, Md.
  i. Edna Gertrude
  ii. Edgar Eugene

iii. Evelyn 10-6-1918
(d) Nina Emma 4-6-1886 to 9-28-1959 m. William Albert Leister (6-18-1885) on 11-25-1908
Both are buried in Mt. Olivet Cemetery, Frederick, Maryland.
 i. Alice Virginia 10-16-1919 m. Alvin Walter Angerhofer (3-18-1918) on 9-28-1940
   a. Nina Johanna 7-1-1941
   b. William David 8-22-1942
   c. Richard Alvin 7-9-1946
 ii. Nina Edith 9-2-1922 married Warren William Reichert
   a. William Warren 10-6-1949
   b. Charlotte Ann 7-16-1951
   c. Susan Jeannette 11-28-1953
 iii. Glenice Alberta 6-9-1924 m. Leo Joseph Ritter (11-7-1920) on 1-22-1949
   a. Martha Lee 9-25-1950
   b. John William 6-19-1952
   c. Andrew Paul 1-28-1955
(e) Johnnie Renn 6-5-1889 to 10-9-1892
   buried in Mt. Olivet Cemetery, Frederick, Maryland
(f) David Henry, Jr. 6-5-1889 to 1965 m. Helen Hightman (6-14-1891 to 4-19-1964)
   on August 10, 1910 in Frederick Co., Maryland
 i. Martha Alice 8-29-1911 to 5-7-1934
 ii. Nina Emma 12-17-1912 m. James Robert Filler (9-14-1903) on 7-24-1940
   a. Janet Lenore 5-31-1943
   b. Martha Mary 11-15-1944
   c. Elizabeth Ann 11-22-1946
   d. James Robert, Jr. 3-17-1952
 iii. Lillian Gertrude 9-4-1914 m. Ford Lee Harwood (6-4-1914) on 12-29-1937
   a. Mary Elizabeth 11-24-1938 m. Joseph Eugene Crampton (9-20-1937)
 iv. Helen Hightman 9-9-1916 m. Clarence William Ryan (12-21-1908) on 10-10-1940
   a. Helen Rebecca
   b. Charles William 7-22-1944
   c. Edith Lee 5-13-1947
   d. Judith Ann 12-20-1948
   e. Doris Elaine 12-31-1953
 v. David Henry III 5-24-1918 to 8-18-1956 m. Eleanor Holkins (d. 8-18-1956) brd in Mt. Olivet Cemetery, Frederick, Maryland

      a. David Henry IV 10-31-1945
      b. John Walter 10-26-1946
  vi. John Ellsworth 7-31-1920 to 1995 m. Betty Jane Hardy (4-14-1935) on 1-9-1952
  vii. Mary Elizabeth 9-3-1922 m. Roy Franklin Simpson on 1-1-1942
      a. Jack David 2-1-1943
      b. Kathryn Ann 11-14-1944
      c. Selva June 7-26-1948
      d. Roy Franklin, Jr. 1-26-1951
  viii. Oliver Charles 9-16-1924 to 8-9-1986 m. Margaret Anne Feather (10-18-1931) on 9-27-1952. brd in Mt. Olivet Cemetery
      a. Oliver Keith 9-11-1954
      b. Lisa Anne 6-12-1956
  ix. William Noah 7-23-1926 m. Anna Valeria Tritapoe (7-9-1933)
      a. William Noah, Jr. 5-8-1958
      b. Karen Lee 11-25-1960
  x. Robert Wesley 4-4-1928 m. Elinor Jane Grimes (2-25-1937) on 6-2-1957
      a. Robert Wesley, Jr. 7-13-1958
      b. Warren Steven 5-25-1959
      c. Elinore Jane 7-3-1960
      d. Michael Lee 11-10-1961
  xi. Albert Richard 8-12-1930 m. Joy Patricia Minnick 11-8-1932 on 4-5-1953
      a. Albert Richard, Jr. 10-15-1953
      b. Joyce Elaine 12-12-1954
      c. Charles Stanley 5-30-1955
      d. Patricia Lynn 12-23-1957
  xii. Warren Delano 8-1-1932 to 6-12-1997 m. Jane E. Stocks
      a. Warren Delano, Jr.
  xiii. Dorothy Ellen 6-1-1934 to 6-1-1934
(g) Blanche Elizabeth 8-18-1892 to 1-9-1896
(h) Lillian Anne 11-28-1897 to 7-3-1906
(4) Laura Augusta 2-1-1856 to 6-29-1945 m. Dewitt Clinton Dixon (7-23-1854 to 3-21-1918) on 8-16-1917
  (a) Howard Eugene 2-8-1885 m. Eva Castle (8-12-1889)
    i. Eugene Dewitt 1-2-1917 m. Evelyn Fink Phillips (11-14-1917) on 6-25-1939
      a. Nancy Evelyn 9-3-1942
      b. David Eugene 2-25-1947
    ii. Dewitt Clinton 7-20-1918 m. Eleanor Norfleet (10-13-1923) on 9-16-1945
      a. Clinton Dewitt 9-19-1949

      b. Lynn Arden 12-31-1950
      c. Stephen Norfleet 1-18-1960
   iii. George Carlton 12-4-1919 m. Eleanor Champ (6-11-1915) 2-14-1942
      a. Penny Castle 4-11-1950
(b) William Edward 8-30-1886 to 2-7-1964 m. Margaret Cleveland Eagle (2-18-1885 to 10-5-1973) on 8-16-1917. She was a daughter of Charles William and Sarah Jane Boyer Eagle. They are both buried in Mt. Olivet Cemetery, Frederick, Md.
     i. Infant 11-8-1918 to 11-8-1918
    ii. Margaret Adele 7-2-1920 m. Louis Tomey
      a. Margaret Adele
   iii. Dorothy Jane 10-11-1921 m. Rudolf Wheatley
      a. Mark Obi
(c) Mary Roelkey 2-9-1888 to 10-18-1893
(5) Lloyd Eugene Duval 2-14-1859 to 1-18-1930 m. Helen Rebecca Dorsey (1863-1930), daughter of James and Elizabeth Dixon Dorsey
(a) James Milburn 8-30-1884 to 2-25-1959 m. Cora Sophia Brunner (9-23-1884) on 1-7-1909
     i. Roy Lloyd 10-31-1909 m. Inez Evelyn Truax (2-8-1910) on 11-1-1930
      a. Judith LoDeane 5-22-1932 m. Kelley Keith Kindig (1-4-1932) on 11-28-1953
      b. John Milburn 3-31-1937 m. Nancy Jo Gugle (5-5-1938) on 6-8-1957
      c. Carol Irene 4-29-1945 m. William Joseph Fisher (4-14-1946) on 4-23-1965
    ii. Milburn Eugene 8-15-1911 to 1-31-1950 m. Eleanor Reed (4-19-1913) on 10-14-1937
      a. Robert Milburn 6-28-1939
      b. James William 7-20-1943
   iii. Paul Lewis 10-27-1913 m. Norma Evelyn Hall (4-1-1918) on 12-4-1938
      a. Patricia Lynn 10-15-1940 m. Joseph Terrell Davis (12-31-1932) on 12-26-1971
      b. Donald Paul 5-21-1943
      c. Kathryn Anne 10-31-1944 m. Thomas William Anderson (6-24-1941) on 12-7-68
      d. Virginia Lee 7-20-1948 m. David Ramey Gibbs (7-9-1947) on 6-22-1968
      e. Norman Lewis 8-29-1949
   iv. Helen Virginia 12-3-1915 m. Russell Harvey Buss (2-29-1912) on 4-17-1937

      a. Roger Harvey 3-4-1943
   v. Dorothy May 12-4-1917 m. Neil Leroy Chase (2-2-1916) on 2-21-1940
      a. Daniel Chase 8-5-1955
      b. Jeanette Eileen 12-29-1948 m. Dean Bradley Frick (2-28-1947)
      c. Jeanine Irene 12-29-1948 m. Jerome Thomas Holderead
         (3-2-1948) on 8-30-69
      d. Larry Neil 2-25-1943 m. Sue Carol Greenlee (2-19-1942)
         on 11-28-1964
(b) Olivia May 2-21-1886 m. Earl Mathias Ahalt (3-1-1890 to 6-28-1966)
   i. Lauretta Rebecca 1-19-1916 to 8-9-1916 brd Lutheran Cemetery,
     Middletown, Md.
   ii. Milburn Roelke 4-6-1917 m. Jessie Magaha (2-21-1917)
     on 12-16-1945
      a. Larry 4-22-1947
      b. Kay Rebecca 10-10-1948
   iii. Charles William 9-9-1918 m. Pauline R. Prebish (10-23-1919)
     on 7-23-1945
      a. Janice Kay 11-8-1944
   iv. Charlotte Ruth 1-17-1921 m. LeRoy Kitchenmaster (3-9-1917)
     on 8-20-1940
      a. Ronald LeRoy 1-2-1945
      b. JoAnn 9-15-1951
(c) Mary Elizabeth 1-30-1888 to 11-2-1966 m. Louis S. C. Darner
   (9-25-1888 to 10-3-1947) on 2-24-1914 in Frederick Co., Md.
   She is buried in Mt. Olivet Cemetery, Frederick, Maryland
   i. Louise Elizabeth 5-16-1914 m. Woodrow Wilson Corbin (9-27-1912)
     on 6-28-1935 Frederick, Frederick Co., Md., son of William F.
     and Rosa Mary France Corbin
      a. William Louis
      b. Carol Elizabeth
      c. Daryll Woodrow
     Louise Elizabeth also married Charles Victor Main
   ii. Helen Madora married Robert Carbaugh
      a. Dorothy Mae
      b. Robert, Jr.
   iii. Edna married Howard Butcher
   iv. Carl F. 8-16-1923 m. Lucille C. Cutsail (8-12-1920)
     on 12-24-1946 daughter of Roy Cleveland and Jane Davis Cutsail
      a. Sally Kay 9-20-1948
      b. Stephen Lee 7-3-1952
      c. Timothy Eric 1-3-1959
   v. Anna Alice 3-22-1890 m. Ernest L. Doub 3-23-1888 on 11-26-1913
      a. Alice Helen 8-18-1914

      b. Elise Marguerite
      c. Ernest Leroy
      d. Betty Rebecca
  vi. Lloyd Eugene 12-24-1893 to 1-18-1964 m. Katie Blanche Eagle (2-6-1895 to 10-22-1977) on 1-8-1918 in Frederick, Frederick County, Maryland. She was the daughter of Charles William and Sarah Jane Boyer Eagle. He is buried at Fort Lincoln Cemetery, Bladensburg, Prince George's County, Maryland. Katie is buried in the Lutheran Cemetery in Burkittsville, Frederick County, Maryland.
      a. Edna Jeanette 10-12-1918 m. Charles Clinton Rogers (11-29-1921) on 7-9-1945
      b. Margaret Eagle 4-20-1921 m. Lawrence McNitt on 10-29-1970
      c. William Lloyd 10-3-1924 m. Betty Jane Carter (8-17-1926) on 4-6-1946
  vii. Helen Dorsey 7-30-1898 to 12-18-1989 m. Clarence Elgin Hemp (4-30-1894 to 8-12-1978) on 3-5-1919. Both are buried in Mt. Olivet Cemetery, Frederick, Maryland
      a. Doris Eugenia 1-17-1921 m. Francis S. Gaither, Jr.
  viii. Laura Dewitt 5-15-1902 to 12-1-1992 m. Ralph Wainwright Hicks (5-15-1879 to 4-7-1954) on 3-20-1936 son of Samuel and Elizabeth Kepler Hicks. She then married Ezra R. Jacoby (12-22-1896) after the death of her fist husband.
  ix. Margaret Myrtle 9-30-1904 m. Roy Steiner Schroeder (12-9-1897 to 6-9-1987) on November 19, 1923
      a. Frances Ann 11-28-1924 m. Bernard L. Gilbert, Jr. 3-1-1924
      b. Margaret Elizabeth 6-15-1927 m. Arnold Frederick Keller, Jr. (5-27-1924) on 4-12-1950.
      c. Nancy Steiner 2-12-1929 m. William Dare Morton, Jr. (8-24-1925) on 6-2-1950

(6) Lewis Albert 7-1-1861 to 10-29-1862 brd Mt. Olivet Cemetery, Frederick, Maryland

(7) John Robert 10-27-1866 to 6-10-1943 m. Verna Viola Karn (7-3-1867 to 3-5-1937) on 12-14-1893 in Frederick County, Maryland. Both are buried in Mt. Olivet Cemetery, Frederick, Maryland.
  (a) Infant d.2-3-1897
  (b) Charles Robert 7-29-1898 m. Alice E. Baker
    i. Charles Robert, Jr.
    ii. Elizabeth Logan
  (c) John Peter 4-8-1901 m. Jean A. Marken
  (d) Olive May 8-16-1905 to 6-2-1992 brd Mt. Olivet Cemetery, Frederick, Maryland

(8) Wilhelmina May 5-5-1869 to 1946 m. George E. Hightman (1872-1955) on 12-12-1892 in Frederick County, Maryland
   i. George Lewis 9-22-1893 m. Martha Bingham (9-24-1894 to 2-4-1958)
   ii. John T. 9-22-1899to 3-26-1902
   iii. Maude H. 9-9-1902 m. George E. Cannon (12-20-1891 to 10-28-1959)
(9) Lawrence Herbert 3-12-1875 to 3-30-1941 m. Mary Ellen Thomas (12-18-1876 to 7-26-1967) on December 21, 1898.
They are buried in Mt. Olivet Cemetery, Frederick, Maryland.

Heinrich Wilhelm Hermann Roelke
son of Johannes Roelke
1828-1916

H. Heinrich Wilhelm Hermann was known as George William "Harmon" Roelke. Harmon married Carolena Wilhelmina Christiana Dorothea Bode who was born in Gottenberg, Germany in 1826. They were married in Cincinnati, Ohio on May 2, 1849.

   (1) Augustus 5-8-1850 to 8-1850 buried in Cincinnati, Ohio
   (2) Clementine Virginia 5-2-1851
   (3) John William 5-18-1854
   (4) Robert F. 4-28-1856
   (5) James Edwin 2-5-1858
   (6) Henrietta Caroline 2-5-1860 m. John W. Reese
     (a) Edna
     (b) George
   (7) Sophie Eliza 8-25-1862 m. Preston W. Smith on August 28, 1891 in Elderado Co., California
     (a) Carolyn Elizabeth
     (b) Mildred
     (c) Vergil Thomas
   (8) Caroline Augusta 12-23-1864 m. Louis Albert Beckstead

Children of Christian Friedrich Wilhelm "William" Roelke
Sarah Jane Roelke
1846-1926

(2) Sarah Jane Roelke was baptized by Daniel Zacharias at the Evangelical Reformed Church in Frederick on 1-17-1847. She is buried in the Sugarloaf Mountain Chapel Cemetery. The rest of her story is in the Cecil chapter as Mrs. George Mortimer Cecil.

Ann Eliza Roelke
1849-1940

(3) Ann Eliza Roelke was born February 12, 1840 and was christened at the Evangelical Reformed Church in Frederick on August 5, 1849. She married Samuel

Lefevre Boyer on November 11, 1875. They had two children. After Boyer's death she married William Henry Funk and had five children. She is buried in Mt. Olivet Cemetery.

(a) Helen Amelia 8-29-1877 to 3-16-1922 m. Elias Daniel DeLaughter (2-18-1870 to 2-1-1937) son of Elias D. & Sarah Ann Stottlemyer DeLaughter
 i. Helen Annie 10-10-1895 to 11-18-1952 m. Raymond Isaac Ford December 4, 1917
  a. Miriam Ann 10-2-1918 to 3-4-1966 m. Howard Cantwell
  b. Dorothy Louise 2-21-1923 m. William Carl Krieger
   I Willam Carl Krieger II 7-20-1953 m. Pamela Dicke
   II Jeffery Ford 5-3-1957 m. DeAnn Deason
  c. Raymond Isaac Jr. 3-12-1925 m. Amelia Deangelis
   I Helen Annie 8-25-1954
   II Raymond Isaac III 10-29-1959
 ii. Rebecca Amanda 1-9-1899 to 7-17-1973 m. Lester Walter Boyer
  a. Ruth Rebecca 11-15-1919 m. Allen Reese Kinsey (10-7-1908 to 10-27-1986)
  b. Lester William 12-12-1921 m. Anna Maria Sterbinsky
   I William Lester 2-6-1959 m. Peggy
   II David A. 9-22-1961
   III JoAnn M. 9-6-1963 m. Carl Toffemaire
  c. Charles Henry 2-23-1924 m. Violet May Schultz
   I Charles Henry, Jr. 6-28-1947 m. Linda A. Williams
   II Katherine Rebecca 1-27-1954 m. William Dykes
  d. Robert DeLaughter 1-2-1926 m. Margaret Ann Strother
   I Robert DeLaughter 4-3-1955
   II Jennifer A. 11-20-1967
  e. Helen Amelia 10-22-1927 m. Marshall Eugene Hooper, son of Walter and Lucy Hanshew Hooper
   I Susan Rebecca 2-23-1948
   II Sarah Lynn 1-28-1959
  f. Martha Jane 10-27-1928 m. Roland Hooper son of Walter and Lucy Hanshew Hooper
   I Anna Louise 5-13-1948 m. Cleo Heavner
   II Donald Walter 7-23-1951 m. Peggy
   Martha Jane then m. Bernard Lee Linthicum (11-21-1934) son of Miel Wright and Irma Sophronia Watkins Linthicum
   III Erma Jane 6-22-1961
   IV Amanda Jean 7-7-1963
   V Ethan Lee 5-17-1967
  g. George Richard 1-19-1933 to 12-17-1977 m. Alma May Martz
   I Elizabeth Anne 10-19-1962

  II Michael George 3-12-1964
  III Rachael Martz 1-5-1968
 h. Marion Thomas 1-17-1938 m. Mary Lorraine Baker on 1-23-1959
  I Brian Thomas 4-4-1965
  II Mark Allen 3-13-1967
  III Donna Lynn 3-19-1971
  i. Samuel Lefevre 9-29-1939 to 12-8-1982 m. Jeannette R. Maier
   I Cynthia D. 7-3-1965 m. Lester Thompson
   II Samuel LeFevre, Jr. 3-24-1967
   III Steven D. 3-25-1968
   IV Timothy D. 9-22-1970
   V Todd Anthony 12-3-1974
 (b) Annie 1873-1938 married Harry T. Heuett and had two children.
  i. Elizabeth Roelke Huett married Millard Reehling
  ii. Roger R. Huett married Charlotte Burger
  Samuel Boyer died and Ann Eliza married William Henry Funk Jr. (1-3-1850 to 4-30-1935) the son of William Henry and Catherine Susanna Zimmerman Funk and had five children.
 (c) Jessie Sier 10-11-1882 to 10-25-1976 m. Walter Abell Cutsail (6-4-1889 to 12-6-1952), son of James Herron Langley and Lydia Ann Kanode Cutsail
 (d) Wilbur Henry Hamilton 2-9-1884 to 9-30-1949 m1. Sadie Syrgley m2. Jane Davis (9-6-1892 to 5-25-1975)
 (e) George Tyler 11-5-1886 to 11-6-1942 m. Susan M. Cutsail (11-25-1895 to 9-2-1973), daughter of James Herron Langley and Lydia Ann Kanode Cutsail
  I Eleanor Anne married H. Payne Slinkman
  II Julia Mae 6-12-1929
  III Julian Hume 6-12-1929
 (f) Edgar Harmon 1-1-1889 to 11-17-1921 brd in Mt. Olivet Cemetery
 (g) Christian Frederick Walter 10-13-1893 to 8-14-1951 brd Mt. Olivet

John William Roelke
1850-1925

 4. John William Roelke was born on November 6, 1850 in Frederick and was baptized on December 25, 1850. He married Sarah R. Dickerson on October 14, 1874. John died at the Springfield State Hospital, Sykesville, Md. and is buried next to his parents in Mt. Olivet Cemetery.
 (a) Blanche Roelke 1876

Mary Ellen "Mame" Roelke
1853-1939

 5. Mary Ellen Roelke was born on February 25, 1853 and was baptized on

12-26-1853. She married Moses Fisher (10-20-1858 to 7-17-1931) the son of Hugh W. and Marian Miller Fisher. Moses was an engineer. They were married on February 21, 1882 and they lived on South Market Street in Frederick. They are buried in Mt. Olivet Cemetery.
    (a) James Roger 8-12-1894 to 7-29-1961 buried at Mt. Olivet R-28.
    He married Mary Starr (11-28-1892 to 10-8-1977).

Christina Roelke
1855-1912

6. Christina "Chrissy" Roelke was born in Frederick on August 30, 1855 and was baptized on 1-1-1856. Her twin brother, Christian Charles, died before this date, and was buried behind what is now Trinty Chapel, according to the records of the sexton. She married Benjamin Franklin Chew (5-15-1854 to 12-7-1911) on April 30, 1878. Benjamin was the child of William Chew and Anna Mary Hauer Chew. Chrissy died on May 3, 1921 and is buried in Mt. Olivet R-34 with her husband.
    (a) Mary Roelkey 12-28-1880 to 6-23-1948 m. William A. Buckey
        (4-2-1877 to 3-14-1951) son of Herman A. and Margaret E.
        Nusbaum Buckey
      i. Mildred LaRue 10-17-1906
    (b) William A. 7-17-1887 to 9-24-1931 m. Annie Stansfield in 1914
      i. Anna Louise 1915
      ii. William A., Jr. 1917

Bettie Roelke
1859-1941

9. Bettie Roelke was born on October 14, 1859 in Frederick and was baptized on 8-26-1860. She taught in a public school before marrying Lewis Augustus Kolb (3-11-1844 to 7-7-1923) on September 20, 1893. Lewis was the child of Daniel Kolb and Caroline Brengle Kolb. Bettie died on April 18, 1941 and is buried in Mt. Olivet Cemetery
    (a) Ada Roelkey 11-3-1896 to 12-13-1952 m. Paul Andrew Hobbs
        (8-20-1896 to 4-21-1967) son of Philip R. and Laura Jane Boyer
        Hobbs. They are buried in Mt. Olivet Cemetery
      i. Mehrl Lewis 6-24-1921 to 10-5-1985 m. Ellen Snooks and then
        m. Clara Elizabeth Handley on October 4, 1954
          a. Gregory Alan 2-2-1954
          b. Pamela Sue 6-8-1956 married Glennard Wetzel
            I Glennard Alan 5-4-1973
            II Robert Wayne 8-20-1976
          c. Merhl Lewis, Jr. 6-4-1966 married Stephanie Miller
            I Shayne Daniel 8-16-1992
      ii. Paul Philip 8-5-1926 to 6-10-1962 m. Mary King daughter of George
        and Annie King
        a. James Kevin

　　　　　c. Anna Louise 12-17-1928 married Sois Richard Ingram (3-27-1924 to
8-29-1992)
　　　　　　　(1.) Roxanne Lee 3-15-1953 married James Graham
　　　　　　　(2.) Michael Paul 7-7-1954
　　　　d. Donald Leroy 4-22-1932 married Patricia Stone
　　　　e. Robert Eugene 6-9-1934 married Barbara Beall
　　　　　　　(1.) Robert Eugene Jr.
　　　　　　　(2.) Paul
　　　　　　　(3.) Bunk
　　　　　　　(4.) Wanda daughter of Kay Hobbs

Johnann Christian Heinrich Roelkey
Son of Johann Conrad Rolcke
1793-1861

Johann Christian Heinrich Roelkey, son of Johann Conrad was born in Oedelsheim, Germany on February 9, 1793. He married Sophie Dorothee Schachtebeck on November 18, 1819. They had one son, Christian Carl Ludwig. Sophie died six days after his birth. Christian married Maria Christena Dreyer on January 29, 1822. They had six children in Oedelsheim, before coming to Frederick, Maryland, where he was known as John Roelkey.

1. **Christian Carl Ludwig** 4-13-1821 to 2-22-1892
2. **John Jr.** 11-16-1823 to 11-30-1897
3. Caroline Sophia Amelia 1-27-1827 to 7-8-1904 married F. W. Soelkey
4. George Heinrich 9-24-1829 to 1-29-1865 married C. Mumford
5. Christina Sophia Clara 1-17-1833 to 9-15-1868 married W. Stevens
6. Dorothee Wilhelmina Sophie 1-15-1835 to 8-19-1923 married J. B. Cook
7. Edward 11-18-1837 to 2-12-1881 married Alice Himbury

Christian Carl Ludwig Roelkey
son of Johann Christian Heinrich Roelkey
1821-1892

1. Christian Carl Ludwig Roelkey married Rebecca Brashears on January 1, 1845 in Frederick. He is buried at Bush Creek Brethern, in Monrovia, Frederick County, Maryland. They had five children.
　　　　A. Charles Wesley 1-15-1846 to 11-13-1870 brd in Bush Creek Brethern
　　　　　　Cemetery
　　　　B. Wilhelmina c. 1847-1935 brd in Boonsboro, Washington Co., Md
　　　　C. Clarence　　c. 1850
　　　　D. John Henry 1-17-1852 to 1-29-1858 brd in Bush Creek
　　　　　　Brethern Cemetery
　　　　E. Carrie L. c. 1853 brd in Fahrney Cemetery, Boonsboro, Washington Co.,
　　　　　　Maryland
　　　　F. Dorcus I. 12-1-1857 to 9-26-1861 brd in Bush Creek Brethern Cemetery

John Roelkey, Jr.
son of Johann Christian Heinrich Roelkey
1823-1897

2. John Roelkey, Jr. married Julia Ann Metcalf (12-12-1844 to 1-18-1848). They did not have any recorded children. She is buried in the Reformed Cemetery in Frederick, Maryland. He married second, Susanna Rebecca Allbright (10-5-1825 to 4-10-1898) on October 10, 1848 in Frederick, Maryland. She was the daughter of Carl Philip and Elizabeth Matilda Rebecca Measell Allbright. They had eight children. They are buried in a vault at Mt. Olivet Cemetery, Frederick.

  A. Almeria 2-10-1850 to 2-12-1851
  B. Clementina 2-10-1850 died in infancy
  C. Infant Son 1-15-1851
  D. Fanny Drusilla 8-20-1852 to 10-4-1922 m. Dennis Casper Ramsburg, Jr. (12-22-1853 to 11-27-1928) on 12-19-1876 in Frederick, Maryland. He was a son of Dennis Casper and Lydia Ann Elizabeth Brengle Ramsburg. They are buried in Mt. Olivet Cemetery, Frederick, Maryland.
    (1) Dennis died young
    (2) Harvey Edward 11-12-1877 to 5-6-1965 m. Elise Ann Eichelberger (1-21-1877 to 5-22-1960) on 3-26-1902 in Frederick Co., Maryland. They are buried in Utica Cemetery, Frederick County, Maryland.
      (a) Earl Eichelberger 1-28-1904 to 5-24-1986 m. Ella Mae Myers (1-27-1910) on 8-19-1940.
        i. Earl Eichelberger, Jr. 5-10-1941
        ii. Richard Charles William 3-14-1943
        iii. Laura Jane 11-10-1944
      (b) Jacob Ray 2-16-1908 to 7-7-1971 m. Ethel Mattie Ramsburg (6-10-1910 to 3-8-1977) on 6-27-1935.
        i. Jacob Ray, Jr. 6-23-1936 m. Norma Jean Wright (7-9-1939) on 1-9-1960
        ii. Martha Ann 8-13-1939 m. Neven Aleksander Popovic on 3-28-1970
        iii. Mary Alice 2-10-1944 m. David L. Harris (1945 to 11-28-1966) in 1964. She then married John Dorsey Forsythe Grove (1-5-1941) on 9-20-1968
    (3) Guy Roelkey 6-17-1882 to 4-27-1943 m. Ethel Virginia Summers (1-1-1892 to 12-6-1944) on 3-27-1913 in Frederick County, Maryland. They are buried in Mt. Olivet Cemetery, Frederick, Maryland.
      (a) Guy Roelkey, Jr. 8-13-1920 m. Mary Ethel Young (9-8-1920) on 5-25-1946 at St. John's Catholic Rectory, Frederick, Maryland.
        i. Thomas Summers 1-12-1949 m. Nancy Marie Sheckles on

12-10-1972
E. Charles Christian Albright 3-9-1855 to 9-5-1902 m. Laura E. Brengle (8-25-1844 to 4-7-1893) on 9-16-1873. She was a daughter of Ezra M. and Laura A. Blackburn Brengle. They are brd in Mt. Olivet Cemetery, Frederick, Maryland.
  (1) Gertrude 7-24-1874 to 12-5-1874 brd in Mt. Olivet Cemetery, Frederick, Maryland
  (2) Elsie Lenora 11-1-1875 to 4-21-1944 m. Robert Emory Zimmerman (4-4-1871 to 7-12-1962) on 1-2-1897 in Frederick, Maryland. He was the son of Henry Otho and Martha E. Albaugh Zimmerman. They are buried in Mt. Olivet Cemetery.
    (a) Walton Roelkey 3-13-1901 to 3-23-1907
  (3) Mary Elizabeth 2-25-1893 to 9-6-1957 m. Joseph Paul Mahoney (5-9-1887 to 2-11-1953) on 1-24-1917 in Frederick Co., Maryland. They are brd in Mt. Olivet Cemetery, Frederick, Maryland.
    (a) Elsie Elizabeth 12-9-1919 m. George Albert Strine, Jr. on 10-27-1945.
      i. George Albert III 11-14-1947
      ii. Monaca Marlene 1-23-1951
      iii. Jay Dwight 7-12-1952
      iv. Jan Paul 5-24-1953
      v. Isabel 1957
    (b) Robert Paul 10-9-1928 m. Hilda Elizabeth Martz (5-26-1931) on 9-29-1948 in Frederick County, Maryland.
      i. Karen Elaine 2-10-1954 married Daniel Altmire (4-24-1951)
      ii. Stepanie Ann 8-3-1955 married John Wilson (12-19-1954)
      iii. Melissa Kay 7-11-1961
F. Elroy Livingston 3-14-1858 to 12-9-1929 m. Genevra Lucetta Zimmerman (1-11-1864 to 3-8-1929) on 10-17-1883 in Frederick Co., Maryland. They are buried in Mt. Olivet Cemetery, Frederick, Maryland.
  (1) Lew Milton 5-27-1885 to 5-37-1939 m. Flora Lillian Gladhill (7-15-1884 to 10-7-1971) on 1-31-1906 in Frederick at the Lutheran Parsonage. She was the daughter of Upton McClellan and Laura Diehl Gladhill. They are buried at Mt. Olivet Cemetery, Frederick, Maryland.
  (2) Margaret Medora 12-31-1893 to 12-8-1951 m. Earl Francis Shriver (11-23-1883 to 12-24-1953) on 3-8-1920 in Frederick, Maryland. They are buried in Arlington National Cemetery, Arlington, Virginia.
    (a) Margaret Roelkey 3-5-1921 to 11-23-1983 m. Landon Clifford Hendricks (1922 to 10-10-1944) on 12-11-1941 in Orlando, Orange County, Florida. She then married

James Walter Knight on 1-10-1945.
(3) Julia Susannah 8-31-1895 to 6-12-1977 m. Edward Irvin Myers (4-11-1896 to 12-5-1979) on 12-5-1918 in Frederick, Maryland. He was the son of George Edward and Mary Elizabeth Stewart Myers. They are buried in Mt. Olivet Cemetery, Frederick, Maryland.
  (a) Edward Irvin, Jr. 9-17-1919 to 9-6-1992 m. Anna Lee Gilliam (9-4-1915 to 1-13-1991) on 1-26-1946 at the Presbyterian Church in Frederick, Maryland.
  (b) Lew Livingston 9-30-1922 m. Helen Elizabeth Gladhill (1-18-1924) on 11-10-1942 at the Parsonage of the Evangelical Reformed Church, Frederick, Maryland.
  (c) Margaret Elizabeth 3-31-1925
G. Celeste Manzetta 6-25-1862 to 2-27-1946 brd in Mt. Olivet Cemetery, Frederick, Maryland
H. Joseph Edward 5-10-1865 to 9-30-1931m. Margaret Worman (12-17-1866 to 1-12-1958) They are brd in Mt. Olivet Cemetery, Frederick, Maryland.
(1) Roberta Celeste 1-8-1894 to 9-26-1976 m. Chauncey Ames Bergh, Alfred Simmons on 12-20-1922, Edward H. Kasting on 2-8-1928, and William H. Hampe on 3-7-1959. She is brd in Mt. Olivet Cemetery, Frederick, Maryland.

Caroline Sophia Amalia Roelkey
daughter of Johann Christian Heinrich Roelkey
1827-1904

3. Caroline Sophia Amalia Roelkey 1-27-1827 to 7-8-1904 married Friedrich Wilhelm Soelkey (aka Zulkey) (12-5-1818 to 10-4-1861) on November 24, 1847 in Frederick County, Maryland. They had seven children. They are buried in Mt. Olivet Cemetery, Frederick, Maryland.
A. Maria Elizabeth 9-15-1848 to 12-8-1851 brd in Mt. Olivet Cemetery, Frederick, Maryland
B. William Henry 11-18-1850 to 3-9-1911 m. Emma Virginia Switzer (4-15-1849 to 3-4-1941)
  (1) Cora Alice 7-26-1879 to 6-23-1961 m. Edwin Bishop
  (2) Margaretta Virginia 4-5-1883 to 1-3-1963 brd in Mt. Olivet Cemetery, Frederick, Maryland
  (3) Oliver Edward 4-4-1887 to 6-28-1889
C. Christian Edward 11-11-1852 to 7-28-1936 brd in Mt. Olivet Cemetery, Frederick, Maryland
D. William Edward 3-24-1855 to 6-11-1857 brd in Mt. Olivet Cemetery, Frederick, Maryland
E. Clara Ada 8-15-1857 to 1944 brd in Mt. Olivet Cemetery, Frederick,

Maryland
F. Alice Olivia 11-22-1859 to 5-25-1942 brd in Mt. Olivet Cemetery, Frederick, Maryland
G. Ann Louise 1-10-1862 to 11-22-1864 brd in Mt. Olivet Cemetery, Frederick, Maryland

Georg Heinrich Roelkey
son of Johann Christian Heinrich Roelkey
1829-1865

4. Georg Heinrich 9-24-1829 to 1-29-1865 married Catherine S. Mumford (1835 to 8-28-1911) on November 29, 1853. They had five children. The family is in Mt. Olivet Cemetery, Frederick, Maryland.
   A. Christian Edward 10-7-1854 to 8-5-1859
   B. Clara Virginia   5-27-1856 to 8-12-1857
   C. Mary
   D. James Kenly   7-22-1862 to 8-8-1862
   E. Henry Ashby   7-22-1862 to 8-7-1862

Christina Sophia Clara Roelkey
daughter of Johann Christian Heinrich Roelkey
1833-1868

5. Christina Sophia Clara 1-17-1833 to 9-15-1868 married William E. Stevens (died 3-9-1869) on December 13, 1854 in Frederick, Maryland. They had four children and are buried in Mt. Olivet Cemetery, Frederick, Maryland.
   A. Marion   d 1873
   B. Edward William d 1873
   C. Emma
   D. Clara May m. Harry G. Smith

Dorothee Wilhelmine Sophie Roelkey
daughter of Johann Christian Heinrich Roelkey
1835-1923

6. Dorothee Wilhelmine Sophie 1-15-1835 to 8-19-1923 m. Benjamin Cook (5-13-1834 to 5-13-1889) on July 4, 1860 in Frederick, Maryland. They had six children.
   A. Clara Maria 7-6-1861 to 10-8-1955 m. Joseph Henry Ferdinand Hahn (5-25-1860 to 11-6-1927) on 10-30-1884 in Frederick County, Maryland
      (1) Edgar Ferdinand 7-27-1885 to 10-8-1970 m. Carrie Elizabeth Hermann (1-21-1886) on 10-3-1907
         (a) Mildred Elizabeth 6-8-1911 to 7-11-1993 m Marion Justice Ingram (7-16-1909 to 5-31-1960) on 9-4-1935
            i. Infant

ii. Betty Jane 2-19-1942 m. Roland V. Lynch (7-13-1935) on
     6-11-1961
  iii. Judy Carol 12-7-1946 m. Andrew Vincent Curreri (3-5-1942 to
     3-31-1992) on 12-12-1964.
 (b) Irving Henry 5-8-1887 to 10-10-1966 m. Hermine Roschen on
     1-26-1909
    i. Irvin Henry Ferdinand 5-6-1917 m. Jessie Hilda Warren
       (11-22-1922) on 8-8-1942.
      a. Jessie Warren 3-2-1944 m. Barry Rodner in June of 1968
 (c) Clara Viola 12-8-1888 to 11-9-1974
 (d) Mildred Elizabeth 10-1-1891
(2) John Henry 2-14-1864 to 12-?-1938 m. Adelia V. Bankerd on
    4-29-1885 and also Carrie Behr and Ruby Becker.
(3) Alice Josephine 7-21-1866 to 1-13-1869
(4) Philip Thomas 3-17-1869 to 3-31-1870
(5) Katherine Elizabeth 2-10-1871 to 3-3-1968 m. J. Frank Baetjar on
    1-14-1897 in Frederick, Maryland
   (a) Ruth 4-14-1898
   (b) Anna Medora 7-7-1899
(6) Joseph Edward 8-31-1874 to 12-17-1937 m. Ida Ellsworth Deunger
    (1872 to 9-25-1966)

Edward Roelkey
son of Johann Christian Heinrich Roelkey
1837-1881

7. Edward 11-8-1837 to 2-12-1881 m. Alice V. Himbury (1840 to 11-17-1915) on March 20, 1860 in Frederick County, Maryland. She was the daughter of John B. and Julia Ann Hooper Himbury.

Heinrich Friedrich Wilhelm Roelkey
Son of Johann Conrad Rolcke
1802-1853

6. Heinrich Friedrich Wilhelm 20-2-1802 to May 1853 married Christena Wilhemina Biene (1802 to 9-13-1875. She was born in Bavaria, Germany. They are buried in Mt. Olivet Cemetery in Frederick, Maryland. They had four children
   A. Sophia Ronna Charlotte Elizabeth 8-26-1829 to 5-1905 m. Conrad
      Murkhardt (11-18-1817 to 5-28-1871) on 1-1-1850 in Frederick
      County, Maryland, buried in Mt. Olivet Cemetery, Frederick,
      Maryland.
      (1) Ernestine Wilhelmina 11-5-1852 to 11-13-1938 buried in Mt. Olivet
          Cemetery, Frederick, Md.
      (2) Clara Sophia 9-17-1864

(3) Emma Clementine 5-12-1867 m. Mr. Stowe
(4) Charles Denton 8-3-1856
(5) Anna Virginia Palmeltio 5-28-1862 to 1-1-1871 brd in Mt. Olivet, Frederick, Maryland
(6) James Cornelius 5-28-1869
(7) Mary E.

B. George A. 11-25-1835 to 8-31-1915 m. first Charlotte Sarah Mix (5-28-1840 to 3-7-1862) on 10-19-1857. They had three children. After her death he married Mary Jane Veney Jordan (4-1-1844 to 3-22-1897) on 4-11-1864 in Frederick County, Maryland. They are buried in Mt.Olivet Cemetery, Frederick, Maryland.
(1) Mary Elizabeth Susan 5-3-1858
(2) Laura Wilhelmina Bertha 5-25-1860 m. Jesse Crum
   (a) Jesse
   (b) Pauline
   (c) Vinona
   (d) Mary
   (e) Frances
   (f) Arthur
   (g) Harold
   (h) Alton
   (i) Evelyn
(3) Ludwig Wilhelm 5-25-1860
(4) Clara A. Virginia 2-17-1865 m. Charles E. Moberly (1865-1941)
   (a) Infant
(5) Eugene George Augustus 1-31-1867 to 11-1-1953 m. Susan Christena Rickerd (5-16-1873 to 2-15-1935) on 4-4-1893 in Frederick, Maryland. They are buried in Mt. Olivet Cemetery, Frederick, Maryland.
   (a) Mary Lillian 1-29-1894 married Nicholas H. Haller
      i. Eugene
      ii. Helen
   (b) Charles E. 9-11-1855 to 9-11-1895
   (c) Lewis George 7-17-1896 to 12-24-1975 m. Fanny Schutzman
      i. Jerry Roelkey
   (d) Franklin 1897 m. Evelyn Magaha
      i. Philip Michael 8-28-1944
      ii. Blaine Franlin
      iii. Susan Marie 9-27-1947
   (e) Roger Eugene 9-8-1898 m. Grace A. Welty
      i. Betty C. 9-25-1926 m. John Helfrich
      ii. Mary m. Seibert C. Shifler

iii. Delores Jean m. Emil Richard Notnagle
(f) Albert Austin T. R. 1-1-1900 to 8-9-1901 brd in Mt. Olivet Cemetery, Frederick, Maryland
(g) Harry Edward m. Madeline Jelariv
   i. Robert
   ii. Dorothy
   iii. Marian
(h) Helena Christina 3-26-1905 1-20-1958 m. Melvin Decker, Clarence H. Yinger on 3-1-1930, and Howard D. Herrold on 3-19-1937.
(i) Edna Louise 4-27-1908 m. Ralph Howard
(6) Lucy M. 4-8-1869 to 1-3-1876 brd in Mt. Olivet Cemetery, Frederick, Maryland
(7) Harry Edward 11-9-1874 to 5-3-1867 m. Bessie Ennis Lane (4-20-1883 to 3-15-1963) They are buried at Mt. Olivet Cemetery, Mt. Olivet, Frederick, Maryland.
(8) Lougene 1876
(9) Florence Christina 8-23-1877 m. Louis W. Bennett on 11-7-1900
   (a) Margaret
(10) George William Marshall 1878 m. Margaret Rosenmarkle (1866-1935) on 10-11-1897 in Frederick County, Maryland.
   (a) Mary Margaret 3-22-1898
   (b) Allen Millard 10-21-1899 m. Ruth Dinterman
      i. Nancy Eaton
   (c) Paul Eugene 1-2-1901
   (d) George Alexander 6-29-1904 m. Grace H. Hoke on 9-18-1935
      i. Sylvia Ann 2-11-1937
      ii. Susan Nora 2-21-1946
   (e) Lawrence William 11-5-1905 m. Ruth Curfman
      i. Carolyn
      ii. Lawrence William, Jr.
      iii. Catherine
(11) Lee Alexander 4-27-1879 to 10-24-1881 brd in Mt. Olivet Cemetery, Frederick, Maryland
(12) Viola May 6-5-1882 to 1-28-1946 m. George Henry Barnes Moberly (11-10-1881 to 9-15-1940) on 2-24-1907 in Frederick County, Maryland. They are buried in Mt. Olivet Cemetery, Frederick County, Maryland
   (a) Florence
   (b) Arthur
   (c) Gerald
(13) Arthur Grover 10-7-1884 to 10-30-1918 m. Edna Estelle Miller (4-6-1884 to 3-7-1967) on 4-29-1909 in Frederick County, Maryland. They are buried in Mt. Olivet Cemetery, Frederick, Maryland.

(a) Gertrude C. 3-17-1910 to Alvin C. Doering, Jr. (2-10-1862 to 10-13-1907) on 10-27-1934 in Thurmont, Frederick County, Maryland.
  i. Cynthia
(b) Hjalmar Ernestine 8-12-1911 to 10-24-1876 m. Nathan J. Baile in 1933, and then married Franklin Lee Thomas (1-19-1908 to 2-1-1978) on 11-26-1943. One child from each union.
  i. Gertrude Marie 1934
  ii. Arnold Lee 6-29-1947
(c) Arthur Arnold 11-9-1913 to 11-16-1917 brd in Mt. Olivet Cemetery, Frederick, Maryland
(d) Winifred Miller 10-27-1918 to 3-6-1983 m. John William Molesworth III (5-16-1915 to 9-6-1988) on 7-1-1936 in Rockville, Montgomery County, Maryland. They are buried in Mt. Olivet Cemetery, Frederick, Maryland.
  i. John William IV
  ii. Carol Ann
  iii. David Arthur 4-10-1957
C. Daniel Edward 6-5-1838 to 1-2-1911 m. first Mary Catherine Young (11-1-1844 to 1-2-1871) on 3-10-1863. She was a daughter of Joshua and Mary Dertzbaugh Young. They had four children. He then m. Virginia J. Orndorff (3-15-1850 to 2-17-1919) in 1871.
 (1) Mary Annetta Sophia 9-20-1864 to 4-1-1937 m. Marshall E. Hagan (3-18-1864 to 8-5-1934). They are buried in Mt. Olivet Cemetery, Frederick, Maryland.
    (a) Carl
    (b) John
    (c) Calvert
    (d) Catherine
 (2) David
 (3) Mary Catherine 5-20-1868 to 5-2-1916 m. Benjamin Franklin Zimmerman (2-20-1871 to 10-5-1950). They are buried in Mt. Olivet Cemetery, Frederick, Maryland.
    (a) Rhudelia Catherine
    (b) Lester Nicodemus
    (c) Tobias E. 1890 to 12-7-1964 m. Mabel M. Ausherman
      i. Dorothy
      ii. Margaret
      iii. Richard E.
      iv. George
      v. Daniel Edward, Jr.
      vi. Francis D. 1879
      vii. Lovaletta 7-24-1882

D. Maria E. H. F. W. 7-30-1843 to 8-25-1854 brd in Mt. Olivet Cemetry, Frederick, Maryland

Oedelsheim Reformed Church

WOLFE

Johann Heinrich Wolfe was born in 1726 in Hundsback ad Rhinum, Germany. He married Maria Margaretta and came to Frederick, Maryland in the mid-1750's. His children were confirmed in churches in Frederick County and married into local families. His eight children were:

   1. Johann Peter 1754 m. Catherine Brunner on 6-23-1780
   2. Johannes   1755
   3. Catherine A. 1756 m. Elisha Griffith on 8-27-1781 in Frederick Co.
   4. Elizabeth   1757 m. Michael Drew on 5-3-1781 in Frederick Co.
   5. Margaret   1758 m. John Smith 1-10-1787
   6. Johann Henry 1760 m. Sarah Hyatt 4-13-1782 Frederick Co.
   7. Jacob   1770 - 5-3-1832 m. Ann Welch 6-20-1795,
                    then Anna Mary Christina Welch
♦   8. **George Friedrich, Sr.**, 1775

      8. George Wolfe, Sr. married Lavinia Hyatt, widow of William Richards. The children from her first marriage are listed in the Hyatt section of this book. George and his family were founders of the Hyattstown Christian Church.

      One of the denominational founders, Alexander Campbell, came through Hyattstown on a preaching tour in March of 1834. His other stops were Beaver Creek, Boonesboro and Williamsport. Groups of believers began meeting in homes and organized by 1840. The founders of this congregation were: Eli Wolfe, William Richards, Jr., Charlotte (his wife), Lavinia Hyatt, Sarah (her daughter), and William E. Anderson. Other early members included the George Wolfe family, including a very young Joel Wolfe.

      Robert H. Ferguson was called as a circuit preacher for Gunpowder, Hyattstown and Rockville. He undoubtedly baptized our Wolfes in Little Bennett Creek, but the church records have been discarded. The building was completed in 1845, a simple log structure, south of town, adjacent to the cemetery on land from the Price's farm.

      A cornerstone was laid for the present structure in 1870 and it was dedicated on August 20, 1871, with about 40 members present. The parsonage was added in 1922. In 1925 the road bed south of town was changed and as a result, the graveyard is now on the east side of Frederick Road. One now enters the cemetery facing the back of the tombstones, and on your left are George Wolfe Jr., Joel and Garrott and their families, fairly near the location that the original church building was. For the older stones of Eli, Josiah and their contemporaries are to the right. The building was moved to the top of Long Hill in 1871 and served as the Montgomery Chapel.

      George Wolfe, Sr. married Lavinia Hyatt, the widow of William Richard's, Sr., the former miller of Hyattstown. When William Richard's died, the deed to the mill property had not been recorded accurately and, by a decree of the chancery of the state of Maryland, the mill and the surrounding 20 acres of "Ivy Reach," "Hard

Struggle" and "Resurvey on Discovery was sold to George Wolfe, Sr. on August 17 1807. All of his children were born at this house, as he was living with the widow of the former owner. George Sr. and Lavinia Wolfe had six children:

    A. **Sarah Ann**   1798 m. Elijah Price, farmer
    B. Elizabeth   1799 m. Caleb Moxley January 22, 1821
    C. **Eli**   1801 to 1871 m. Caroline Ann Hyatt
    D. John   1803 died young
♦   E. **George Jr.** 8-20-1806 to 10-27-1868) m. Mary Davis
    F. Josiah   12-26-1812 to 4-18-1849 m. Ann Lee Beall 1838

A. Sarah Ann Wolfe (1798) married Levi Price and lived near Hyattstown, in Frederick Co., Md. They are buried on the family farm. He was a son of Thomas and Hannah Price.

    (1) Charles 2-20-1838 to 7-27-1896 m. Sarah Warfield Day
    (2) Daniel 1832 m. Laura V. Watkins
    (3) Elizabeth 9-3-1834 to 8-22-1932 m. George Wallace Davis 1862
    (4) George Wolfe 9-15-1840 to 5-16-1918 m. Eunice Ann Day
    (5) Levi 11-1835 m. Laura Virginia McElfresh (see that section)
    (6) Thomas 1826 m. Sarah Eleanor Phillips
    (7) William H. 2-11-1827 to 4-13-1896 m. Ann R.
    (8) Eli 4-5-1831 to 2-29-1904 m. Ann Rebecca Burgee

C. Eli (1801 to 6-1871) was a farmer and the Magistrate of Hyatt's Town. He married Caroline Ann Hyatt (1802 to 4-1862) of Jesse Hyatt and Ann Riggs. They had seven children.

    (1) Dr. John Hammond Riggs   1829
    (2) Dr. James Milton DDS   1830
    (3) Ann Clarinda   8-13-1833 m. Jesse Hyatt in Poolesville
    (4) Catherine Davis Wolfe   1-27-1835 m. Luther L. Hyatt
    (5) Jesse Hyatt   10-4-1837 to 5-1-1921 farmer & Justice of the Peace m. Laura Dorcas Hyatt (7-30-1848 to 9-28-1930)
        (a) Maggie Boone Dorsey Wolfe 6-3-1879 to 6-17-1932 m. Charles P. Ryan (1881)
          i. Mary Hyatt Ryan 1909 to 1-7-1996 m. Townsend W. Kirtland
          ii. James Wolfe Ryan 1912
        (b) Norman Hyatt Wolfe 7-4-1880 to 3-21-1969 m. Dora M. Padgett (1874-1940)
    (6) son   1839 died infant
    (7) Mary Dorcas   1840 m. Theodore Benton

E. George Jr. (8-20-1806 to 10-27-1868) was married to Mary Davis in 1828 by Rev. James Day. They had seven children. He was a carpenter and lived at Mt. Zion, present-day site of Old Georgetown Road at Democracy Blvd. They attended

the Baptist Church, which is now called Wildwood, and a one-room school which was on the site of Walter Johnson High School. Their Bible records are in my possession.
  (1) William 3-28-1830 m. Sarah E. Mary Eller, Hester Lawson
    (a) E. Gertrude Wolfe 1859-1939 m. Charles F. Grubbs
    (b) Ollie Ruth Wolfe 2-9-1872 to 4-14-1925 m. George Frederick Linthicum
    (c) George Wolfe 1873
    (d) James Clifford Wolfe 4-6-1875 to 8-19-1908 m. Louise Stone
    (e) Beulah m. Mr. Fishback.
  (2) Eli   11-11-1832 to 2-15-1870
  (3) Mary Elizabeth 2-13-1834 died young.
◆ (4) **Joel Hamilton** 5-17-1837 to 2-25-1910 m. Anna Mary Linthicum
  (5) Lavinia 2-30-1840 to 8-6-1926 m. James Milton W. Davis
    (a) William
    (b) Nicetas m. William H. Dutrow
    (c) Elbert Davis
  (6) Zacharieh 10-6-1842 m. Henrietta Dorsey
    (a) Grace Wolfe
  (7) Susannah Rebecca 6-25-1846 to 7-1895 m. Augustus Flack in 1864.
    (a) Bruce 1866
    (b) Lawrence 1868
    (c) Valerie
  (8) George Davis III 9-22-1849

  (4) Joel Hamilton Wolfe (1837-1910, attended Mt. Zion schoolhouse and Mt. Zion Baptist Church. He and his wife were founding members of the Barnesville Baptist Church. They lived in Sellman when the first two boys were born, and then purchased a house in Barnesville, next to William T. Hilton. He was to married Anna Mary Linthicum on February 3, 1865. Sometimes Joel would accept goods for his services instead of cash. There are records of people giving him carriages, buckboards, etc. After mortgaging the Barnesville house, he sold it and moved to Comus. The land where the Comus Inn is now, was patented in 1790, and sold to the Johnson's. The well house dates to 1794. The chicken house is the building which was later used as the "antique shop" and the "wedding chapel" was the barn. The smoke house is unused. When Joel and Annie Mary purchased the two-story chinked log cabin, it was too small for their growing family, so in 1879 Joel hired his former neighbor, noted area builder, William T. Hilton, who incorporated the log cabin into a frame house. An addition was added in 1890. The house was moved back from the original location closer to the road, to its present location in 1960. The stumps of the trees that you can see by the road are in the 1900 family photograph as full grown trees. In 1903 Joel sold the property back to the Johnson family, and sold the blacksmith shop to his former apprentice, Henry Kennedy. Joel and Annie had seven children. Annie died in childbirth with the seventh child. Her tombstone reads:

♦   (a) **Garrott Davis**   6-24-1866 to 1-17-1941 m. Lillian G. Cecil
     (b) **George Maurice**   1-19-1868 to 6-21-1951 m. Mary Frances Beall
     (c) **Myrtle Mayfield**   1-9-1870 to 7-12-1934
     (d) **Myra Hannah**   1874 to 7-27-1940 m. Aquilla Walker
     (e) **Mary France**   2-22-1880 to 11-11-1955 m. James R. Nutter
     (f) Ethel   1-7-1881 to 8-26-1881
     (g) infant   8-30-1889 to 8-30-1889

(a) Garrott Davis Wolfe attended the Mountain School diagonally opposite his house (which is now Comus Inn). Garrott Davis Wolfe and Lillie Cecil Wolfe were married in the parlor of the Cecil house on the road between Comus and Hyattstown, by Thomas J. Cross The witnesses were family and friends. They lived first in a small log cabin near Thurston, where their first child was born. They were living in Montgomery County when the second child was born, but the other children where born at 1542 Columbia Street, Washington, DC . They had eight children. They are buried in Hyattstown Christian Cemetery.

♦   i. **John Linthicum**   12-24-1888 to 3-1-1977
     ii. **Janie Rolke**   11-12-1890 to 4-9-1892
     iii. **Mrya Estelle**   9-24-1892 to 8-9-1956
     iv. **Lillian Gertrude** 3-28-1895 to 8-19-1967
     v. **Garrott Walker**   8-24-1897 to 2-13-1960
     vi. **Alice Pauline**   4-15-1901 to 4-27-1992
     vii. **Cecil**   8-1-1903 to 11-21-1985
     viii. **Charles Lewis**   9-22-1907 to 2-16-1994

i. John Linthicum Wolfe attended Polk School at 7th & P in Washington, DC. In 1906 John was in the eighth grade, that was the highest grade in grammar school at that time. His report card lists the subjects that he was taking: Arithmetic, Grammar and Language, Penmanship, Reading, Spelling, History and Civics, Alge

John and Nettie Lenora Beall were married on September 3, 1913 in the Brightwood Park Methodist Episcopal Parsonage, by Charles S. Cole. The witnesses were Minor Cecil and Gertie Clifford. They had three children. They are buried in Rock Creek Cemetery.

     a. John Kavanaugh   8-5-1914 m. Mary Alexander Hodge
♦   b. Ethel Louise   4-22-1918 m. Lester William Hebbard
     c. Ralph Elmer   10-8-1923 to 8-8-1945

John later was the Superintendent of the Brightwood Station and then Supervisor of carriers at the Benjamin Franklin Station and was later Supervisor at the main Post Office. He retired after 50 years in 1957. He was a member of the Stansbury Lodge #24 and Ruth Chapter of the Eastern Star #1, and a member of Berwyn Presbyterian Church, after they moved to New Carrollton.

     a. Jack attended the University of Maryland and invented the "Drinking

Bird." Ethel has one of the prototypes. He married Mary Alexander Hodge on 12-30-1939. Jack worked for G. E. in New York. They had three children.
    I. Joyce Ann   6-19-1947 m. John Smothers on March 29, 1969. had Laura Jane 2-28-1984.
    II. Ralph Douglas 9-23-1949 to 9-8-1993 m Betty Gilbreath, had Lucy 8-11-1983 and Jack 9-5-1986
    III. John Richard   3-31-1952 m1 Virginia Gordan 8-1975-1990 m2 Sandra Whitsell 9-7-1990.

    b. Ethel worked for the National Geographic, for Dr. Forster, a dentist, Stone's Mercantile Agency and retired from NIH as a printing specialist. She married Lester William Hebbard on April 17, 1937. They had two daughters.
    I. Louise Ethel   5-21-1938 m1. Donald Arthur Cuttler (10-29-1933 to 6-11-1977) buried at Ft. Lincoln-Masonic Section November 26, 1958 had Dona Lou 9-27-1961 m2. William Monell Ehlers April 12, 1980
    II. Peggy Ann   5-21-1943 m. Denton J. Wolford

    c. Ralph Wolfe graduated from McKinley High School and attended Maryland University for two years before World War II. He went to Pensacola for training, and then served in the Naval Air Corp. Ensign Wolfe's last message was "Strafed and beached three enemy motor torpedo boats, continuing mission assigned."

    ii. Janie Roelke Wolfe (11-12-1890 to 4-9-1893) was named for her grandmother. She was born in Montgomery County and contracted diphtheria. She died when she was two and a half. She was buried in the Hyattstown Christian Cemetery, in the family plot. Grandmother Wolfe taught her children to pray "and take us to live with Janie."

    iii. Myra Estelle Wolfe (9-24-1892 to 8-9-1956) was born at 1542 Columbia Street and died in Bethesda. She is buried at Forest Oaks, Gaithersburg. She attended Business High School and worked in a photography studio. I am so grateful that she took so many pictures at the farm and of the family. She married Robert Hamilton Walker (1-24-1885 to 1938). They lived on New Jersey Avenue, and had a house in Washington Grove. Her sons were born in Sibley Hospital.
    a. **Samuel Hamilton**   10-17-1914 to 2-9-1994
    b. **Robert Custis**   11-30-1916 to 10-13-1982
    c. **Richard Garrott**   8-12-1919 to 2000

    Samuel moved to Florida in 1961 where he worked as an architect with local contractors. He helped design the Pinellas County Courthouse, was a member of the AA and Vintage Thunderbird Club of America, was a graduate of George Washington University, member of Sigma Chi, and served in the Navy in World War II. He married Betty Jarvis and they had Albert, Edwin, Beverly (m. Morrano) and Karen

(m. Summers). Bobby m. Bette Burch and they had Robert H. Walker and Christy. Dick m. Dorothy Chiswell on August 2, 1942. They had two children. Richard Garrott Jr. 10-2-1945 m. Barbara Goswell, had Kristenn & Scott. Joan Lynn Walker 2-28-1951 m. Robert H. Pope, had Zach & Zeb.

The Walker immigrants were three brothers who were forced to flee from Scotland to France, temporarily. Isaac was married to Mary Stuart, who eventually came also. They had four children, and moved to Kentucky. His brother Charles had a son Zachary.

The third brother, Nathan, was born in 1756 and died 12-28-1842. He married first, Nancy Baggerly, and they had three children. Henry B., Nathan and Elizabeth Ann. He married second, Elizabeth Thomas on April 10, 1810. They had seven children.

   A. Jonathan Thomas   8-4-1811
   B. Nathan   12-8-1812 to 11-1839
   C. Catherine   4-30-1814 m. John Beall
   D. Jane   7-20-1815
   E. Samuel Hamilton   2-24-1817
   F. Charles E.   12-15-1818
   G. Mary Thomas   11-28-1820

A. Jonathan married Jane Amelia Benson of Cephas Webb Benson and Annie Harvey Benson. Jane was born on 7-3-1813. This information was excerpted from a history compiled for their fiftieth wedding anniversary. They were married on October 13, 1833. They had twelve children.

   (1) James Thomas   8-10-1834 m. Maria Gittings 3-20-1860
   (2) Elizabeth Jane   9-18-1836 m. William Wharton Lester 2-9-1858
   (3) Martha Ellen   6-2-1838 to 6-19-1839
   (4) Charles Henry   12-8-1839 m. Mary Creaser 7-17-1862
   (5) William   7-8-1841 to 7-14-1841
   (6) John Newland   7-30-1842 m. Louise Duvall 10-6-1874
   (7) Samuel Hamilton   6-7-1844 m. Sallie Brady 11-1-1853
      (had Robert Hamilton, see above)
   (8) George Newton   11-7-1846 m. Elenia P. Brannan 5-2-1862
   (9) Oscar Reese   9-15-1848 to 12-22-1851
   (10) Francis Davis   10-25-1850
   (11) Alice Cemelia   12-21-1852 m. Grafton CD Townsend 5-17-1877
   (12) Edward Spedden   6-4-1855 m. Sophronia Duckett 5-17-1877

   iv. Lillian Gertrude Wolfe (3-28-1895 to 8-19-1967) was born at 1542 Columbia Street, and attended Business High School. She married Edward Brooke Harry. Sr. His grandparents were Rebecca French (1838 to 5-8-1880) and John Henry Harry (1-18-1838 to 1915). They were married in 1861 and had John Bernard Harry (9-27-1867 to 11-6-1972) who married Sabra Woodward on June 4, 1894. John and

Sabra had six children
- A. Edward Brooke   4-5-1895
- B. Ida Adele   2-18-1897
- C. Sabra Amelia   2-13-1902
- D. Lawrence Woodward   10-7-1903
- E. Alice Elizabeth   10-20-1906
- F. Helen Rebecca   6-23-1908 to 4-24-1997

Ed and Lillian resided at 4303 River Road, Washington, and had three children.
  a. Mary Elizabeth   3-29-1923 m. John Sanford
    I. Peter B.   10-4-1945 had Cameron Sanford 10-6-1985
    II. John Woodward 3-4-1948 m. Maryelle Gravier (10-18-1950) on 4-3-1971. They had Valarie Elizabeth 4-12-1975 and Caline Francois 7-27-1979
    III. Edward Brooke Jr. 7-24-1924 m1 Betty Lee Payne (1-17-1923 to 8-3-1984) on January 31, 1945. They had three sons.

Edward Brooke III 5-10-1954 m. Terri Jeanette Sheaffer had
  G. William 3-14-1980 & Daniel Sheaffer 10-25-1983.

Jason Dean 5-3-1957 m. Karla Cleek (5-22-1957) on August 4, 1979. They had four children.
- Drew Erikson 9-19-1983
- Lane Edward 9-8-1987 to 10-26-1989
- Hope   10-13-1990 to 10-13-1990
- Hannah Lee   2-6-1992

David Kent 11-25-1958 m. Jamie Sue McCaslin (4-20-1962) on June 14, 1986. They had two children.
- Dylan Kent   7-9-1989
- Lillian Paige 11-12-1991

Edward Brooke m2 Marilyn J. Spaan (8-16-1939 to 9-1996) on June 3, 1993 m3 Sally

    III. John Bernard 10-18-1928 m. Jane Weiss (9-16-1929) on October 5, 1957 They had three children.
- John Bernard III 7-16-1958 m Amy Rachel Meyerson
- Jennifer Lynch 5-27-1960 m. Austin Damien Cullen
- Janet Elizabeth 8-24-1963

  v. Garrott Walker Wolfe (8-24-1897 to 2-13-1960) was called "Happy" after a comic strip character (Happy Hooligan). He was a graduate of Business High School. He married Mercer Smith, and his brother John and sister-in-law Nettie were the attendants. They resided at 6510 5th Street and had a summer cottage at Breezy Point. Happy worked for the IRS Collections Office as a Planning Officer. He was a member of The Presbyterian Church of the Pilgrims, Stansbury Lodge, Almas Temple, played in the Shriner's Band and was an avid amateur radio operator. They are buried in Rock Creek Cemetery.

vi. **Alice Pauline** (4-15-1901 to 4-27-1992) attended Central High School, and in a German class met Kenneth Allen. She failed the class, but found a life long partner. They were married on June 5, 1920. They first lived in TB, (near Brandywine) where he farmed and built a mail order house. They eventually moved to Brooklyn and raised their five daughters there.

    a. **Lillian Cecil**   3-17-1922
    b. **Margaret Isabel**   11-1-1924
    c. **Dona Lee**   9-28-1927
    d. **Sara Jane**   7-29-1932
    e. **Pauline Marie**   6-5-1934

a. Lillian Cecil Allen was born in Sibley Hospital in Washington, DC. She married Frank Frye on July 23, 1943. They had three sons.

    I. Paul Allen   8-17-1944 m1 Sherilyn Brunnenmeyer 1-6-1963
        Patricia Lynn 10-16-1963 had Brittany Nicole 4-8-1987
                          Kimberly 3-1-2001
        Michael Darren 5-24-1968 m. Rhonda had Dallas Michael
                7-17-1994 m2 Barbara Kyle (8-1-1948) in 1969
                        Shannon Cathleen 2-11-1971
    II. Peter Jay   2-7-1949 m1 Doris Ann Perks 5-2-1967
                Paula Ann 2-9-1968 m. Timothy John Flanangan
                8-1-1987 had Somer Leighlan 10-11-90
                m2 Bonnie Jean Anthony Urquhart 5-23-1980
    III. Thomas William 11-10-1953 m Patricia Ann Corbin
        on 2-24-1993

b. Peggy Allen (11-1-1924 to 5-22-1994) was born in Sibley Hospital in Washington, DC. She married Jack Curtwright McClure, Jr. on February 21, 1943. They had two sons. After Jack died in 1964, Peggy married Kenneth Johnson on March 12, 1982. He died 9-19-1989.

    I. Jack Curtwright III 5-10-1944 m1 Marilyn Mermel had Adam 9-20-1970
        m2 Katherine Rogers
    II. Kenneth Allen 10-15 1947 m1 Glynda Howard had Vicki Raquel
        7-16-1968
        Kenny Jr. 4-15-1970 m1 Kristy Parrish 5-27-1989
        had Chelsea 11-2-1989
        m2 Beverly Arredondo 9-9-1989 had Ryan James 7-23-1993

c. Dona Lee (9-28-1927) was married to Leonard Tyson Murphy from 1948 until he died in 1963. She married Fred Erb on July 5, 1964, he died March 3, 1997.

d. Sara Jane (7-29-1932) was born in Columbia Hospital For Women, Washington, DC. She was a school nurse, worked in an ambulance, was an ob nurse in Holmes Regional Medical Center in Melbourne, Florida. She married LeRoy C. Harris (12-31-1930) on August 29, 1953. They had four children and were married until 1979. She married Raymond J. Mayerle (1-18-1929 to 5-31-1997) on May 5,

1984.
    i. Susan Janet   4-15-1956 m1 Mark Snyder 9-20-1975-1979
                                   m2 Cab Carlan on August 20, 1993
    ii. Ellen June   4-22-1957 m1 Brian Murray
                                   m2 Thomas Vallone 1979-1983
    iii. Karen Jane   7-4-1960   m1 Stephan Parish on July 8, 1978 to 1987
                                   had Shannon Cathleen 8-28-1982
    iv. Lee Allen   7-20-1961 m. Linda Jean Hadley July 8, 1989 had
                                 Lee Allen Jr. 7-16-1992

    e. Pauline Marie Allen (6-5-1934) was the only daughter to be born in Brooklyn. She was married to Fred Schramm from February 27, 1954 to November 9, 1988. They had two sons. She married Frank Burkhart December 20, 1973, he died in March of 2000.
        i. Donald Allyn 11-22-1954 to 4-20-1992
        ii. Gary Edward 2-21-1958 m. Joyce Rotramel had Gary E. Jr. 6-9-1979

    f. Cecil Wolfe (8-1-1903 to 11-21-1985) married Pierre McFarland Bealer (8-10-1897 to 7-11-1976) on June 16, 1920.
        i. Ernestine 6-28-1924 m1 Ray Barnett (6-30-1920 to 5-29-1954).
            I. Leigh Cecil   8-25-1946 m. John Vincent Walker
                Edwin Bradley 5-26-1979
                Laura Newman 11-28-1981
            II. Judith Lynn 10-25-1947 m. Dennis Alton Dutterer
                Andrew Dennis 9-15-1978
                Emily Barnett 2-6-1982
            III. Robert Alton 5-22-1952 m. Mary Bailey Fellars May 8, 1981
                Rainey 8-12-1983
                Elizabeth Bealer 11-3-1986
Ernestine m2 Roland Tcherkezian (1-17-1929) on July 10, 1956.
            IV. Mark Bealer   9-13-1958 m. Lisa Bates September 25, 1981.
                Mark Jr. 10-4-1987
                Matthew Allen 6-8-1989
                Kathleen Bates 12-31-1991
                Luke Wolfe 11-10-1995
            V. Harold Pierre "Happy" 6-17-1963

    g. Charles Lewis Wolfe (9-22-1907 to 2-16-1994) enlisted in the Marines from 7-27-1931 to 3-12-1934. Following that, he was in the National Guard 6-21-1940 as Company Clerk. The Army was next, on 1-6-1941 as 1st Sergeant Headquarters Battery, 2nd Battalion, 260th Co. He served at McChord AFB and was assigned to Dutch Harbor, Alaska where his company's designation was changed to 380th AA. He met Evelyn June Gipple (6-4-1917) on a blind date that a friend had set up on Christmas Eve, 1942. They were married on April 2, 1943 in Takoma, Washington. He was transferred in 1944 to Riverside, CA, then to Camp Livingston, LA to train NCO's to be reassigned to the Battle of the Bulge. In 1945 he was Sgt. Major at Madigan Army Hospital, and later a Personnel Officer. He shipped out for Korea in July of 1950, and by 1953 was in Bayreuth, Germany. June of 1956 was Ft. Still, OK, and then on to Hawaii as the Personnel Officer of the 21st Artillery, where his two sons joined the Army. He was discharged after returning to Madigan Army Hospital after 32 years, 8 months of service.

    i. Thomas Edward 12-10-1939 m. Lynn Marie Loomis
       (8-29-1946) on August 6, 1965
         Alisa Marie 12-28-1966
         Jolie Sue 11-15-1969
    ii. Jo Ann 11-13-1943 m. Jared Dean Burbank (8-11-1939)
       on January 27, 1964.
       Jared Dean Jr. 4-12-1965
       Deborah Dawn 10-11-1967 m. Joe Trembly (4-6-1961) on
         January 29, 1993 Had Taylor Noelle 3-2-1996
    iii. Charles Lewis Jr. 5-13-1945 m. Linda Lou Neat (12-5-1949)
       on October 27, 1972
       Kelly Lou 1-13-1975
       Randall Lewis 1-2-1976 m. Tanya Lieb (2-27-1976) on April 2,
       1995   Jacob Lewis 12-12-1995.

(b) George Maurice Wolfe (1-19-1868 to 6-21-1951) He courted Mary Frances Beall in Greenfield, by riding his horse around Sugarloaf Mountain. They were married in the living room of her home on April 22, 1896. They moved to Linden where he had a store and ran the Post Office when the B & O railroad started the town. Later, Maurice was the Superintendent of Grounds and Maintenance, and the Manager of Purchasing for the National Park Seminary. They had three children. They are buried in Mt. Olivet Cemetery, Frederick, Md.

    i. James Newton   2-7-1897 to 8-30-1897
    ii. Mary Frances   2-28-1903 to 4-28-1995
    iii. Margaret Beall   8-30-1905 m. Howard Reford Aldridge
       on April 27, 1929
       a. James Reford 9-16-1931 m. Patricia Marie Baker
         March 27, 1971 had Edward 7-18-1972 d. 1973 and
         Elisabeth Beall 11-18-1975
       b. William Francis 12-7-1945 m1 Diane Robeson had Kevin
         Michael 7-6-1972 and Michelle Lee 9-7-1974
         m2 Nickie 6-7-1989

Frances attended the Seminary and she and her sister attended Rockville High School and University of Maryland. Frances worked for the Agriculture Department, and gave lectures on nutrition at area schools. Frances also went to homes in rural areas to document what health standards and modern conveniences the lady of the house had.

(c) Myrtle Mayfield Wolfe (1-9-1870 to 7-12-1934) attended the Comus School and was a member of the Comus Southern Methodist Church before transferring to the Barnesville Baptist Church. After moving to Washington, DC she became a nurse. She completed her training in 1909, and I am very glad to have her class ring. She lived on Westminster Street and worked for Dr. Hadley at the Homeopathic Hospital. She was a patient, kind, warm person, and I think that really shows in her portrait. She is buried in the Wolfe family plot in the Christian Cemetery, Long Hill, Hyattstown, Her tombstone is inscribed "I Know That My Redeemer Liveth."

(d) Myra Wolfe attended the Comus School and then became a school teacher at the Hyattstown School. Myra represented the Barnesville Baptist Church at annual conference for several years, and was active in the Sunday School. Myra retired from teaching and married Aquilla Ridgeway Walker (b. 1876). He got a job with Kanakee Coffee Company in Washington, DC and moved to 8th Street. Her father, Joel, was staying there when he died. Myra cried so profusely at his funeral that her face turned black, from the dye of her veil running. Myra and Quill are buried in Glenwood Cemetery. They had three daughters.

   i. Helen   1903 m. Mr. Day. She died in FL
   ii. Margaret Ridgeway 1906 m. Mr. Grace brd. Glenwood
   iii. Annie Mary   1915

(e) France (2-22-1880 to 11-11-1955) attended Comus School and then went into nursing, obtaining her degree from the Homeopathic Hospital in Washington, DC. She married James Richard Nutter (3-13-1882 to 2-18-1957) on February 14, 1912 in the living room her sister's home, 913 Westminster Street NW. He ran the Capitol Ltd. for the B & O Railroad. They lived in Brunswick, where their two children were born. They are buried in Cumberland, Allegheny Co., Md.

   i. Mary Margaret 9-24-1913 to 2-1998
   ii. Richard Wolfe 12-25-1918 to 2-11-1919 brd Hyattstown Chr. Cemetery

Garrott Wolfe's Family

John L. Wolfe Family

Home of Joel Wolfe in 1900, Comus

5505 Fifth Street, N. W.

LINTHICUM

The name Linthicum is found in the southern part of England spelled as Linscombe. The people in this region were extremely proud that their part of England never had succumbed to William the Conqueror. You may find some records that say our Linthicum was from Wales, but he only departed from Wales, (he was not Welsh). Many of the neighbors from his home town, eventually became his neighbors in Anne Arundel County. Thomas arrived in America on the ship "Margaret Shields" in 1658. Thomas was born in 1640 in Devonshire, England; and died 11-10-1701 in Anne Arundel County. He married Jane and they had five children in All Hallows Parish

♦
1. **Thomas Jr.** 10-31-1674
2. Mary 1676 m. Richard Snowden
3. Hezekiah 1677 m Milcah Frances on October 5, 1697
4. Jane 1680 m. Thomas Rutland d 12-14-1731
5. Richard 1682

Thomas Jr. was the builder of Linthicum Walks, pictured in this book. It located on Rt. 424 between 450 and 3, next to the school. He also owned several other estates in the area. He married Deborah Wayman whose father Leonard Wayman signed a petition requesting another parish be divided in Prince George's County, which was denied by King George III. Leonard Wayman was born in 1660 and was married to Dorcas Abott. Deborah and Thomas Linthicum were married on June 22, 1698 and had thirteen children, all born in All Hallow's Parish, Anne Arundel County, in the South River Hundred.

A. Dorcas 8-15-1700 m. Francis Hardesty on February 14, 1719
B. **Thomas III** 9-28-1701 to 12-4-1766
C. Mary 9-29-1703 m. Edward Wayman November 13, 1716
D. Gideon 2-15-1704 to 1770
E. Leonard 8-5-1705
F. Deborah 9-11-1707
G. Assaiel 5-11-1708
H. Ann 5-11-1711
I. Elizabeth 8-30-1712
J. Ruth 2-5-1713
K. Edmund 3-30-1714 to 1767 m. Elizabeth
L. John 1719
M. Hezekiah 11-7-1723, a school master m. Sarah Bateman 1750

B. Thomas III (9-28-1701 to 12-4-1766) married Sarah Burton (11-7-1706) on April 28, 1724. Sarah was the daughter of Joseph Burton (1685). They had eight children born in All Hallow's Parish.

    (a) Thomas IV   6-1-1725 to 4-8-1799
    (b) Joseph   4-30-1727
    (c) Burton   1730
    (d) Hezekiah   1732 m. Lydia Andrews
    (e) Deborah   1734- to 1803
♦   (f) **Zacharieh**   1735 to 1808 m1 Sarah Prather
                                m2 Mary Ann Clagett
    (g) Jane   1737
    (h) Aseal   1739

(f) Zacharieh Linthicum (1735 to 1808) married Sarah Prather and second, married Mary "Ann" Claggett on October 31, 1803. Sarah Prather was the daughter of John Prather (1705) and Rachel Odell (1717). They were married in 1738. Rachel Odell's grandfather Thomas Sr., an Irish Catholic, came to America in 1680 at the age of 20. He married Sarah Ridgely born 1660 in Devonshire, England. Her father was the Honorable Henry Ridgely (1625-1710) and her mother was Sarah Warner. Thomas Odell and Sarah Ridgely Odell had five children born near present-day Laurel.

♦   1. **Thomas, Jr.**   1-7-1692
    2. Henry   1694
    3. Ann   1703
    4. Rignall   1705
    5. Sarah   1709

1. Thomas Jr. married Mary "Margaret" Beall, a Presbyterian, and he became an Elder in the church. Margaret's grandfather was Alexander Bell, a physician in Fife, Scotland. Alexander and Margaret Ramsey Bell's sons, who all immigrated to Maryland over a period of ten years, spelled their name Beall. They were all active in the early beginnings of the Presbyterian Churches of Prince George's County.

    A. Alexander   1649-1744
    B. Andrew   1651
♦   C. **James**   1652-1725 m. Sarah Pierce
    D. William   1653
    E. Robert   1657

C. James Beall's arrival in Maryland is listed in Liber 15 folio 340. James and Sarah Beall had seven children: Mary "Margaret," John, James, Nathaniel, Sarah, Joseph, and Zephaniah.

(f) Zacharieh Linthicum had seven children. The first five were born in All Hallow's Parish and the last two in Frederick County. He was the promoter of subscriptions for "Sugar Loaf Hundred" during the Revolution and raised $1,333.00.

(1) John 1770 d. in Kentucky m1 Anne Seeder (1804-1896) m2 Priscilla Magruder. His 2 sons founded the Linthicum Institute in Washington, DC.
(2) Thomas Prather 7-20-1771 to 6-8-1850 m. Nancy Williams 4-24-1798
(3) Hezekiah   1773 m. Mary Hickman October 26, 1801
♦ (4) Frederick   1774 to 1835
(5) Elizabeth   1775 m. John Magruder
(6) Sarah   1777 m. William Mackelfresh
(7) Mary   1778 m. James Magruder

(4) Frederick Linthicum (1774 to 1835) married Rachel McElfresh on November 28, 1801. She had three children, and died (3-7-1808). He married her sister Betsy McElfresh on October 6, 1809. They had five children all born in Frederick County.
    a. **Philip**   12-1802 to 11-1846
    b. Lydia   1804 m. Jones
    c. Eleanor   1806 m1 Miel Burgee m2 Joseph N. Chiswell
    d. Ann   1810 m. William Beall
♦   e. **John Hamilton Smith** 3-2-1812 to 3-22-1896 m. Julia Ann Garrott
    f. Elizabeth   1815, single
    g. **Frederick**   10-14-1826 to 3-10-1896 m. Sarah E. Wright
    h. **Otho Norris** 1833 to 3-10-1870 m1 Hannah Garrott
                        m2 Elizabeth Hodges

Philip Linthicum
(1802-1846)

Philip Linthicum was born near Hyattstown, Md and christened on 12-21-1802. He married Mary Elanor McElfresh (1803-1874) on 2-3-1825. She was a daughter of Charles and Elizabeth Chiswell McElfresh. All four are buried in the family cemetery off Fire Tower Road near Hyattstown. They had ten children:
    1. Carrie Belle 10-1846 to 1-10-1919 m. Thomas S. Davis
       A. Mary Genevieve 3-17-1874
       B. Carrie Eleanor 1880
    2. Charles Philemon McElfresh 12-6-1825 to 8-13-1853
          m. Margaret Eleanor McElfresh (9-24-1824 to 5-28-1919) on 7-20-1851. She was a daughter of Philemon and Eleanor Stewart McElfresh.
       A. Charles Philemon 1852-1921
       B. **Cassidy** 4-1854 to 1939 m. Rachel Eleanor McElfresh Dutrow
    3. Edward
    4. Frances d. 9-1923
    5. George W. 1840 to 1-18-1912 m. Catherine Tacy Webb in 1860

    (a) Eleanor Elizabeth 6-26-1862
    (b) Cora Kennedy 11-16-1863
    (c) Edwin Ernest 10-6-1866
6. Hamilton Smith, Sr. m. Sophronia Galliher (1834) on 4-13-1858
    (a) Richard 3-30-1859
    (b) Edwin 3-1861
    (c) Benjamin F. 10-28-1863
    (d) Hamilton Smith, Jr. 3-20-1867
7. Philip
8. Rachel Eleanor
9. William
10. John d. 5-25-1892 m. Eliza Helen
    (a) Charles d. 12-28-1905
    (b) Frank d. 4-4-1910
    (c) Bernard
    (d) Leonard 10-12-1873 to 5-8-1931 m. Clara Church on 10-9-1902
        i. Madeline 5-15-1904
        ii. Elsie 9-15-1906
        iii. Bernard 5-19-1908
        iv. Mary 6-19-1924
    (e) Joseph 9-12-1922 m. Charlotte Youtz (d. 2-13-1929)
        i. Genevieve
        ii. Eleanor
        iii. John
    (f) Lelia Mary 5-12-1879 to 3-24-1928 m. William Pfarr 12-6-1879
    (g) Edward d. 2-1-1918 m. Jenny Coyle (d. 1927)
        i. Roy
        ii. Edward

    B. Cassidy Linthicum (4-1854 to 1939) married Rachel Eleanor McElfresh Dutrow (1856-1951) in 1880. They are both buried at Hyattstown Cemetery beside the Methodist Church. She was the daughter of John Dutrow and Elizabeth McElfresh Dutrow.
    (1) John Dutrow 7-17-1881 to 8-8-1953 m. Leona May Davis (3-20-1885 to 10-9-1960) on 2-15-1908. They are buried at Monocacy Cemetery, Beallsville, Md. They had six children:
        (a) Margaret Eleanor 12-11-1908 to 2-8-1993 m. William Marshall White (10-20-1908 to 4-4-1991) on 8-23-1930. They are buried at Monocacy Cemetery, Beallsville, Md. He was the son of William White and Mary Bowman White.
            i. Maryanne 10-4-1937 m. Duane Elto Warne 10-20-1961
            ii. Barbara Jane 10-2-1938 m. Michael Belecancah on 11-11-1961
        (b) Katherine Elizabeth 6-1-1910
        (c) Leona May 5-12-1912 to 1975 m. Travis Lyle m2 Ellis Lupton

(d) Anne Linthicum 10-21-1913 m. Douglas Schuyler Hardin (6-8-1914 to 5-5-2001) on 8-5-1938.
    i. Patricia 1939 m. James Michael McGraw 1962
    ii. Wayne D. 1941 m. Anita Pacen 1965
    iii. Richard W. 1943 m. Annabel Restly 1973
    iv. Dwight S. 1946 m. Shirley Bruffey 1978
(e) Charles Wallace 4-16-1915 to 1-18-1994 m. Helen Virginia Beall (4-30-1922) in 1946, daughter of Leslie and Bessie Lewis Beall. He is buried in Bethesda Methodist Cemetery, Browningsville, Md.
    i. Margo Lane 1951 m. Paul Stiles 1970, Thomas Lewis 1979, Richard Young 1987.
        a. Todd Michael 1973
(f) Frank Cassidy 9-4-1916 m. Violet L. Anderson (1-25-1902 to 9-16-1992) in 1949. She is buried in Hyattstown Cemetery, Hyattstown, Md.

(2) Laura E. 9-1885
(3) Margaret E. 7-1889
(4) Louise W. 3-1890
(5) Paul Cassidy 6-23-1893
(6) Philip Sheridan 2-26-1897 to 12-31-1981 m. Annie Mary Miles (3-29-1898 to 11-24-1992) on 1-25-1922 at Bethesda Methodist Church, Browningsville, Md.
  (a) Donald S. 1921
  (b) Philip Lee 1925 m. Dorothy Lou Poole (10-18-1926 to 1-17-1993)

John Hamilton Smith Linthicum
(1812-1896)

John Hamilton Smith Linthicum (3-2-1812 to 3-22-1896), son of Frederick Linthicum, was born in Hyatt's Town. He is buried in the McElfresh Burying Ground. He married Julia Ann Garrott (5-17-1810 to 10-23-1887) of Nicholas and Martha Burgee Garrott on April 5, 1832. They had ten children all born in the vicinity of Hyattstown.

    i. **William Thomas**   3-1-1833
    ii. **James Garrott**   11-23-1834 was a physician m. Mary Wilson
    iii. **John Warren**   11-25-1836 to 1917 m. Sarah Amanda Hendry
    iv. **Charles Frederick**   12-17-1838 to 6-3-1864   see below
    v. Zacharieh   1839 died young
    vi. Hannah Frances   12-11-1840 single
    vii. **Martha "Mattie" Elizabeth** 2-18-1844 m. John Howard King
♦   viii. Anna Mary   7-3-1846 to 8-30-1889 m. Joel Hamilton Wolfe
    ix. Nicholas D.   1849 died infancy
    x. **Julia Ann**   10-21-1850 to 12-27-1931 m. Noah Watkins

i. William Thomas Linthicum (3-1-1833 to 7-3-1897) was married in Ijamsville to Sarah Ellen Crawford. They had eight children (the sixth one is female).
    a. Annie Elizabeth   2-27-1858 died infancy
    b. Mattie S.   7-17-1860 m. Rev. Daniel W. Maylan 1892
    c. Charles Frederick   7-7-1862 m. Sarah Snyder 1888
    d. Wilbur S.   1-31-1865 m. Claire Tiers
    e. Edward Garrott   9-4-1866 m. Gertrude Dronenberg 1897
    f. Ollie Dorsey   7-25-1868 to 6-6-1900 m. Gehb
    g. James Warren   5-25-1870 to 10-26-1903 m. Ella Bowen 1896
    h. Herbert Wilson   6-25-1872 m. Laura Vinson

ii. James Garrott Linthicum (11-23-1834), physician, married Mary Wilson and had John Webster (11-26-1861) who was also a physician. He married Grace Allen Jones in 1882.

iii. John Warren Linthicum was a Confederate Soldier. He married Sarah Amanda Hendry and they had six children.
    a. Charles Hamilton   7-12-1868 to 1916 m. Osie Delilah Burgee 1893
    b. Warren   6-15-1871to 9-22-1872
    c. Wesley R.   8-25-1873 to 9-15-1874
    d. Garrott D.   1875
    e. Thomas S.   1877 m. Bessie Davis (1884-1976)
    f. Burwell Hendry   8-24-1878 - 1944
    g. Elmer K.   6-20-1884 to 7-17-1885
    h. Stanie Frances   1-1887 m. Joseph F. Donaldson
    i. Mary Eleanor   1-30-1887 to 1954 m. William Kindley Davis
        I. Edith M.
        II. Verna Louise
        III. Warren George

iv. Charles Frederick Linthicum was a Confederate Soldier. He was the Company Chaplain, the Adjutant General to General Richard Garnett, and afterward to Eppa Hunton. He volunteered for a dangerous mission observing enemy troop movement following the first day of battle at Cold Harbor (near Richmond). A fellow soldier also volunteered, but Charles said "send me, for I know Christ, and the other fellow doesn't." He was fatally wounded on the mission, and is buried in Hollywood Cemetery, Richmond, VA.

vii. Martha Elizabeth Linthicum married John H. King. They had six children.
    a. Julia Helen   7-4-1874 to 3-22-1943 m. Wm Upton Bowman 1902
    b. Carrrie Frances 5-30-1876 to 8-29-1943 m. Reverdy Mason Purdom 1898
    c. Reginald Windsor 2-17-1878 to 8-10-1952 m. Ida May Grimes

    d. Mary Lorena   10-13-1880 to 5-1-1964 m. Luther Green King 1899
    e. Myrtle Estelle   5-13-1883 to 1-6-1964 m. William Ernest Watkins
        (9-14-1881 to 1-6-1915 brd Browningsville) 1909
    f. Maude Edna   10-20-1886 to 6-16-1950 m. Joseph Felix Aycock
x. Julia Ann Linthicum (10-21-1850 to 1950) was a school teacher from 1869 until 1871 in Hyattstown. She married Noah Watkins of Cedar Grove and had thirteen children. The farm was located off present day Rt. 27 (Ridge Road) just south of the cemetery at the intersection of Davis Mill Road on the East side.
    a. Garrott Webster   10-9-1872 to 1947 m. Vertie A. Mullinix (1873-1959)
    b. Leah J. 8-2-1874 to 1960 m. William G. Iglehart (1867-1935) 4-30-1895
    c. Herbert Hamilton 8-25-1876 to 10-5-1880
    d. Mary Avondale 2-25-1878 to 2-15-1958 m. Franklin Monroe King
        (1876-1932) on 6-8-1898
    e. Nora Linthicum 1-9-1880 to 12-27-1931 m. Charles H. Barber
        (1873-1953) on 4-6-1898
      I. James H.   1916 to 12-14-1916
      II. Monroe F. 8-23-1918 to 12-28-1918
      III. Julia   11-22-1899 to 8-15-1983 m. John D. Purdum (1896-1965)
        had Nora Elaine Purdum
      IV. Anna   10-3-1914 m. Guy Linthicum had Mary Ann
    f. Bessie   1-9-1880 to 6-10-1880
    g. John Lester Clark   12-25-1881 to 3-25-1966 m. Bessie T. Wallach
        (5-13-1892 to 4-20-1967)
      I. Ernest C. 8-18-1927
      II. Jack
      III. Janet
    h. Clinton Cleveland   10-29-1883 to 12-12-1911
    i. Arthur Linthicum   4-5-1885 to 3-16-1957 m. Esther Pearl Luhn
        (6-7-1885) in 1909
      I. Noah Luhn 3-4-1910 to 7-26-1910
      II. Arthur Linthicum, Jr.   3-22-1912 to 5-16-1992
        m1 Ethel Blanche Gue (3-12-1912 to 12-4-1964)
        m2 Hilda Mae Hyatt (3-28-1920) on 10-8-1966
      III. Ollie c. 1913
      IV. Elizabeth c. 1914
      V. Virginia c. 1917
      VI. Oliver Randolph 9-14-1917 m. Margaret Snapp
        had Arthur Leroy, Jane and Ronald W. Watkins
      VII. Herbert c. 1919
      VIII. Lillian c. 1920
    j. Maude Ethel   12-5-1886 m. Edgar W. Davis (1883-1966) in April, 1908
      I. Laura Emma 1-21-1909 m. Ira Leroy King
      II. Julia E. 1-24-1910 m. James W. Purdum

    III. Edgar, Jr. 1912 m. Anna M. Young
    IV. G. Howard 8-8-1918 to 6-26-1920
    V. James 1-26-1921 to 6-3-2000 m. Lela Jane Krow in 1976
    VI. Louise 1923 m. Roland Martin had Delores, Cynthia, Guy
    VII. Betty 1925 m. Edward Vaught had Linda and Danny
k. Raymond Ridgely 12-26-1888 to 8-16-1913 m. Nelle Cosgrove
    I. Nelle Evelyn 1912 to 1-22-1918
l. Grace Louise 3-2-1891 m. Ralph Butterwick, had Mary
m. Frances "Marian" 7-15-1895 to 7-1-1985 m. Filmore Cleveland Brown
    (1893-1979) on 7-20-1914
    I. Francis Earl 2-9-1915 m. Glenrose Mary Flair on 8-18-1937
    II. Julian Wilson 4-14-1918 m. Mary Virginia Purdum on 9-2-1937
    III. Doris Wilson 4-9-1925 m. Forrest Chapman Beane
    IV. Ruth Evelyn 3-25-1931

Frederick Linthicum
1826-1909

    Frederick Linthicum, son of Frederick Linthicum, was born 10-14-1826 near Hyattstown, Md., and died 2-13-1909 in Thurston, Md. He married Hannah Frances Garrott (4-12-1827 to 1860) in 1844. She was a daughter of Nicholas Garrott and Martha Burgee Garrott. He then married Mary Elizabeth Hodges (4-11-1835 to 2-13-1910) on 12-17-1861. She was a daughter of Thomas Hodges and Matilda Bennett Hodges. Frederick and Mary Hodges Linthicum are buried in the Mountain Chapel Cemetery, Comus, Md.
    1. Bradley 11-13-1851 to 2-10-1869
    2. Garrott Davis 1-31-1854 to 2-17-1937 m. Mary Evelyn Lewis (1860 to 3-213-1931) in 1880. They are buried at Hyattstown Cemetery.
        A. Bertha E. 2-26-1881 to 8-3-1964 m. Bernard Gingell
        B. Annie R. 10-1883 to 1976 m. Harvey J. Green (1885-1966)
        C. Nellie 5-1886
        D. Charles F. 2-13-1888 tp 9-27-1918
        E. Nettie E. 6-25-1891 to 10-20-1996 m. Owen F. Wright
            (7-9-1884 to 5-10-1954)
        F. Harvey J. 6-4-1893 to 11-12-1967
        G. Myrtle A. 8-25-1895 to 7-1974
        H. Hattie A. 1897-1974 m. Russell G. Moore (1891-1961)
        I. Daisy Ethel 1899-1977 m. Luther Marshall McDonough
            (4-23-1899 to 3-28-1969). He was a son of Luther McDonough and Mary Remick McDonough.
            (1) Luther Marshall, Jr. 5-2-1934 to 1-10-1994
            (2) Kenneth
            (3) Betty Marie m. Merton A. Rhinecker (1926-1999)

(4) Mary Ann m. Davis
J. Olivia Pauline 5-5-1902 to 10-1980 m. Edgar Guy Jewell (9-1-1901 to 3-2-1984). They are buried at Monocacy Cemetery, Beallsville, Md.
   (1) Olivia 11-24-1923 to 1992 m. Kenneth Thurston King
K. Garrott 1906
2. George Frederick 3-3-1856 to 8-31-1931 m. Irene Alverta Tabler (11-20-1857 to 8-27-1897) on 4-2-1879. She was a daughter of William Tabler and Harriet Smith Tabler. He married second, Ollie Ruth Wolfe (2-9-1872 to 4-15-1925) on 11-9-1897. She was a daughter of William Wolfe and Hester Lawson Wolfe.
   A. Samuel 11-1881
   B. George 10-1883
   C. Grover D. 11-18-1888 to 2-22-1958 m. Mary V. Carlisle (8-29-1892 to 8-19-1947).
      (1) Guy 9-30-1916 to 1-24-1989 m. Anna Barber
      (2) Fred
   D. Fitzhue Lee 5-17-1889 to 2-11-1890
   E. Smith 10-1883
   F. Mabel aft. 1897
   G. Alverda aft 1898

Otho Norris Linthicum
1833-1870

Otho Norris Linthicum, son of Frederick Linthicum, was born in 1833 in Thurston and died March 10, 1870 in Browningsville. He married Sarah Elizabeth Wright (1835-1906). They are buried in Bethesda Methodist Cemetery, Browningsville, Md.

1. Florence Elizabeth 12-28-1858 to 1928 m. Lycurgus B. Layton (1841-1912)
   A. Harry 1877
   B. Sarah E. 1878 to 12-31-1935 m. Clarence E. Davis
      (1) Lois Lillian 5-23-1911 m. Howard Raymond Watkins 1928
         (a) Marjorie Ann m. Charles Jacob Green, Jr.
            i. Charles Raymond
            ii. Rita Lynn
            iii. Kevin
         (b) Bradley Parker
   C. Lenora F. 1880
   D. Raymond Ridgely
   E. Grace Louise
   F. Frances Marian
2. Sarah Eleanor 10-5-1860 m. J. P. Saffold

3. Otho Lee 7-5-1862 to 1896
4. Miel E. 2-28-1865 to 9-8-1928 m. Mary L. Purdum
    (1-18-1866 to 9-16-1956) on 4-25-1887, daughter of Joshua H. and
    Martha B. Burdette Purdum
    A. Earl Kindley 11-22-1893 to 7-31-1984 m. Ada M. Oagle
        (8-27-1894 to 10-25-1959)
        (1) Edwin Lee
    B. Ethel H. S. 3-26-1897 to 4-25-1967 m. Ivan Thompson Lawson
        (11-21-1886 to 9-14-1973), son of Caleb Crittendon and Alice
        Norwood Lawson
        (1) Arthur
        (2) Hanford
    C. Miel Wright 1901 to 10-2-1975 m. Irma Sophronia Watkins
        b.3-29-1903, daughter of Alonzo C. and Mary L. Boyer Watkins
        (1) George Morsell 4-4-1926
        (2) Miel Wright, Jr. 4-10-1928
        (3) Joseph 4-21-1930
        (4) Bernard Lee 11-21-1934 m. Martha J. Boyer
    D. Purdum Burdette 3-27-1906 to 11-28-1973 m. Edna Wilson Hyatt b.
        11-26-1905, daughter of William E. and Mildred S. Boyer Hyatt
        (1) Mary Mildred 5-9-1930 m. Jeremiah Elsworth Brandenburg
        (2) Shirley Hyatt 7-10-1931
        (3) Debora Kay 9-16-1950
5. Joseph Hamilton 9-28-1966 to 1-7-1942 m. Margaret Jemima Roberta
    Walker (1-7-1866 to 5-1-1913) on 12-23-1889, daughter of George W.
    and Rachel Browning Purdum Walker.
    A. Walker S. 9-5-1891 to 9-26-1930
    B. Paul 1893-1894
    C. Rosia Rachel 11-11-1899 to 1-23-1979 m. Sherman C. Kline
        (1-22-1901 to 3-10-1985)
    D. Eleanor 7-30-1902 m. Everhart
6. George M. 7-28-1869 to 1-20-1948 m. Flora J. Purdum
    (8-9-1868 to 6-13-1953) on 12-27-1899
7. William M. Frederick 1856-1860

McElfresh

Johne Macklefreishe married Jonet Thomsone in South Leith, Mid Lothian County, Scotland on 11-30-1654. Their son David came to Londontown, Anne Arundel County, Maryland. Londontown is presently the site of several archaelogical digs and perhaps in the future will have some reconstructed areas to visit. One of the streets there is McElfresh Street. David McElfresh, Sr. married Alice Jones in 1694 and had seven children. David McElfresh, Jr. (10-27-1702 to 3-1737) married Mary Elizabeth Leeke (91-7-1707 to 2-16-1732) on 3-3-1721 and had four children. After her death David married Martha Sellman (1712-1792) on 10-8-1733. Their son, John Hammond McElfresh was born in 1735 near the South River, Anne Arundel County, Maryland. He married Rachel Hammond in 1758 and moved to Frederick County, Maryland. They had eight children:

1. John, Jr. 1759-1789 m. Rachel Dorsey 3-4-1778, Jane Cumming 1780
2. Philip 1761 to 5-8-1833 m. Lydia Griffith (3-7-1755 to 4-24-1811) on 2-22-1781. She was the daughter of Greenberry Griffith and Ruth Riggs Griffith.
   A. John c. 1781 m. Rachel Maynard
   B. Ruth c. 1783 m. Ignatius Griffith
   C. Philip
   D. William M. 1878 m. Sarah Linthicum (1777) 12-21-1802
   E. Caleb c. 1790 m. E. Shipley
   F. Rachel c. 1791
   G. Rhoderick c. 1793 m. Linthicum
   H. Rachel Smith m. Frederick Linthicum
3. Thomas 1763-1791 m. Martha Phelps on 9-30-1784
4. Sara 5-10-1770 to 10-183 m. Henry Wood
5. Henry 7-21-1771 to 6-22-1846 m. Ariana Hammond (9-15-1768 to 7-7-1827) on 3-6-1790 daughter of Philip and Barbara A. Hammond
   A. Corilla Eleanor 1791 to 5-6-1806 m. Smith
   B. Rachel C. 1792
   C. Henry Jr. 1794
   D. John Hammond 11-27-1796 m. Theresa Mantz (12-22-1794 to 5-29-1846)
      (1) Casper Mantz 8-9-1824
      (2) Ariana 4-7-1828
      (3) Anna 3-14-1821
      (4) Francis
   E. Ann 6-10-1801 to 4-4-1878 m. John Norris (10-9-1803 to 12-19-1873)
      (1) William Lee 1830 m. Rachel C. Welsh
      (2) Henry M. 1-5-1835
      (3) Ariana McElfresh 1845-1927 m. Charles Barrick

        (12-10-1840 to 10-12-1912)
        (a) Charles H. 2-9-1870
        (b) Hattie 8-15-1873
  6. Joseph 1773-1801 m. Sara Howard
♦ 7. **Charles Thomas, Sr.** 1776-1835 m. Elizabeth Smith Chiswell
  8. Rachel 3-25-1775 to 3-15-1842 m. John H. Smith on 4-4-1792
    A. Philemon McElfresh, Sr. 2-2-1794
    B. John H., Jr.
    C. Ann

    7. Charles Thomas McElfresh, Sr. (1774-1835) was born near Thurston, Frederick County, Maryland. He was married three times and had ten children. His first wife was Ann Smith (1755-1799) whom he married 11-25-1789. They had two children. She was a daughter of Philemon Hamilton Smith and Elizabeth Rawlings Smith. His second wife was Elizabeth Smith Chiswell (10-28-1780 to 3-7-1808) whom he married on 2-5-1800. She was a daughter of Joseph Newton Chiswell (4-13-1747 to 4-9-1837) and Eleanor Chiswell White Chiswell (4-29-1750 to 3-23-1831). They had six children. His third wife was Elizabeth Pitts whom he married 2-10-1809. She was a daughter of Thomas Pitts and Susannah Lusby Pitts.
    A. Elizabeth Smith 1792 m. Frederick Linthicum (see previous chapter)
    B. Philemon Smith 9-27-1793 to 8-4-1841 m. Eleanor Stewart
       (10-20-1797 to 11-12-1864) on 10-4-1815.
       (1) Elizabeth Ann 9-10-1817 to 9-30-1907 m. John W. Dutrow (3-28-1811
          to 3-29-1900) on 5-8-1837
          (a) Philemon 10-21-1843 to 4-17-1923 m. Carrie M. (9-2-1841 to
             10-20-1931)
          (b) John P. 1848
          (c) Rachel Eleanor McElfresh (1856-1951) m. Cassidy Linthicum
             (previous chapter)
       (2) Charles M. 8-1819 to 6-19-1887 m. Mary Louisa Turner (1826 to
          8-4-1904) m. 2-17-1853. They were married in Frederick Co., Md. and
          are buried in Pikesville, Md.
          (a) Charles Fisher 8-19-1854 to 7-30-1857
          (b) James Philemon 2-28-1857 to 5-26-1887
          (c) Katie Ann 10-26-1859 to 9-17-1917
          (d) Ellen Stewart 6-25-1862 to 1-28-1888
          (e) Mary Juliet 3-31-1865 to 4-5-1865
          (f) Bessie Berry 6-16-1867 to 1-1-1937 m. Frank Bolgiano
             i. Charles Walton
          (g) John Fisher 10-29-1872 to 6-26-1926 m. Bessie Simmons (7-23-1875
             to 1-24-1967) on 9-16-1896. She was a daughter of William H. D.
             Simmons (12-24-1841 to 8-23-1901) and Eliza P. Harris (4-9-1844
             to 12-1928)

    i. John Lister 1-18-1899 to 5-27-1973 m. Gertrude Ogden Kenney (5-22-1899 to 7-21-1986) on 6-4-1923
        a. Gertrude Elizabeth 10-6-1924 m. Robert Edgar Gilbertson (7-31-1921 to 5-25-1997) on 6-14-1947.
            I. Robert Edgar, Jr. 8-31-1949
            II. Linda Marie 9-15-1951 m. George Randolph Stevens
            III. Jean Elizabeth 10-20-1955 m. Thomas Charles Lenard
        b. Mary Louise 10-30-1929 m. Donald Kay Wand (10-22-1929) on 5-30-1952
            I. David Michael 10-13-1954 m. Ana Madrid
            II. Kenneth Gordon 8-28-1957 m. Kathie Green
            III. Karen Louise 1-6-1959 m. Vincent Whittles
            IV. James 1-6-1959
    ii. Charles William 7-8-1906 to 2-23-1963 m. M. Elta Baker (7-24-1906 to 7-21-1986)
        a. Joanne 2-20-1929 m. Robert Zorn
            I. Trent 5-25-1950
            II. Donna 2-19-1952
            III. Kurt 6-8-1954
(3) Margaret Eleanor 9-24-1824 to 5-28-1919 m. Charles Philemon McElfresh Linthicum (12-6-1825 to 8-13-1853) on 7-20-1851. He was killed in an explosion on the B&O. She married Eberle E. Harris (2-1-1838 to 11-22-1920) in 1875
    (a) Charles P. Linthicum 1852
    (b) Cassidy Linthicum 1854 (see previous chapter)
    (c) Charles McElfresh Harris 6-6-1876
    (d) Margaret E. Harris 6-18-1877
(4) Annie M. 8-4-1825 to 2-23-1895
(5) John Pitts 7-28-1828 to 1-26-1906 m. Jemima Welch (7-7-1848 to 6-30-1893) on 9-27-1864, daughter of Abner and Susannah Barrett Welch. They were married in Bourbon Co., Kansas
    (a) Abner Philemon 10-24-1865 to 2-5-1895
    (b) Mary Susanna 7-13-1867 to 11-5-1945 m. Henry Thomas Pyle on 12-28-1887
        i. Anna
        ii. Thomas
        iii. Eleanor
    (c) Charles Lewis 4-1-1870 to 1-2-1961 m. Sarah Lurcretia Prowse (11-10-1875 to 11-10-1968) on 8-11-1898 in Emporia Kansas
        i. Carrie Louise 5-1899
        ii. John William 1-1903
        iii. Charles Floyd 11-1907
        iv. George Lewis 4-1-1909 to 10-17-1983 m. Dorothy G. Ward

(2-5-1911 to 4-28-1998) in April 1938 in Kansas.
  i. Sara Ann 7-4-1939 m. D. J. Bolt
  ii. James Dale 2-5-1946
 v. Mary Lucretia 8-1914
(d) Elizabeth 4-1-1870 to 6-21-1870
(e) Anna Louise 11-11-1872 to 12-28-1953 m. Fred Warren
(f) B. Norris 2-3-1876 to 10-23-1845 m. Mary Archer
(g) Jeanette 8-27-1878 to 2-23-1887
(h) Lenora Carrie 10-19-1880 to 9-22-1917 m. Arthur Warren
(i) Eleanor Rebecca 11-3-1883 to 5-2-1954 m. A. M. Thompson
(6) Susannah 1830
(7) Rachel 2-2-1834 to 10-20-1918
(8) Mary Hamilton 10-23-1836 to 11-7-1911 m. Edmund Wagner McElfresh, Sr. (10-10-1835 to 12-30-1921) on 7-7-1860 (see following section)
C. Rachel Ann 6-2-1801 to 7-11-1875 m. Somerset Richard Waters (8-24-1796 to 3-3-1860) on 12-30-1817, son of Richard and Margaret Smith Waters.
 (1) Charles Richard 9-27-1821
 (2) John Thomas 1-19-1824
 (3) Somerset Richard, Jr. 4-3-1826 to 11-30-1874 m. Rachel Ann Davis (1-28-1834 to 12-6-1896) a daughter of Samuel and Hannah G. Davis
  (a) Fuller 7-22-1853 to 1-8-1908 m. Gidonia L. Showacre
  (b) Somerset Rawlings m. Lillian Spignall
  (c) Alice m. William A. Gartrell 1881
  (d) Robert Fowler m. Mary Caroline Landwehr on 9-10-1927
  (e) Lucy
  (f) Samuel Davis 1851 to 11-181913 m. Florence Owings
 (4) Margaret Eleanor 6-20-1829 m. George H. Davis
 (5) Ignatius 10-9-1831
 (6) Casper Quin 1832
 (7) Hannah Virginia 4-10-1836 to 11-28-1896 m. James H. Steele on 1-12-1882
 (8) James Kenna 4-10-1838 to 12-10-1916 m. Anna Mary Hill in 1862
 (9) Sarah A. Norris 1-4-1840 to 12-6-1905
D. Edmund c. 1802
E. Mary Eleanor 1803-1874 m. Philip Linthicum (see previous chapter)
F. William Walter c. 1804
G. Sarah Ann 5-24-1805 to 11-6-1852 m. William T. Glaze (1799)
 (1) Basil T. 3-9-1833 to 1-12-1913 m. Mary Elizabeth Lewis
  (a) Sarah E. 1877
  (b) William H. 3-28-1878 to 8-27-1916 m. Annie M. (10-8-1871 to 3-13-1950
  (c) Basil Russell 5-29-1887 to 8-6-1863 m. Bertie May King (6-26-1886 to 12-11-1975)

H. Margaret Chiswell c. 1806
I. Infant son
J. Charles Thomas, Jr. m. Fannie S. Waggoner on 9-27-1832, daughter of Edmund and Zeriah Beall Waggoner
  (1) Sarah 1834
  (2) Edmund Wagner, Sr. 10-10-1835 to 12-30-1921 m. Mary Hamilton McElfresh (10-23-1836 to 11-7-1911) on 7-7-1860 (see above)
    (a) L. Louisa 12-1-1860 to 11-1-1950 m. Louis F. Conrad (12-15-1860 to 7-4-1843)
    (b) John Philemon 7-7-1862 to 3-15-1948
    (c) Edmund Wagner, Jr. 5-20-1864 to 3-30-1945 m. Jane Elese Simmons (3-24-1880 to 2-11-1916), daughter of William H. D. and Eliza P. Harris Simmons. They are buried in the McElfresh cemetery.
      i. Bessie Louise 10-26-1909 to 6-29-1952 m. Rufus Burkett Hipkins (7-18-1911)
      ii. Rachel 1911
      iii. Emund Wagner III 9-19-1914 to 11-8-1945
      iv. Infant b&d 2-11-1916 brd. McElfresh Cemetery
    (d) Charles Philemon 1866-1936 brd. McElfresh Cemetery
    (e) Nigel Dorsey 7-2-1867 to 2-8-1934 m. Lottie Dixon (2-1-1888 to 6-13-1927), daughter of Dallas Dixon, brd. in McElfresh Cemetery
    (f) Thomas Still 10-30-1872 to 1-17-1919 m. Ann Beall House (8-15-1874 to 4-18-1953) on 2-6-1912, daughter of John Thomas William House and Lucinda Rebecca Beall
      i. Lucy Mary 1-16-1913 m. John Elwood Kelley (3-22-1913)
        a. John Elwood, Jr. 7-26-1938
        b. Linda Lee 4-25-1940
      ii. William Thomas 7-21-1916 m. Verna Louise Gardner (8-26-1922 to 11-9-1983) on 12-23-1944 in Louisville, Ky.
        a. Patricia Louise 3-17-1951
        b. William Thomas, Jr. 6-19-1954 m. Elizabeth M. Kempson
    (g) Rachel 2-28-1870 to 10-28-1952 m. Charles H. Smith (2-25-1864 4-17-1937)
    (h) Mary Frances 5-13-1874 to 8-20-1949 m. Harry C. Anderson (9-2-1876 to 11-10-1948) son of Charles Thomas and Eliza A. Hurley Anderson
      i. Clifton E. 8-6-1902 to 9-13-1991 m. Roxye Moselle Norwood (12-9-1904 to 8-23-1997) daughter of Edward Livingston and Carmye Fay Day Norwood
        a. Steven E. m. Pat
        b. Jean
      ii. Louise Conard 10-27-1911 m. William Wharton O'Keefe (12-31-1912)
  (3) Laura Virginia 5-1837 to 3-24-1902 m. Levi Price (11-1835 to

3-24-1902), son of Elijah Price and Sarah Ann Wolfe Price
   (a) Ernest Elijah 7-16-1864 to 8-19-1929 m. Betty Blanche Buxton
   (b) Levi, Jr. 1867
   (c) Bessie 1869 m. William Soule Hammond 9-13-1895
   (d) Minnie Blanche 1873 m. Walter Gardner Smith 9-21-1892
   (e) Laura Estelle 5-10-1874 to 1954 m. John Gardner (1873 to 12-31-1926) son of Edward Grafton and Rachel Ann Benton Gardner
      i. Edward Otis 1900
      ii. Ella Lael 1-7-1906
      iii. Minnie Eudora 8-20-1907 m. Paul F. Wire
      iv. Laura Rachel m. Beeser
   (f) Charles 1875
   (g) Cada 6-30-1876 to 7-6-1876
   (h) Sadie 2-13-1879 to 2-22-1879
   (i) Daisy V. 1881 m. Richard Bagby 6-2-1896
   (j) William Otis 1889
(4) Rosetta 1842
(5) Zeruiah Belle 1844-1874 m. Grimes
   (a) Mary Elizabeth 5-5-1866 to 8-25-1928 m. Samuel Lewis Shipley (10-25-1860 to 5-24-1948) in 1886. He was a son of John Robert and Mary Ellen Snowden Shipley
      i. John W. 9-21-1888 to 10-9-1976 m. Cora M. Sheckles c. 1915
         (a) infant
         (b) infant
         (c) infant
         (d) Kenneth
         (e) Thelma
         (f) Edna
      ii. Edward Lewis 10-13-1890 to 6-8-1895 m. Anna E. Sheckles (5-1-1900 to 3-24-1988) daughter of Nathan E. and Edith May Bowen Sheckles
      iii. Walker 4-1892
      iv. Franklin W. 4-1896
      v. Violena Shipley 10-27-1899 to 9-4-1979 m. Walden Vincent King (7-7-1894 to 2-20-1978), son of John Brewer and Emily Lavinia Burns King. They are buried in Clarksburg, Md.
         a. Mary Esther King 7-3-1919 m. Forrest Norwood Haney (10-27-1918 to 9-4-1981) on 10-16-1936, son of Ritchie Emanuel Haney and Helen Pearce Haney
            I. Mary Eloise 6-28-1940 m. Thomas Leslie Woodfield (6-20-1939)
               Alethia Kae 1961 m. Michael Watkins
               Tarra Lee 1966 m. Kevin M. Pumphrey
            II. Mickey Ilene 7-31-1952 m. Larry Greene (1949) on 12-20-1974

Christopher A. 1979
Britnie Ann 1985
III. Ricky Dean 7-31-1952
b. Lillian Mae 1-3-1921 m. Clarence Ellis Hood
I. Dixie Jane 8-30-1941 m. William T. Flynn 11-28-1959
II. Glenn Ellis 2-10-1947 m. Charlotte J. Ramsburg 11-24-1971
III. Dennis Rex 9-26-1952
c. Merhle V. 1925-1946 m. Lucy I. Savage (1927)
vi. Maurice Alton 7-13-1904 to 9-10-1979 m. Nora May Brown (3-7-1912 to 2-26-2000) on 2-15-1930, daughter of Roby Harriman and Virgie Estelle Price Brown.
(a) Fred Alton 3-2-1931
(b) Carroll Wilson 7-28-1932
(c) Donald Lee 9-5-1934
(d) Robey Lewis 8-31-1937
(e) Maurice Linwood 10-10-1942
(f) Norita Mae 12-15-1944
(g) Mary Ellen 10-26-1948
vii. Zerah Belle 10-11-1906 m. Marshall Luther Beall (1904 to 1-30-1991) son of Luther Caleb and Della Mae Beall.
(a) Raymond Chapman 1928 m. Marie Louise Thatcher
I Linda Louise
II Susie Marie
(b) Della Mae 1930 m. Gideon A. Doolin (1929-1996)
I Ruth Ann 1951
II Esther Mae 1953
III Martha 1955
IV Gideon Arthur 1960
(c) Ralph Lewis 9-11-1931 to 2-14-1932
(d) Mary Louise 1935 m. Lee Ballew
(e) Edith Eileen 1937 m. Richard Robert Wolfe (1939)
(f) Dallas Marshall 1938 m. Jane Williams
(g) Jerry Samuel 1946 m. Cheryl Walls
I. Christi
II Andrew
viii. Addie E. 7-18-1887 to 12-26-1966 m. James W. Watkins (5-25-1864 4-17-1924) c. 1913, son of Josiah W. and Mary Ann Beall Watkins
(a) Jessie I. 8-26-1912 to 8-25-1996 m. William Richard Davis (6-23-1907 tp 11-25-1985)
(b) Iris 11-16-1914 to 5-24-1984 m. Ora Henning King (7-18-1910 to 9-26-1968) son of Elias Vinson and Jemima Elizabeth Purdum King.
I Oliver Henry 8-12-1941
II. Gloria m. Phil Winter

Iris then married Emory Edwards
   (c) James Oliver 7-19-1921 to 2-9-1949
   (d) Ruth Estelle M. 7-28-1919 m. Walter E. Haines, Jr. (9-19-1915 to 6-3-2000) on 8-15-1936, son of Walter E. Haines and Rosie Mabel Smith Haines. He is brd. at Mt. View Methodist, Purdum, Md.
(6) Mary 1846
(7) Annie 1848
(8) Colvin Hughes 5-17-1849 to 3-13-1922 m. Hester Ida Lawson (2-11-1854 to 9-28-1921), daughter of James Uriah and Catherine E. Turner Lawson
   (a) Colvin Hughes c. 1877 m. Sophronia Burdette (11-25-1881) on 11-10-1901, daughter of Caleb Joshua and Roberta King Burdette
      i. Fannie Wagner 8-4-1903 to 4-6-1988 m. William Maurice Watkins
         a. Dorothy Janice 4-6-1924 m. Edward W. Mullinix
         b. Ruth Evelyn 10-25-1926 m. John C. Beall
         c. Robert Lee 10-29-1932 m. Ardis M. Hanson
      ii. Annie Sophronia 2-11-1906 to 6-3-1988 m. Raymond Fout Day (4-26-1905 to 12-25-1987) on 12-25-1928
         a. Dorothy Jean 10-16-1929 m. Willis Webster Beall
         b. Raymond Harold 12-12-1930 m. Shirley A. Woodfield
         c. Barbara Ann 7-20-1938 m. Ralph Eugene Kemp
      iii. Marjorie Rebecca 7-17-1910 to 12-27-1982 m. Claude Edward Burdette (10-9-1905 to 4-8-1994) on 11-20-1920
         a. Hazel Mae 5-21-1932 m. Ernest Eugene Hoyle (8-4-1928) on 3-16-1951
            I Richard Eugene 7-8-1952
            II. Kenneth Edward 12-24-1957
            III. Mark Joseph 2-2-1959
            IV. Scott Warren 9-18-1960
            V. Steven Michael 7-25-1966
         b. Donald Edward 5-1-1935 m. June Watkins
         c. Grace Rebecca 6-30-1937 m. Robert Say Snapp
         d. Clifford Warren 6-9-1941 m. Verla Phyllis Jones
         e. Claude Michael 6-1-1943 m. Eunice Elaine Staub
      iv. John Hughsie m. Evelyn Rippeon
         a. John Calvin 1934
         b. Evelyn Irene 1935
         c. Kenneth Ray
         d. Ann Louise 1937
         e. Margaret Virginia 1938
      v. Lindsey Leo 10-8-1918 to 9-1-1999 m. Virginia Mae Burdette (1923) on 9-9-1940
         a. Linda Mae 5-6-1943 m. Meredith Alexander

b. Terrence Lee 7-17-1949 to 1-11-1997 m. Linda Jean Hilton
　　　　i. John Terrence 1-24-1978
　　c. Cora Bonita 4-8-1957 to 1-7-1958
　　d. Joyce Ann 4-11-1960 m. Steven Farkas
(9) Frances 1850

Charles M. McElfresh Family

Hyatt

Charles Hyatt is listed in English records as Hyet, born 1668. He died in Queen Anne Parish, Prince George's County in 1726. He and his brother, Peter, were founders of the Rock Creek Church. Charles was the church warden in 1706 and 1716. He married Sarah Tewksbury, daughter of William Tuckberry. She was born on his estate "Mavron Hills" in 1672. Charles inherited "Tewksbury" from his father-in-law in 1726, and later "Mavron Hills." He also purchased "Bazingthorp Hall." The Tewksbury property is currently under development and is located between Laytonsville and Damascus. Charles sold his half of "Tewksbury" to Benjamin Duvall. Sarah and Charles had nine children, the first three were born in St. James Parish, Anne Arundel County, and the remaining in Queen Anne Parish, Prince George's County. This was prior to the erection of Frederick or Montgomery County, which is were the property is currently.

♦ 1. **Seth**   9-20-1694 to 1750 m. Alice 1717
   2. Susannah   10-19-1697
   3. Ann   11-30-1698 died in infancy
   4. Ann   3-11-1706 died in infancy
   5. Peter   1-30-1707
   6. Ann   3-10-1711
   7. Elizabeth   3-22-1714
   8. Penelope   4-20-1716
   9. William   2-18-1717 m. Elizabeth Walker 1746, had Seth whose 9th child founded Hyattsville, PG Co., Alpheus m. Audella Beebe & had Hannah, Alpheus III, Anna & Verill. Anna (1876) m. Archer Huntington, and founded Brookgreen Gardens, Myrtle Beach, SC

1. Seth and Alice Hyatt (9-20-1694 to 1750) had six children all born in Queen Anne's Parish, Prince George's County. His farm "Maiden's Fancy" between Mt. Airy and Kemptown, was used as the dividing line when the new county called "Frederick" was carved out of Prince George's. The official wording reads: "On December 10, 1748 Frederick County was erected with the dividing line to begin at the lower side of Mouth of Monocacy Creek to the East side of Seth Hyatt's plantation." Tewksbury was part of the land that became Montgomery County after 1776.

   A. Seth Jr.   10-5-1718 m. Jemima Jones
   B. Shadrack   2-25-1720
♦ C. **Meshach**   1723 -1807 m1 Sarah 1749, m2 Susannah Hobbs 1762
   D. Avarilla   1725 m. John Prather
   E. Abednego   1727
   F. Daughter   1729 m. Neale Clark

C. Meshack Hyatt (1723-1807) was born in Kemptown near Old Bartholows Road. The farm is still there, with a few tract houses on the back section. The farm house is very old and in a steep hillside. He and Sarah had four children, and his second wife, Susannah Hobbs, had eight more.

    (1) Meshach   1750
    (2) Abednego   1752
    (3) Shadrach   1753
♦   (4) **Eli**   10-16-1754 m. Mary Ann Warfield July 25, 1780
    (5) Sarah   1761
    (6) Jesse   1-14-1763 to 1-12-1813 m. Nancy "Ann" Riggs 1792
    (7) Elizabeth   1767 m. Zachariah Davis 1784
    (8) Susan   1768 m. Rev. O'Hugas
    (9) Joseph   1769 m. Cutsail, wounded in Battle of North Point, 1814
♦   (10) **Lavinia**   1771 m1 William Richards, m2 George Wolfe, Sr.
    (11) Ezra   1773
    (12) Sophia   1775 m. Joshua Todd
    (13) Catherine   1776 m. Mr. Hinton

Jesse Hyatt laid out the town that bears his name in 1798. He offered 105 quarter acre lots along the "Great Road" in 1809. See "The History of Hyattstown" by same author for details on Hyattstown.

(4) Eli Hyatt (10-16-1754 to 7-28-1815) married Mary Ann Warfield of John on July 25, 1780. They had eleven children in Frederick County.

    (a) John   1782
    (b) William E.   12-18-1783 to 2-17-1848 m. Peggy Kinna
♦   (c) **Elizabeth**   10-15-1785 to 5-13-1855 m. U. Talbott m2 George Davis
    (d) Asa   12-13-1787 to 8-20-1848 m. Mary Ann Phillips
        (1786-1889) on 5-12-1812
        i. Isabella
        ii. Theophilus
        iii. Sarah Ann
        iv. Mary Ann 12-3-1824 m. Warner Welsh, Jr. (1818-1875) 5-27-1843
        v. Leah Ann Willson
        vi. Sarah Elizabeth
        vii. Willson Lee
    (e) Susana 1790 m. John Phillips
    (f) Samuel 4-28-1792 m. Mary Purdum (1799-1841) on 10-28-1815
    (g) Polly 4-8-1794 m. Elisha Riggs Hyatt in 1814
    (h) Charlotte 3-29-1796 m1 William Fowler m2 William Richards Jr.
    (i) Eli 3-28-1798 m. Miranda Waters (1801-1859) on 12-31-1818
    (j) Mary Ann 6-26-1800 m. Ralph Norwood on 8-9-1816
    (k) Lloyd 1-11-1803 m. Miranda Richards (1810-1880) in 1831

(10) Lavinia Hyatt of Meshach married William Richards in 1790. They had

three children born in the miller's house in Hyattstown. After his death, Lavinia married the assistant miller, George Freidrich Wolfe.

    (a) Meshach   1791 m. Nancy Purdum
    (b) William Jr.   m. Charlotte Hyatt
    (c) Susan   1795 m. Thomas Duvall

Hyattstown Grist Mill

Davis

Jenkin David was born in Wales in 1654, and died in Uwchland, Chester County, Wales in August, 1727. People did not have standardized last names at this time. He married Martha in 1695 and had five children.

- 1. **Jenkin Davies**   1675-1748 m. Mary
- 2. David   1680-1730
- 3. Evan   1685 m. Rachel
- 4. Martha   1690

Jenkin Davies (1675-1748) was born in Cilcennin, Cardingshire, Wales and died in Terre Hill, East Earl Township, Pa. He married Mary in 1695 in Cardingshire, Wales. They immigrated from the family home in Esgerwen, in 1704, and cousin Jane Evans has their Bible. They and some of the family members are buried in the Old Welsh cemetery on the Elton Eby farm near New Holland, Pa. (near Lancaster). They had seven children, some Davies and some Davis:

    A. Catherine Davis 11-6-1696 to 1750 m. Rees Davis
    B. David Davies 1-20-1698 to 1746
    C. Jaen Davies 1-14-1701 to 1738
    D. Evan Davies 6-28-1703 to 1799 m. Thamar
-     E. **John Davies** 1-25-1705 to 3-21-1774
        m. Elizabeth Anderson 1748
    F. Zaccheus Davis 2-21-1709 to 3-25-1788 m. Joanna Morgan
    G. Sarah Davies 5-28-1713 to 9-1-1735 m. John Edwards

E. John Davies and Elizabeth Anderson were married in Lancaster in 1748. They are both buried in the Welsh Graveyard, New Holland, Pa.

    (1) Martha Davies 1749 m. Robert Wallace August 3, 1768
    (2) Sarah Davis 1750 m. Joseph Kittera
-     (3) **Richard Davis** 1751 to 12-16-1791 m. Catherine Hinkle
    (4) Isaac Davis 4-4-1754 to 1-5-1838 m. Lydia Carter

(3) Richard and his brother Isaac jointly ran the family farm on Martindale Road on the Conestoga Creek near Terre Hill, East Earl Township, Pa. The old house is still there. The spring house was two stories, but almost totally in ruins in 1997. The covered bridge beside the house was washed away in Hurricane Agnes in 1972. Old photographs of the house, bridge and outbuildings are in the author's possession. Near the mill on the Conestoga Creek is Hinkletown, named for George Hinkle. His daughter Catherine Barbara Hinkle married Richard Davis. She was a member of the Bergstrasse Lutheran Church in Ephrata. In early 1790 Richard decided to relocate, sold his half of the 900 acre farm to Isaac for 400 pounds sterling, and packed his then six children, wife and Jesse Wright into a wagon, and struck out for Maryland. He purchased 229 acres of land in the New Market District of Frederick County, near

Monrovia. He ran a farm and opened a general mercantile store near the present-day railroad bridge in Monrovia. Just up the track from this store is the Monrovia Friends Burying Ground where he is buried. In December of 1791 he traveled to Baltimore to purchase supplies for the store. On the return trip his team and wagon overturned, and he was crushed by a hogshead of molasses. His wife was brought to him, and died shortly thereafter. Catherine remarried to Jesse Wright and had more children.

♦ (a) George   2-3-1775 to 5-6-1850 m. Elizabeth Hyatt
(b) Jonathan   1777-1800 m. Mary Smith
(c) Sarah   10-24-1785 m. William E. Salmon
(d) Mary   1787 m. Samuel Penn January 25, 1804
(e) Isaac   1789
(f) Richard, Jr.   1790-1820 m. Elizabeth Penn June 19, 1812
(g) Catherine   1791 m. Samuel Talbot

(a) George and Elizabeth were married by Reverend Dade on August 12, 1803 in Frederick County. They are buried in the Friends Burying Ground in Monrovia, Frederick County, Maryland.

    i. Julia Anne   12-30-1804 to 1-28-1885 m. Ezra Greentree
    ii. Mary   4-24-1806 to 10-26-1885 m. George F. Wolfe, Jr.
    iii. Katie   1807 to 1810
    iv. Mary Ann Rebecca 8-16-1808 to 11-13-1894
        m. William Thomas Duvall
    v. William D. 4-27-1809 to 3-8-1877 m1 Charlotte Duvall
        m2 Ann E.
    vi. Eli 11-5-1810 to 10-6-1887 m. Rachel Morsel on 8-18-1831
        in Clarksburg, Montgomery Co., Md
    vii. Isaac Howard 6-12-1818 to 3-5-1901 m. Catherine S. Miles
    viii. Catherine   1820-1822

Henckel

The name Henckel is Teutonic in origin. The family descended from an heiress of that name, a daughter of Heinrich, who married Petrus de Thurzo of Donnersmarck in 1400. He took her name and thus the two families have the same coat of arms. Johann Henckel, Bishop of Breslau had a nephew who was the chaplain to the court of Queen Marie, wife of King Ludwig II of Hungary. The records documenting the exact line of descent were destroyed in the 1552 fire in Neudeck. Originally the word Henckel referred to the handle of a tool or luggage. As a surname, it was derived from "son of Heinrich."

Matthias Henckel, son of Casper, was born in 1605 in Allendorf ad Lumbda, Germany. He had at least two children: Georg and Jacob. George was born c. 1635 in Allendorf ad Lumbda and died 1-29-1677 in Mehrenberg. Georg Matriculated in the fourth class of Giessen, July 25, 1650. He was made preceptor of the school at Mehrenberg in 1662. He married Anna Eulalia Dentzer May 2, 1666 in Steinberg. She was a daughter of Othmar and Louisa Wagner Dentzer. His sixth child was born posthumously.

♦
1. Elizabeth Catherine   4-1667
2. **Anthony Jacob**   10-1668
3. Johannes Christian   4-1671
4. Johann Konradus   2-1673
5. Johann Georg   11-1675
6. Philip Conrad   7-1678

2. Anthony Jacob Henckel was born in October, 1668 in Mehrenberg, Germany. He matriculated May 5, 1688 from Giessen University. He was examined by the Theological Faculty January 16, 1692 and ordained Febraury 28, 1692 at Escelbronn. He was called as Pfarrar of the Lutheran Church at Escelbronn by Baron John Anton of Pfeltz. At this time in Germany Baron maintained their own churches for their subjects and chose their own pastors according to their political alliances and religious affiliation. Rev. Anthony was married to Maria Elizabeth Dentzer on April 25, 1692. He was next called to be the Pfarrar at Monchzell by Baron John Melchior of Vestenburg, February 23, 1693. In 1695 he became the Pfarrar of Daudenzell and it's neighboring church, Breitenbronn by Baron von Gemmingen.

On April 9, 1708 Catholics endeavored to gain the use of the Breitenbronn Evangelical Lutheran Church building half of the time. Rev. Anthony resisted. He refused to recognize an order by the Catholic Church to allow them partial use of the building, and a Catholic priest broke in to the church with an axe. Rev. Anthony reported this to the patron in a petition on April 23, 1708, who dropped the contest. Rev. Anthony was recalled to Monchzell where Baron John Melchior von Festenburg was using lands belonging to the church and keeping the tithes for himself. Rev. Anthony reported this to Prince Ernest Ludwig, and the Baron denied the charges.

The prince did not bother to have the charges investigated, so the Baron attacked the character of Pfarrar Henckel, and in October of 1714 Rev. Anthony was called to Neckergemond and Zuzenhausen. His successor renewed the charges, and the Prince appointed an investigator who reported that the Baron was guilty. But Rev. Anthony resigned on June 3, 1717 and joined William Penn's colony of German Lutherans in Penn's Woods. During his German pastorates he baptized 151 children, performed 51 burials and 22 marriages.

Near present-day Philadelphia Rev. Anthony founded the St. Michael's Lutheran Church. He also reorganized New Swamp Church, preached at Trappe, Goshenhoppen and Tulpehocken. He purchased 250 acres for his family and kept accurate precise records for the baptisms, funerals and marriages of the area. His diaries have been lost, but the ledgers are preserved at Mt. Airy Theological Seminary along with his ministerial robes, baptismal pitcher and bowl and Bible. He died following a fall from his horse on Chestnut Hill, and was buried in the St. Michaels Cemetery. Maria and Anthony had twelve children:

    A. Johann Nicholaus   2-19-1692 to 5-14-1693
    B. Johanna Frederica   3-29-1694 to 1739
        m. Valentin Geiger 1716
    C. Johann Melchior   1-30-1695 to 9-27-1706
♦   D. **Johann Gerhard Anthony** 1-12-1697 to 1736
        m. Anna Katherine 1720
    E. Maria Elizabethe   12-31-1699
    F. George Rudolphus   10-19-1701 to 1788
    G. Anna Maria   2-9-1703
    H. Johann Justus   2-10-1705 to 1778
    I. Benigna Maria   9-30-1707 to 12-22-1708
    J. Jacob Antonius   7-9-1709 to 12-22-1708
    K. Maria Catherine   5-10-1711 to 10-1785
    L. Johanna Philipp   4-26-1713

D. Johann Gerhard Anthony was born in Daudengall, Germany and died in 1736 in East Earl Township, Pa. He was a graduate of the University of Giessen, founded in 1607. He married Anna Katherine and had five children:

    (1) Maria Margaretha 1722 to 11-16-1809
        m. John George Yundt 1745
    (2) Maria Elizabeth   1724 to 1809
♦   (3) **George**   1727 to 3-13-1778 m. Barbara Rowland
    (4) John   1730-1780
    (5) Susannah Margaretha 1736-1809

(3) George was born in Colebrookdale Township, Berks County, Pa and died in Hinkletown, Earl Township, Pa. He married Barbara Rowland daughter of Jacob and Barbara Rowland. He operated the stone Inn at Hinkletown, and built the first

bridge over the Conestoga Creek from the Phildelphia Road to the Road to Paxton. At the nearby Ephrata Cloisters, George nursed wounded soldiers following the Battle of Brandywine. Here he and nearly 200 soldiers contractred swamp fever and died. The Hinkle farm is now run by an Amish family who sell roadside vegestables and fruit. George and Barbara had eleven children:

    (a) Susannah Barbara   1-6-1750
♦   (b) Catherine Barbara   5-1753 to 1823 m. Richard Davis
    (c) John Jacob   1-22-1755 m. Elizabeth Edwards
    (d) John   1760 to 4-12-1828 m. Catherine
    (e) Mary Magdelena   5-18-1761 to 3-9-1808 m. Leonard Diller
    (f) Anna Maria   1763 m. Johannes Wolff December 28, 1782
    (g) George   7-2-1764 to 3-13-1769
    (h) Jonathan   1767 m. Catherine Meyer October 2, 1787
    (i) George   1769 m. Susannah Goetzinger
    (j) Samuel   1772-1832 m. Ann Lightner
    (k) Henry Gerhard   12-1773 to 4-11-1774

The Davis House near Hinkletown, Pa.

Old Store in Monrovia, Maryland

Davis Home in Monrovia, Maryland

MATTINGLY

Thomas Mattingly arrived in St. Mary's County in 1663 with his wife Elizabeth and four children: Judith, Thomas, Cezar and Elizabeth. They came seeking religious freedom, as they were Catholics, and in England they were persecuted. The name Mattingly developed from "Matthew's lea," a lea being a meadow. Thomas II had William in 1696, and we are from that son.

Thomas William Mattingly's father was born circa 1800 and was a Catholic in St. Mary's City, Maryland. He was a tenant farmer, and had nothing of his own. When the local church was being rebuilt following a fire, the priest required that each family pay for a pew. As he had no money, and could not abide this ruling, he left St. Mary's and went to Mt. Harmony, in Calvert County, where he joined the local Methodist Church. In a community called Chaneytown, he married Mary Priscilla Howes (10-9-1838 to 9-30-1922). She is buried in Congressional Cemetery, with the Mahones.

Elisha Howes is listed in the 1840 census as having 12 slaves, an overseer, 4 agricultural laborers. His son Samuel (5-16-1804 to 8-18-1859) had a smaller farm, but did own slaves. He had two daughters, Emily and Ann Elizabeth by his first wife, and then married Priscilla Ann French. The French family moved to Calvert County from the Piscataway District of Prince George's County. Jacob and Rebecca were Priscilla's parents. Priscilla and Samuel had Mary "Mammy" Priscilla Howes.

Thomas William Mattingly was born 8-27-1827. The Mattingly's raised tobacco and Thomas went to Baltimore, where he was the janitor of tobacco warehouse #3. He fell to his death on 6-6-1884 and was brought back to Mt. Harmony for burial. The family moved to Washington, DC. Thomas and Mary had nine children.

1. **Sallie Rebecca** 10-4-1858 to 6-16-1934 m. Anthony Malone
2. Joseph Samuel 4-28-1860 to 8-28-1861
3. Mary Angelica 10-12-1862 to 11-12-1863
4. Thomas William Jr. 9-1-1865 m. Sally, served in World War I
    (a) Eva Gertrude 4-1894 to June 4, 1894
    (b) Mary m. Wadell
5. Rosa Lee   2-17-1868 to 8-21-1931 m. James Foust (6-16-1862 to 11-9-1950) had a farm on PG/Calv line.
    (a) Mary Priscilla 2-23-1886 to 1970 m. Herman Bookholtz Lovett on 12-2-1916
        i. Rose Elizabeth 1918 m. Joseph Dudley Walton
        ii. James Herman 1921 m. Lillian Bolduc
    (b) Thomas James 1889-1911
    (c) Rosabelle 4-30-1909 to 1970 m. Adam Miles Noll (1908-1972) on 6-24-1933
6. **John Fielder**   5-2-1870 to 1944

◆ 7. **Hettie Priscilla**   8-12-1872 to 8-14-1958
 8. Ashton Roy   5-17-1875 to 5-24-1875
 9. Robert Lee   8-1876 m. Geneva Bailey
    (a) Robert Jr.
    (b) Mary Wardell

1. Sallie and Anthony Malone lived first at 417 D Street and later on Niagara Street, that is now Piney Branch Road near the fire house where he worked, with Lee Beall. In later years, Mammy lived there, too and the photographs of the Mattingly family were taken at this location.
    A. Mary Elizabeth   5-4-1883 m. James Owen Dove
       (1) Rebecca Elizabeth 2-28-1917
           (8-27-1911 to 4-20-1997) on 12-23-1944
           (a) Judith Elaine 11-2-1945 m1 Robert Lee Bennett (11-10-1936) m2 Darren Baze (4-3-1960) on December 23, 1989
               i. Margit Elaine 3-11-1985 m. Kinsella
                  a. David Anthony 1-7-1985
                  b. Briana Elaine 4-6-1987
                  c. Kristoffer Thomas 6-1-1989
                  d. Thomas Zane 3-28-1991
                  e. Samantha Nicole 2-11-1993 to 7-1993
                  f. Holly Ann 9-5-1995
           b) James Anthony, Jr. 11-22-1947 m. Della Conrad July, 1973.
       (2) James Anthony 4-16-1918 to 4-14-1990 m. Gweneth Crawford

    B. RosaBelle   8-9-1885 to 5 12-1894 brd Congressional
    C. William Fielder   2-7-1891 to 12-4-1932 m. Virginia Bishop
    D. Herbert Anthony   11-27-1892 to 7-1904 brd Congressional
    E. Hettie Ellen   2-26-1900 m. Francis Owens lived 1120 E Street had Richard "Dick" Francis c. 1920
    F. infant buried at Congressional Cemetery
    G. infant buried at Congressional Cemetery

6. John Fielder Mattingly married Margeret Dole Goodman. She was called "Bessie." He was a train engineer and they had four children all born in Washington, DC.
    A. John Fielder "Jack"   7-25-1898 to 2-1979 died in Sterling, VA
    B. Thomas "Dr. Tom"   9-22-1899 to 4-1977 m. Grace Laura Carnahan
       (1) Thomas, Jr. 1927
       (2) Grace Marie 1929 m. Roy Clark
       (3) Richard 1931
       (4) Phyllis 1933 m. Richard Evans

C. **Evelyn Levely** 3-11-1904 to 11-10-1998
D. Margaret 6-28-1910 to 1-1974, single

C. Evelyn married Wilbur Wingate St. Clair at the Second Baptist Church, SE Washington on October 6, 1926. They had three children.
   (1) Wilbur Wingate Jr.5-16-1929 m. Denia Stern
      (a) Deede
      (b) Thomas John
   (2) Barbara Jean 3-5-1932 m. Alfred S. Llorens (1931) on 9-11-1954
      (a) Mary Beth 2-22-1959 m. Schafermeyer
      (b) Jean Marie 4-10-1960 m. Pete Seward
      (c) William Alfred 9-27-1961 m. Marcia Awong
      (d) John St. Clair 4-22-1964
   (3) Marylyn Elizabeth 2-26-1938 m. Larry Doan on 5-17-1975

C. William Fielder Malone and Virginia Dorothy Bishop (8-11-1891 to 2-19-1976) were married March 16, 1914 at Ellicott City, Md. They had 6 children before he was killed in a railroad accident in the Washington Terminal.
   (1) Elizabeth Rose   2-17-1915 m. Otto Neilson, Jr.
      (a) Patricia Anne 3-17-1934 m. Manuel John Martufi
      (b) Otto III 12-24-1935 m. Georgia R. Facer
      (c) Ralph Ernest 5-20-1944 m. Margaret F. Galbraith
   (2) Virginia Evelyn   2-5-1918 m. Edward Heller
   (3) William Fielder, Jr. 9-25-1920 to 2-9-1981 m. Catherine Thompson
   (4) June Louise   9-16-1922 m. George Whitmer
   (5) Robert Anothony   10-8-1924 m. Melba Dougherty
   (6) John Bishop   1-28-1929 m. Louise Hawkins

7. Hettie Priscilla Mattingly (8-12-1872 to 8-14-1958) married Theodore "Lee" Beall on April 5, 1894. Rev. Rice of the Trinity M.E. Church, 4th St, SE performed the ceremony. When their first child was born, they were renting part of 2202 I Street, NW. Later, they lived at 9th and Illinois Avenue. Lee was a fireman at Engine Co. No. 1 at 16th and K Streets, and later at Brightwood Station, #8. Lee was initiated into the Stansbury Lodge on April 9, 1906, passed on May 14, and raised on June 11. At the time Nettie completed grade school, they were renting rooms from Mrs. Green on Madison Street between 9th and Georgia Avenue, NW. Mrs. Green's husband, Lieut. Green worked at engine company 22. When her mother-in-law, Catherine V. Beall, died they were living at 614 Longfellow Street. They lived there until 1911, when they purchased 5505 Fifth Street.

   The following article is from "The Evening Star" Saturday, June 17, 1911, page 1. Lee Beall, 47 years old, driver of No. 22 engine company's horses, died at Garfield Hospital about 10:45 o'clock this morning as a result of a fracture of the skull, the injury having been received when a horse that he was exercising was struck by a street car and he was thrown to the roadway. The accident happened about 8:30 o'clock when the horse shied in front of the southbound car about 100 yards north of the quarters of the company at Brightwood.

The horse was so seriously injured that Dr. C. Barwell Robinson, the District veterinarian, found it necessaary to kill it. Hezekiah Dodson, motorman in charge of the car, and L. Robinson, conductor, were taken to the tenth precinct police station to be detatined until Coroner Nevitt can finish the investigation.

Theodore Beall, father of the deceased, said this morning that his son's death was foretold in a dream he had Thursday night.

"It was plain as day," said the aged man, "and a gray horse did it."

The horse, which is gray, has been in the department since May 10, 1910, and had never become accustomed to noises of street cars and automobiles.

Beall was riding the horse and leading another, giving them exercise. He had gone as far north as the Brightwood Hotel, and was returning to the engine house when the accident happened. The animal shied in the direction of the car tracks. The car struck it and threw it to one side. Beall was thrown upon his head, the force of the contact with the road being severe enough to inflict a fracture of the base of the brain.

Dr. A. V. Parsons of Takoma Park and Dr. C. B. Heinecke, the latter Beall's family physician, attended the injured man before he was taken to the hospital. He was accompanied to the hospital by George A. Tarbell, a neighbor and Dr. Heinecke. Dr. Charles S. White and Dr. W. H. R. Brandenburg, the latter a surgeon in the fire department saw the the injured man at the hospital.

Beall's condition was so critical that the surgeon's decided it was useless to perform an operation. Mrs. Beall, who was hurried to the hospital by Dr. Parsons shortly after the accident, was with her husband when he died.

The deceased is survived by his widow and two children--Nettie, sixteen and Lee, thirteen years old. Last night his daughter received her diploma at the graduating exercises of the high school and this morning her father hurried to his home at 614 Longfellow Street to extend his congratulations.

It was stated by all the witnesses that the street car was not going fast and that Motorman Dodson brought it to a stop almost instantly. Dodson is well known to the members of the fire company and they stated that they did not blame him for the accident.

Coroner Nevitt directed that a jury be summoned to hear testimony Monday morning in order to determine the question of responsibility for the accident.

This afternoon an autopsy was performed at Garfield Hospital and the body was ater removed to the home.

It is probable that members of Stansbury Lodge, No. 24, and Royal Arch Masons will have charge of the funeral, the deceased having been identified with both organizations.

Chief Wagner hurried to No. 22 engine house as soon as he heard of the accident, reaching there shortly after the injured fireman had been taken to the hospital. He later went to the home of the fireman and from there to the hospital, where he saw Mrs. Beall. He directed that the flags on the buildings of the department be placed at half-mast.

Driver Beall was a native of Prince George's County, Md., having been born between Upper Marlboro and Queen Anne in 1864.

In July 1883, he was appointed a member of the fire department, and many years of his service were spent as a member of No. 1 engine company. He received a promotion the second year he was in the service.

In 1888 he was a victim of the fire at the George W. Knox Express Company's stables on B Street, NW. He sustained severe burns about his face and hands, while Mr. M. R. Fenton and D. O'Donoghue, members of his company, were burned to death, and S. E. Mastin, another member of the company, was crushed to death.

The following article is from "The Evening Star" Tuesday, June 20, 1911, page 4. Funeral services for T. Lee Beall, driver of No. 22 engine company's horses, who was killed as a result of being thrown from one of the horses in a collision with a street car Saturday were held at 10 o'clock this morning at his late residence, 614 Longfellow Street, NW.

Rev. Charles F. Cole, pastor of the Brightwood Park Methodist Church, officiated. Interment was made in Rock Creek Cemetery. The pallbearers were Masons from the following fire department companies: Capt. Warren, truck No. 6; Lieut. Green, engine co. No. 22; Private [Oliver] Bassford, engine No. 22; J. L. Glascock, engine No. 10; C. C. McKay, engine No. 7; R. D. Crompton, engine No. 21; Lieut. Steele, truck No. 4; and T. Phipps, No. 4. All of the pallbearers wore the Masonic apron over their uniforms.

All of the members of No. 22 engine company attended the funeral in a body. Chief Wagner had arrenged a detail of firemen from other companies to occupy the quarters of No. 22 company so that the department would not be out of service.

Many floral offerings were sent to the house, both from members of No. 22 engine company and the other fire department companies in the District.

Hettie Priscilla Mattingly and Theodore "Lee" Beall had two children.
- ♦ 1. Nettie Lenora   1-18-1895 to 2-17-1984 m. John Linthicum Wolfe
    2. Lee Stone   11-11-1897 to 11-13-1978 m. Rose Alpha Morett
        A. infant daughter
        B. Betty Anne 2-13-1931 to 1-23-1999 m1 Alexander Montcalm Daly, Jr.
            on July 24, 1950 m2 Virgil Settle in 1999
            (1) John Joseph 10-30-1952
            (2) David Lee 2-16-1959
            (3) Donald Alexander 9-26-1964
        C. Lee Morett 7-29-1933 m. Susan McKinsey

Mattingly Family

Mattingly Reunion

Thomas Mattingly, center, Priscilla Howes Mattingly, right

Beall

Ninian Beall, was an endentured servant of Richard Jackson. He was freed on December 24, 1698, in Calvert County, Md. Originally from Scotland, of the Clan MacMillan, he was not the famous Colonel Ninian Beall of Prince George's County, Md. Ninian was the name of the patron saint of the MacMillan Clan, who had been Druids. The Bell's were their priests and resided in the forest surrounding the MacMillan castle. So many of the Bell's chose Ninian as a name for their sons. The author's Ninian ancestor came to Prince George's County, married Catherine, and died there in August of 1780. They had 12 children:

1. Catherine   m. Zacharieh Brown had Lithe
2. Mary   m. Price
3. Richard
4. James
♦ 5. Ninian, Jr.
6. Thomas
7. Benjamin
8. Ann   m. Nichols
9. Elizabeth   m. Barrett
10. Eleanor   m. Brown
11. Martha   m. Nichols
12. Margery   m. Brown

5. Ninian Jr. (1723) married Catherine and had
   - A. Nathan   1745 to 5-1818
   - B. Andrew   1749 to 8-1781 m. Margaret
   ♦ C. **John**   1749 m. Eleanor (or Ellender)
   - D. Ninian III   1751 m. Ann Nancy Cecil
   - E. Elizabeth   m. Oliver Barron 5-28-1800
   - F. Zadock aka Shadrick m. Agnes
   - G. Aaron
   - H. Teressa
   - I. Leathe   m. Samuel B. White 2-21-1781
   - J. Catherine   m1 John Baynes, m2 William Beanes

C. John was a Second Lieutenant in the Revolutionary War, commissioned on January 3, 1776. He married Eleanor and had eight children:

   - (1) Naomi   1780 m. William Mullican
   - (2) **Elizabeth**   1782 m. James Shaw
   - (3) Leathy   1784 m. Peter Plunkett
   - (4) Teressa   1787 m. Alexander McBee 12-24-1810
   ♦ (5) **Theodore**   11-1789 m. Catherine E. Free b. 1813
   - (6) George   3-1791 m. Amelia Hayes 10-20-1813

(7) Brooke   1795 to 5-1843 m. Asenath G.
(8) Alley   1796

John died when Theodore Beall and his younger siblings were very young. His older sister, Elizabeth, had already married master brickmason, James Shaw. Shaw took in Elizabeth's three younger siblings when Eleanor Beall died soon after her husband. The Shaw's had eight children of their own, who resided between Bladensburg and present-day New Carrollton, Maryland:

    (a) Rezin   m. Elizabeth Beall 12-21-1842
    (b) Matthias
    (c) Zachariah m. Mary Ellin Ryon 10-4-1846 lived in Bladensburg, Md.
    (d) George Washington, Bladensburg Dist. New Carrollton
    (e) Emmerline   m. John S. Hall 11-7-1849 of Governor's Bridge
    (f) Maria   m. Hall lived on Brick Church Rd, Mulliken's Station
    (g) Mary Ellin 1813 m. William T. Beall 12-19-1841 brd. Whitfield Chapel

    5. Theodore learned bricklaying while bonded to his brother-in-law. In return, James acquired the land that should have gone to the Beall sons, including Theodore's portion. It took many years before he was able to buy some of it back. Theodore Borp Beall, (3-4-1833 to 10-22-1912) met Catherine Virginia Jones, and they were married on August 13, 1860. On October 18, 1867 they purchased "Waring's Lot", "Williams Range"and "Woodland" for $1,000.00 from Evan & Mary Branson of Henderson Co., Kentucky. On December 28 of the same year they purchased two more adjoining pieces of property, both part of "Elverton Hall." These 221 acres were purchased for $8,840.60 from Charles and Emily Hill. The "Elverton Hall" property was mortgaged on January 18, 1877, when after ten years, Charles Hill had received no payments from Theodore Borp Beall toward the cost of the land. They were given 9 promisory notes to pay off the land, one for $1,000.00 and the other 8 for $980.58 each. Each one was due one year after the preceding one. On February 9, 1880 they were unable to pay the interest on the notes. On June 3, 1882 they still owed 7 of the notes to William B. Bowie, who had assumed the notes from F. Snowden Hill, Charles C. Hill's son, for a total of $789.29. They were given another year to pay off the interest, and resume paying the notes, with the condition that if they could not, the property would be forfieted. The Beall property was across Brick Church Road from the mansion, Elverton Hall, which had an interesting history. Although George Washingon never slept there, it was the sight of many balls and jousting tournaments. It had a marble floor entrance and was quite elegant in it's day. The property of Theodore Borp Beall is presently an airport. He died in Glenn Dale, Prince George's County, Maryland, at his daughter's farm. He and Catherine are buried in St. George's Episcopal Cemetery. Although there is no stone for him at this time, he is buried next to CV Beall's large obelisk. Catherine died in Washington, DC at 614 Longfellow St. NW. They had four children, three of whom lived on the above mentioned property:

    (a) Owen Albert Beall   10 1860 to 1909 m. Ida A.

   i. Fanny E. 10-1891
   ii. Altha B. 8-1897 m. Simpson, had Betty m. McKay
   iii. Eutha May 6-1899
  (b) Infant
♦ (c) Theodore Lee 2-29-1864 to 6-11-1911 m. Hettie P. Mattingly
   buried at Rock Creek Cemetery, Washington, D. C.
  (d) Mary Ann 2-3-1867 to 12-28-1929 m. Norval Clinton Harvey

  The lineage of Theodore Borps Beall's wife Catherine was from James Jones and Mary A. Bryan Jones. They had six children. Mary was born in Ireland. The Jones lived in Marlborough, and James was a manager on a farm.

  1. Sarah A.   1831
  2. George W.   1834
  3. Edward   1835
  4. Richard F.   1836
  5. Mary A. R.   1838 m. John D. Nally
   (a) Philip F. m. Ann Rebecca Beall
   (b) Frances L. m. James Washington Beall 5-27-1872
   (c) Sarah (12-6-1860 to 11-7-1882) m. Norval Clinton Harvey
    She is buried at Mt. Carmel, in Bowie, Maryland
  6. Walter   1843
  7. Catherine Virginia 10-1845 m. Theodore Borp Beall

  4. Mary Ann Beall married Norval Clinton Harvey (1856 to 11-1924), of Thomas F. (9-17-1828 to 1-4-1909) and Amelia (11-3-1832 to 2-27-1896). They are all buried in St. George's Episcopal Cemetery. They had six children in Glenn Dale, and ran a dairy farm between there and Seabrook.
  (a) Nelson E. 1887
  (b) Harry O. 1889-1960 m. Mary Lee Beall of Albert
  (c) Florence V. 1892 m. George H. Harrison lived in Virginia
  (d) Frederick L. 1894 lived on Chestnut Stree in Bowie, Md
  (e) Lena A. 1895 m. Jack Drescher, lived in Brookmont, Md
  (f) Nellie R. 1902 m. Maxwell B. Caplan, moved to Phila, Pa.

Owen Beall and Theodore "Lee" Beall

MAHONE

Daniel and Willis Mahone came to Virginia from Waterford, Ireland. They married the Hatton sisters cicra 1730 in York County, Virginia. Daniel and the former Miss Hatton had at least 6 children.

    1. Major   1731
    2. John   1733 had Milley m. Wm Padgett 12-24-1789, Amherst Co.
    3. Daniel   1735
♦   4. **William**   1739 to 1795 m. Susannah d. 1807
    5. daughter
    6. daughter

4. William and Susannah had at least 6 children in Surray Co., Virginia
♦   A. **James**   1767
    B. Nancy   1770
    C. Sally   1772 m. Michajah Mountfort March 9, 1797
    D. William, Jr.   1780 m. Nancy Jordan May 16, 1801 had Gen. Billy
    E. Patsy   1782 m. Benjamin Pittman Jan. 2, 1802

A. James had at least 2 children:
♦   (1) Thomas B.   1785
    (2) John W.   1788

(1) Thomas B. married first, Edda Callaway on April 10, 1810 in Amherst Co.; Levi Hamilton [Dudley] Callaway was the witness. They had at least 2 children:
    (a) Martha   1819 m. Marquis White July 14, 1842
    (b) Chiswell D. d. 11-27-1864 of Thyphoid m. Mary A. Gruber

Thomas B. remarried Mary Scott c. 1835. They had at least 2 children in Rockingham Co., Virginia.
    (c) L. Warren
♦   (d) **Charles Wesley** 12-1-1844 to 10-27-1909 m. Rebecca Francis Reedy 8-2-1868 in Augusta Co., Virginia. She was a daughter of Solomon Reedy and Polly Duvall, who had at least three children:
    1. Rebecca Frances   2-3-1848 to 5-24-1923
    2. David F.   d. 11-23-1880
    3. Levi   1853 to 8-20-1880

(d) Charles and Fanny had nine children.
    i. Mary Regenia "Gertrude" 5-2-1869 to 1938 m. Andrew. F. Callan
                                (5-11-1898 to 1935)
♦   ii. **Mary Cora Lee**   12-26-1870 to 4-12-1946
    iii. E. T. L.   2-23-1872 to 9-8-1872
    iv. **Florence B.**   8-30-1873 m. James A. Bragg 10-28-1898
    v. Sarah E. B.   10-30-1875 to 9-9-1901

    vi. Pearl E.   9-3-1877 to 4-2-1934 m. Wm E. Elliott 2-8-1911
    vii. Charles E. B. 12-29-1880 to 5-19-1901 m. Lucy
    viii. J. Will A.   5-20-1883 m. Maude Creasy 12-25-1904
    ix. **Charles Ashby Lawrence** 1-10-1889 to 12-20-1929
        m. Lettie Hunter Terry 1-23-1908

    ii. Cora Lee had Elaine Beatrice Mahone (9-10-1890 to 3-24-1974) who married Ralph Hebbard, and were the parents of Lester William Hebbard. Cora married John Henry Nagengast on December 1, 1895. They had two children.
        I. John Charles April 1896-1901
        II. Katie Pearl 8-17-1899 m. Kenneth Buker

    John Henry Nagengast, a cooper, was the son of John and Ursula Nagengast, of Springfield, Ohio. They had immigrated from Germany. John Henry's first daughter was Mary Catherine, born in Pennsylvania, her mother was Barbara. After John Henry Nagengast died, Cora Lee moved to Richmond, where her mother was running a boarding house. One of the boarders was William Elliott. Cora's sister Pearl married him. Another boarder was Frank P. Waktins, whom Cora Lee married after 1924, in the living room of 703 Longfellow Street, NW, Washington.

    Florence and Belle worked for S. P. Greenstone, a cigarmaker in Lynchburg in 1892, while Charles Wesley Mahone was a cooper for J. T. Yates, and later, a foreman. Several of Charles brother's and nephew's also worked there.
In 1904 Pearl worked for a shoe factory called Southland, where later, Ashby, Elaine and Katie also earned money.

    Elaine Beatrice Mahone and her sister, Katie spent part of their time at their grandmother's boarding house in Richmond. By that time, Fanny was a widow and was running the boarding house for a living. Elaine then went to live with her Aunt Gert, in Washington, DC. She met Ralph Hebbard at church youth group from Metropolitan Presbyterian Church, SE Washington, DC.

    II. Katherine Pearl (8-17-1899 to 10-5-1988) married Kenneth Cook Buker (8-24-1896 to 10-19-1989) on June 17 1919 in Washington, DC. They had three children:
        Barbara   6-26-1920 m. Edward Alonzo Burgoon 2-1942
            Barbara Eileen 2-1943
            Kathleen Anne 11-6-1946
        Kenneth Cook, Jr.   10-23-1922 m. Anne Caroline Engle 6-28-1947
            Ruth Anne 7-16-1950 m John Giles Foushee 2-26-1972
            Mary Katherine 11-7-1953 to 1-14-1995 m. Dwight Allen Sparks
            Ken Cook III 3-17-1957 m. Lori Kinnear
        Joyce Elaine   6-23-1930 m. Claude Wickers had
            Linda Joyce 11-6-1951 m. Craig Russell
                Brian Patrick 3-14-1980
                Shannon Marie 6-4-1984

                Dale Howard 8-18-1954
                Brandt Frederick 1-14-1957 m. Troye Dick 9-17-1990
        iv. Florence B. Mahone married James A. Bragg and lived in Norfolk, Va. They had three children:
                I. Charles   1899
                II. Robert   1901
                III. Ada   1903 m. Sidney Campbell
                    Muriel
                    Delcy Ann
                    Sylvia Aurelia

    ix. Charles Ashby Lawrence Mahone (1889-1929) married Lettie Hunter Terry and lived in Richmond, Virginia. They had three children:
                I. Lester Gay 7-1909 m. Nell Wright had Lenny, Jerry, Lanney, Gayle, Mickey and Gay.
                II. **Charles Jeffries** 12-1-1911 to 7-1961 m. Hester Garthright
                III. Edith 7-1912 m. John Herndon had Frances J. and Malcolm

II. Charles Jeffries Mahone married Hester Garthright (9-18-1912) in April of 1928. They had three children:
        Lester 10-10-1931 m. Viola Henley, had Kathy and Connie
        Francis 6-3-1933
        Robert 3-9-1943 had Robert Douglas and Elizabeth

Elaine Mahone

Pearl, Florence and Cora Mahone

Hibbard - Hebbard

Robert Hibbard was born in Salisbury, England in 1613. He arrived in Massachusetts on "The Arabella" 6-12-1630 with Governor Winthrop. The Winthrop delegation left from Yarmouth, England 4-7-1630. Robert was a member of Rev. Higginson's church, in Salem. He was a saltmaker and brickmaker. He married Joanna Loffel circa 1640 and died in 1684. They had nine children.

    1. Mary   9-27-1641
    2. John   11-24-1642
    3. Sarah   7-26-1644
♦   4. **Robert Jr.** 3-?-1648
    5. Joseph   5-7-1649
    6. Joanna   12-23-1651
    7. Elizabeth 3-6-1653
    8. Samuel   5-4-1658
    9. Abigail   3-21-1665

    4. Robert Hibbard, Jr. Of Wenham, Massachusetts, married Mary Walden (d. 4-29-1710). They had twelve children, including a set of twins.

    A. Mary   1674
♦   B. **Robert III**   7-8-1676 to 6-26-1742
    C. Joseph   1678
    D. Josiah   1680 died as an infant
    E. **Nathaniel** 1680 (see page 96)
    F. Ebenezer   1682
    G. Martha   1684
    H. Josiah   1686
    I. Sarah   1690
    J. Hannah   1691
    K. Abigail   1692
    L. Lydia   1694

    B. Robert Hibbard III married Mary Reed on December 3, 1702. Robert was made a townsmen in 1698. They had ten children in Windham, Massachusetts.

♦   (1) **John**   10-30-1704
    (2) Robert IV 4-30-1706
    (3) Josiah   9-30-1708
    (4) Samuel   5-2-1710
    (5) Mary   12-14-1711
    (6) Joshua   10-19-1713
    (7) David   3-9-1716
    (8) Martha   9-9-1718

(9) Seth   4-19-1724

(1) John Hibbard married Martha Durkee on September 22, 1725. They lived on "Canterbury Farm" in Little River, Canterbury, Connecticut. They had thirteen children.

    (a) Martha   12-21-1725
    (b) John   12-9-1727
    (c) Ebenezer   8-20-1730
♦   (d) William   1-20-1732
    (e) Anna   8-13-1734
    (f) Mary   9-30-1736
    (g) Daniel   9-29-1738
    (h) Jedediah   10-15-1740
    (i) Lemuel   2-8-1742
    (j) Sarah   2-4-1744
    (k) Elizabeth   2-15-1746 to 4-5-1753
    (l) Elizabeth   11-26-1751 to 11-26-1751

(d) William Hibbard (1-20-1732) married Dorothy Burnam on October 16, 1750. His children spelled their last name Hebbard. They had seven children born in Canterbury, Connecticut.

    i. Lucy   11-13-1752
    ii. Andrew   10-30-1754
♦   iii. **Rufus**   1-7-1758
    iv. Ebenezer   9-20-1761
    v. Joseph   10-2-1763
    vi. Dorothy   10-12-1766
    vii. Araunah   1-14-1770

iii. Rufus Hebbard (1-7-1758 to 4-17-1846) had twelve children:
    a. Annice   4-11-1778 to 7-6-1790
    b. William B.   10-15-1780
    c. Jeptha   7-8-1782 m. Polly had Frances Caroline 12-19-1808
    d. Olive   6-24-1784
    e. Lucy   10-28-1786
    f. Hezekiah H.   7-23-1788
    g. Dorothy Burnham   12-26-1792
    h. Mary Cleveland   12-6-1794
♦   i. **Ebenezer Bradford**   10-27-1797
    j. Rufus Jr.   11-17-1798
    k. Lydia   7-2-1801
    l. Moses   7-15-1807 to 1-7-1809

i. Ebenezer Bradford Hebbard (10-27-1797 to 8-1-1839) was a physician and married a physician's daughter. Ebenezer may have studied under her father. He left Woodsboro to go to Naples, Illinois, and died there. His family returned to Walkersville, and are buried in Isreal's Creek Burying Ground. He married Christiania Smith Sim on December 2, 1823. Their family Bible is the posession of the author. They had seven children.

    I. William Fletcher 10-20-1824 Leitersberg, Washington Co. died 11-7-1824
    II. Mary Elizabeth   5-23-1826 Reisterstown
    III. Harriett Sim   2-9-1829 Taney Town
    IV. Maria Louiza   9-17-1830 Taney Town died 7-25-1831
    V. Susan Rebecca   1833 Taney Town died 2-21-1833
    VI. Henry Bradford   3-21-1835 Westminster died 11-4-1837
♦   VII. **Thomas William** 3-27-1837 Woodsboro died 9-20-1890 Lansing, MI

    VII. Thomas William married Mary E. Edwards (1839) of Ann E. and James (1813) Edwards. James Edwards was a hotel keeper in Isle of Wight, NY. Thomas William Hebbard is buried in Mt. Hope Cemetery. The following is from the Lansing State Republican Newspaper, September 22, 1890: Thomas William Hebbard, ex-justice, ex-city treasurer, and a businessman who has gained honor and respect by years of upright, energetic and conscientious methods, died, Saturday night, at his home, from a paralytic stroke. At 4 o'clock in the afternoon Mr. Hebbard was waiting on a customer at his grocery store on Michigan Avenue, East. He attempted speech but could not make a sound. Turning quickly around he walked rapidly to the rear and sat down in a chair. A clerk, alarmed by his strange action, followed him and spoke to him receiving no reply, but a nod of the head on his volunteering to go for a doctor. The physician announced paralysis of the left side, and a hack was hastily called and the unfortunate paralytic taken to his home, whre he made several fruitless efforts to communicate a farewell to his family by means of writing. He could not speak a word, though seeming to understand all that was said, and at 8 o'clock he passed to his long rest, speechless, with his wife and son at his bedside. The death was a sad one, and doubly so to his scores of firm friends who deeply sympathize with the afflicted family

    The funeral will be held from the house tomorrow afternoon at 2 o'clock, Rev. J. M. McGrath officiating. The service will be conducted by the Masonic Order, of which he was an honored member of long standing,

    Thomas W. Hebbard was born March 27, 1837 in Woodsboro, Frederick County, Maryland. His youth was that of most young men of his period and station, marked with no unusual event nor distinguished by any remarkable traits [his father died when he was very young-author's note]. In 1845 he came to Michigan, locating at Milford, and moving to Ovid in 1860, where he married Miss Mary E. Edwards of that place. In 1862 he came to Lansing and entered a livery business, starting the firm of Giles and Hebbard. Subsequently, he engaged with John A. Kerr in the Republican Newspaper Office, then a weekly. He spent five years in the Saginaw Valley buying staves for a New York lumber firm, was appointed to the City Treasurer's Office in 1874 to fill a vacancy caused by the death of Treasurer Loomis, after which he entered the grocery business with N. J. Roe. In 1877 he built the Hebbard Block, now occupied by Page & Turney's Grocery Store, where he conducted a grocery in partnership with Ald. Henry Klocksiem, retiring in 1879, when he began business in his present location.

In this position Mr. Hebbard was quiet and retired, remarkably so, since he never was known to talk of his affairs, especially business affairs to anyone. His excellant business habits were careful and methodical, and all details were left in excellant shape. Indeed, within ten minutes of his sickness, everything was accounted for, showing the excellence of his business methods.

Mr. Hebbard leaves a wife and one son, William T. His death is a loss among Lansing businessmen and will be deplored as much. He was a mason and Knight of Maccabee, as well as a member of the St. Paul's Vestry. The remains will be buried at Mt. Hope with all masonic honors.

William Thomas Hebbard
son of Thomas William Hebbard
(1864-1930)

William Thomas Hebbard (7-23-1864 to 11-25-1930) married May Louise Blood. He was a Knight's Templar, tool and die maker, ran a machine shop and hardware store, where many of our good knives came from. He also worked for the Oldsmobile plant, setting up the assembly line and making tools for them, before they became a part of General Motors. He moved his family to SE Washington, DC to work in the Navy Yard. He was a civilian machinist, and made machine guns for battle ships. He took photos of the US Capitol and every statue in Washington on sensitized glass plates. He developed them in his attic and hand tinted them for a customer in England. The summer before he died, he purchased a cottage on the bay, which was a wonderful place for the family to enjoy. He married May Louise Blood on October 12, 1886 and they had four children.

♦ 1. Ralph Leroy 8-24-1887 to 6-27-1980 m. Elaine Beatrice Mahone on 10-12-1908. Ralph sold umbrellas at Grover Cleveland's second inauguration when he was ten years old. He remembers when the Potomac River was frozen solid, and when the canal barges came in with produce to Center Market.

    A. Russell Eugene 7-15-1911 to 6-1978 m. Yvette Gershon
    B. Lester William   7-21-1914

B. Les attended Tech High School and North Dakota State School of Science. He joined the Police force on 12-1-1938 and retired in 1964. He had a second career at NIH as a security specialist until 1977. He married Ethel Louise Wolfe.

2. Carl Bradford   1888 to 10-3-1918 m. Edith Cannon

3. Myrtle Frances "Polly" m. Joseph Quinn
4. Mary Alzina   4-18-1894 to 7-30-1970 m1 Edgar L. DeMoreland
   A. Robert Edgar 1916 m. Virginia VanSise (2-26-1916)
      (1) Donald 1-11-1939 m. Jerilyn Louise Hetrick
         (a) Stephen Donald 9-7-1967
         (b) Douglas Robert 11-12-1970 m. Angela May Patti
           i. Sean Douglas 10-19-1996
      (2) Grace 7-4-1943 m. Larry Haskins
         (a) Denise Caryl 9-29-1965 m. David W. Norfolk
         (b) Dawn Marie 4-14-1967 m. Michael W. Smith
         (c) Dana Samanatha 6-23-1970 m. Todd J. Hanson
   B. Jack   1918-1948
Mary Alzina Hebbard m2. Oscar Reynolds, St. Petersburg, FL

Nathaniel Hibbard
son of Robert Hibbard, Jr.
(1680-1725)

Nathaniel Hibbard married Sarah Crane and had at least two children.
1. **Nathaniel Hebbard, Jr.** 1709-1790
   A. Nathaniel III 1-18-1740 to 5-30-1803 m. Mary Abbe
   B. **Elisha** 1745-1825 m. Elizabeth Osborn
2. Paul Hebbard   1711-1791

   B. Elisha Hebbard (1745-1825) was born in Greenwich, Connecticut and married Elizabeth Osborn.
      (1) Nathaniel Hebbard 1778 m. Abigail Sherwood
         (a) Betsie
         (b) **Elisha, Jr.** 1802
         (c) Hiram
         (d) Horace
         (e) Harriet
         (f) Jane Ann
         (g) William
         (h) Nathaniel
         (i) Henry

   (b) Elisha was born in New Fairfield, Connecticut and married Olive Ferry. They had eight children.
         i. **Alonzo** 6-11-1827 to 7-29-1887 m. Margaret Ann Chitry
         ii. Jane A. 12-8-1829
         iii. Jane A. 10-4-1831
         iv. Nathaniel 11-17-1833

    v. Josephine 3-30-1836
    vi. Elisha G. 7-2-1839
    vii. Oliva G. 4-23-1842
    viii. William 4-15-1825

    i. Alonzo Hebbard married Margaret Ann Chitry and died in New York. They had seven children:
- a. **Franklin Pierce** 5-26-1853 to 3-18-1938
- b. Elisha 12-3-1854 to 1-24-1856
- c. Alonzo, Jr. 11-23-1856 to 1-22-1930 m. Adelia Dean Murphy on 6-10-1891 in Mt. Vernon, NY
- d. Ella 4-7-1859 to 6-11-1945 in New Rochelle, NY
- e. Edgar Crawford 11-21-1864 m. Francis Edgar Marsh on 1-7-1904 in NY.
  - I. Mary Edgar
  - II. Jean
- f. Jennie 4-19-1871 m. Melvin Thomas MacLaury on 10-14-1907 m2 John Hopfengartner
- g. Harrison W. 8-28-1884 m. Gertrude Spencer 6-1-1904
  - I. Gertrude Margaret, East Orange, NJ

    a. Franklin Pierce Hebbard married Carrie Marie Merchant (10-3-1855 to 11-17-1927) on 12-24-1876. He was born in Beverly, Massachusetts and died in New Rochelle, NY. They had seven children:
    I. Franklin Barton 10-8-1877 to 12-25-1961 m. Helen Harrison 3-17-1908
    II. Carrie Edith 7-2-1879
    III. May 5-27-1881 to 8-11-1976
    IV. **LeRoy Blanchard, Sr.** 10-13-1883 to 7-8-1968
    V. Edna 8-21-1888 to 1-7-1952
    VI. Russell Edgar 10-1-1892
    VII. Marguerite Merchant 11-25-1895 to 8-22-1974

    IV. LeRoy Blanchard Hebbard, Sr. was born in Bedford Park, NY and died in Dover, New Hampshire. He married Edwina Rhoby Grant on 8-13-1927. She was the daughter of Roscoe Ernest Grant and Etta May Hurd Grant and was born in Acton, Maine. They had three children:
    Louise Myra 6-4-1928 m. Howard Albert Davis m2 Robert Craig Lawrence
    LeRoy Blanchard, Jr. 10-23-1929 m. Beverly Jane Ellis 6-13-1953
    Richard Earle 3-21-1934 m1 Thelma Carraway m2 Carol Nichols
        m3 Lucille Gagnon

Russell and Lester Hebbard

The Hebbard and Wolfe Families

Hebbard and Blood Reunion

Lester Hebbard Family

Blood

James Blood (1588-1641) had Richard (1617). Richard Blood arrived in New England prior to 1642 and was an original proprietor of Groton, Massachusetts. He married Isabel and they had six children.

    1. Joseph   m Mercy Butterworth
◆ 2. **James**   9-7-1646 to 9-13-1692 m1 Elizabeth Longley (1669-1685) m2 Abigail Kemp (1666) December 20, 1686, daughter of Sarah Foster and Samuel Kemp.
    3. Sarah   6-1648
    4. Nathaniel   4-1650 m. Hannah Parker 6-13-1670
    5. Mary   d. 4-19-1662
    6. Hannah   3-1663 m. Joseph Parker, Jr. 11-19-1684

2. James Blood had seven children. The first four are Elizabeth Longley's and the last three are Abigail Kemp's.

    A. Richard   3-29-1670 to 7-8-1670
    B. Mary   9-1-1672 to 3-4-1756 m. John Shattucks
    C. Elizabeth   4-27-1675 to 10-20-1759 m. Samuel Shattucks 1695
    D. Hannah   4-27-1675 to 1-6-1675
◆ E. **James B.**   8-12-1687 m. Katherine Nutting
    F. John   3-16-1689
    G. Martha   10-20-1692 m. Thomas Jewell 12-6-1712

E. James B. and Catherine Nutting Blood had nine children in Groton, Massachusetts.

    (1) Eleanor   9-12-1712 m. Jonathan Lampson
    (2) James   10-26-1714
    (3) Josiah   1-20-1716
    (4) Sarah   1-20-1716   died inf.
    (5) Elizabeth   3-22-1718 m. Nathaniel Bowers 2-8-1742
    (6) Solomon   3-13-1720 to 1745
◆ (7) **Simeon**   9-15-1723 m. Sarah Gilson
    (8) Silas   9-8-1725
    (9) Lois   8-25-1727 to 9-27-1814 m. Abraham Parker 3-16-1748
    (10) Simon   8-4-1729
    (11) Sampson   10-16-1731
    (12) Eunice   6-22-1735

(7) Simeon Blood and Sarah Gilson Blood had seven children. He was born in Groton/Dunstable, Massachusetts and died in New Hampshire.

    (a) Amy   1749 to 6-11-1785 m. John Brown
    (b) Lois   1750-to 7-13-1832 m. Joseph Brown

(c) Mary	1754	m. Joseph Scott, Jr.	
(d) Deborah	1755 to 8-26-1829 m. Joel Waite 5-11-1775		
(e) Abel	1758 to 8-19-1852 m. Hannah Hale 12-20-1781		
(f) Simeon	1760	m1 Rhoda Youngman	
		m2 Mary Giles-Hutchins	
♦ (g) **Lemuel**	1761 to 4-21-1834 m. Lucy Hale (8-30-1765 to 8-14-1843) daughter of Hannah Lovewell & Joseph Hale.		

    Lemuel and Lucy were married on May 2, 1782. Lemuel had been a Revolutionary War Soldier. He is buried in a private yard on the South Acworth Road on the banks of the Cold River on Alstead. He was a farmer in Deering, Springfield and then Acworth, New Hampshire. They had Ezra Faxon Blood on 10-28-1798.

    Ezra served in the War of 1812 and then at the age of 21 he moved to Brownville, New York where he was engaged in a nail factory with Asa Whitney. In the spring of 1824 a Quaker named Musgrove Evans visited the land in Michigan that would become Tecumseh. He returned to Jefferson County, New York to organize a party of settlers, enlisting the support of his brother-in-law, J. W. Brown, and Ezra Blood. They set out with 14 men and their families, and at Buffalo discovered that steamboat tickets to Detroit would cost them each $20.00, so it was more practical to charter the sailing vessel (the Red Jacket or Erie, depending on which source you read). As soon as the harbor was clear of ice they set sail for Detroit, disembarking the last week in April.

    The women and children were left with goods and the men started for Tecumseh on foot, taking with them one pony and a French boy to transport their baggage and goods. They followed the St. Joe trail to Ypsilanti. This was a narrow, well beaten Indian trail, three to six inches deep. From Ypsilanti they followed the trail to Saline and then to the Raisin River. They they crossed the river, left the trail and headed southwest toward what would be the Evans Creek.

Here they found three Indian wigwams, deserted but good enough to sleep in. The next day they explored the section of county adjacent to the creek and came to the conclusion that this was the place for their settlement. After several days of exploration their supplies were exhausted, so they headed for Monroe, where they were to meet the rest of the party. Following the Indian trail, they arrived just at nightfall. The entire population greeted them, as it was peculiar to see men arriving from the west. Here they met the women and children of the party, who had just arrived on the "Fire Fly" from Detroit.

    Evans hired 30 men and they cut a road to the settlement. They built a log cabin twenty feet square, with a room upstairs for the children. They could not add a floor until the following November, when they built a sawmill, at which time they also added 2 shanties, fireplace and chimney. The bed was made in each corner of the house by sticking two poles into a hole in each wall and supporting the outer ends of the poles where they crossed each other with a block of wood. Thus, a good bedstead was made out of two saplings with a single leg. They used benches instead of chairs, and they had one plow. Mr. Fulsom borrowed Evan's plow, hitched on an ox team and with Ezra to hold the plow turned the first furrows in the virgin soil of what would become Lenawee County. They built smudge under the table to drive away mosquitoes. They attended church in Monroe, walking barefoot until just before reaching the church, then stopping to put their socks and shoes on before going inside. This was to save the souls of the shoes.

Ezra was a carpenter of some note and in 1832 erected the Walker Tavern at Cambridge Junction in the heart of the lovely Irish Hills. This historic building entertained many notables during it's period of activity including Daniel Webster, Henry Clay and James Fenimore Cooper and his family stayed there for several months when he began gathering material for "Oak Openings".

Ezra F. Blood
(1789-1887)

Ezra F. Blood, son of Lemuel Blood, married Alzina Blackmar of Eleanor Rice and Charles Blackmar (12-25-1774 to 8-22-1834) who were married in 1790. Alzina was born 4-25-1810 and was the first public school teacher in Tecumseh, Michigan. She was married to Ezra on January 12, 1830. In 1850 the census lists the worth of their farm as $1,350. Their six children were born in Tecumseh, MI.

    1. Mary A.   1832
    2. Mary Jane   1835
    3. Charles H.   1837 to 6-11-1918
    4. William A.   1840
♦   5. **Leroy C.**   10-19-1842
    6. Orville   1847 to 10-25-1915 in Lapeer, Michigan

5. Leroy C. Blood married Frances E. "Fanny" Conklin (7-23-1843 to 1-26-1915) of Hudson W. Conkling (12-24-1821 to 10-25-1910) and Caroline Gray (1824 to 10-9-1909), who were married in December of 1842. Hudson's parents were Samuel Conkling (4-11-1797 to 12-9-1883) and Julia Corvin (1800 to 9-7-1876). Leroy and Fanny were the parents of two children:

    A. May Louise Blood (1865-1947), who married William Thomas Hebbard. She played the piano while her children played other instruments for evening sing-a-longs. She sewed, canned and crocheted.
    B. Wilbur C.
        (1) Eunice 1-1888 to 8-3-1888
        (2) daughter who m. O. J. Holland and they lived in Chicago.

BRADFORD

The name Bradford was derived from crossing a broad ford. The earliest record of this name is Robert Bradfuth of Bentley, England (1450-1523). He had Peter Bradfouth (1474-1542) who had William Bradford (1527 to 1-10-1595) of Austerfield, Yorkshire, England. William had four children.

♦ 1. **William II** 1559 to 1591 m. Alice Hanson on 7-21-1584
   2. Robert 6-25-1561
   3. Thomas 1565
   4. Elizabeth 7-16-1570

1. William and Alice Bradford had four children who were orphaned in 1591.

   A. Margaret 3-8-1585
   B. Alice 10-30-1587
   C. **William II** 1589 Baptized 3-19-1589
   D. Roger 1590

C. William Bradford III married Dorothy May in 11-1613. The sailed from England for the New World but Dorothy Bradford drowned in Cape Cod Bay on 12-7-1620 while William Bradford was scouting. He then married Alice Carpenter on 8-14-1623. William was chosen as Governor in 1621 and remained so until 1657 with the exception of 1633-34, 1636, 1638, and 1644. Alice and William had three children born in Plymouth Colony. He assuredly would have known Robert Hibbard, who arrived in 1630, as there were not many Englishmen there at the time. Eight generations later, their descendants would marry.

   (1) John 1618 in the Netherlands
♦   (2) **William IV** 6-17-1624 to 12-12-1671 m1 Alice Richards 1650
                            m2 Mary Wiswell m3 Mary Holmes
   (3) Mercy 1626
   (4) Joseph 4-? 1630 to 7-10-1715

William Bradford IV had fifteen children by his three wives.
   (a) John 2-20-1653 Plymouth m. Mercy Warren
   (b) William V 3-11-1655 to 1687 m. Rebecca Bartlett
♦   (c) **Thomas Joseph** 1657
   (d) Alice c. 1659 -1745 m. Wm. Adams m2 James Fetch (1649-1727)
   (e) Mercy c. 1660 m. Samuel Steele
   (f) Hannah c. 1662-1738 m. Joshua Ripley
   (g) Melatiah c. 1664 m1 John Steele m2 Samuel Stevens
   (h) Samuel c. 1667-1714 m. Hannah Rogers
   (i) Mary c. 1668-1720 m. William Hunt
   (j) Sarah c. 1669

(k) Joseph   c. 1669
(l) Israel   m. Sarah Bartlett
(m) Ephraim   m. Elizabeth Brewster
(n) David   m. Elizabeth Finney
(o) Hezekiah   m. Mary Chandler

c. Thomas Joseph Bradford married Anna Fitch c. 1711 and one son. He then married Priscilla Mason of Major John Mason, hero of Pequot War. They had James, Jerusha and Mary. James married Edith Susannah and had six children in Norwhich, CT.

    i. Thomas   11-14-1712 in Norwich, CT.
    ii. John   1-30-1715
    iii. Jerusha   6-27-1716
♦   iv. **William**   7-1-1718
    v. Sarah   8-27-1720
    vi. Anna   1722

iv. William Bradford married Zerviah Lothrop in 1739 and one daughter, He then married Martha Warren in 1743 and had nine children. He then married the widow Stedman in 1759 and had five children and then married Mary Cleveland and had three children. The eighteen children were born in Connecticut.

    a. Zerviah   9-6-1740
    b. Mary   3-1-1744
    c. William   3-4-1745 to 3-31-1808 Minister, Canterbury, CT
    d. Ebenezer   5-29-1746
    e. David   5-8-1748
    f. Joshua   10-17-1751
    g. Abigail   9-2-1753
    h. James   2-1-1755
    i. Olive   7-13-1756
    j. Josiah   11-25-1757 m. Elizabeth
♦   k. Lydia   7-2-1760 m. Rufus Hebbard
    l. Beulah   9-3-1763
    m. Moses   8-6-1765
    n. Joseph   1-22-1767
    o. Benjamin   3-29-1768 to 12-16-1843 Lt. in War of 1812
    p. Keziah   6-11-1770 to 6-20-1770
    q. Zerviah   6-11-1770 to 9-23-1775
    r. Samuel   11-5-1772

Bibliography

Across the Years in Prince George's County, Effie Gwynn Bowie, 1947, Richmond, VA
Ancestral Colonial Families, Luther Welsh, 1932. Kansas City, Mo.
Atlas of Montgomery County, G. M. Hopkins, 1879, Phila., Pa.
Circling Historic Landscapes, Sugar Loaf Regional Trails. Maryland-- National Capital Park and Planning Commission, 1976, Silver Spring, Md.
Family History of the Cecils, Anice Lee Cecil, Ethel Hebbard, John L. Wolfe, Edie Eader, C. Douglas Cecil,
Family History of the Davis's, Jane Evans Best, Ethel Hebbard
Family History of the Haneys, Eloise Haney Woodfield
Family History of the Hebbards, Lester and Ethel Hebbard
Family History of the Linthicums, Ethel Hebbard, Kitty Linthicum
Family History of the McElfresh's, Ann Bolt, Betty Gilbert, Kitty Linthicum, Mary Lou Ballew
Family History of the Mahone's, Lester Hebbard, Peggy Hebbard, Edith Herndon and Butch Mahone
Family History of the Mattingly's, Ethel Hebbard
Family History of the Roelke/Roelkeys, Margaret E. Myers
Family History of the Shipleys, Mary Lou Ballew
Family History of the Thompsons, Mary Thompson McDonough
Frederick News, The, September 10 & 12, 1902
Genealogical Companion to Rural Cemeteries, Dona Cuttler, 2000
German Evangelical Reformed Church Registers, Frederick & Odelsheim, Germany
Scharf's History of Western Maryland, J. Thomas Scharf, 1882, Philadelphia
Sunshine of Your Smile, The, Sara Jane Allen Mayerle, unpublished manuscript
Urbana District History and Legends, Urbana Historical Society, 1976, Urbana

INDEX

J. Lizzie, 27
V., Rebecca, 2

Abott, Dorcas, 69
Adams, William, 123
Adamson, Rebecca, 2
Adkins, Ralph, 36
Ahalt, Charles, 40
Ahalt, Charlotte, 40
Ahalt, Earl, 40
Ahalt, Janice, 40
Ahalt, Kay, 40
Ahalt, Lauretta, 40
Ahalt, Milburn, 40
Albaugh, Martha, 48
Aldridge, Edward, 65
Aldridge, Howard, 65
Aldridge, James, 65
Aldridge, Kevin, 65
Aldridge, Michelle, 65
Aldridge, Nickie, 65
Aldridge, William, 65
Alexander, Meredith, 86
Allbright, Carl, 47
Allbright, Susanna, 47
Allen, Dona, 63
Allen, Kenneth, 63
Allen, Lillian, 63
Allen, Margaret, 63
Allen, Pauline, 63, 64
Allen, Sara, 63
Allnutt, Elizabeth, 3
Allnutt, Edwin, 3
Allnutt, Ernest, 3
Allnutt, James, 3
Altmire, Daniel, 48
Anderson, Charles, 83
Anderson, Clifton, 83
Anderson, Elizabeth, 91
Anderson, Harry, 83
Anderson, Jean, 83
Anderson, John, 17

Anderson, Louise, 83
Anderson, Mary, 35
Anderson, Thomas, 39
Anderson, Robert, 35
Anderson, Steven, 83
Anderson, Violet, 73
Anderson, William, 56
Andrews, Elizabeth, 27
Andrews, James, 8, 10
Andrews, John, 27
Andrews, Lydia, 70
Andrews, Kathleen, 10
Andrews, Lenora, 25
Angerhofer, Alice, 37
Angerhofer, Alvin, 37
Angerhofer, Richard, 37
Angerhofer, William, 37
Archer, Mary, 82
Arredondo, Beverly, 63
Ausherman, Mabel, 54
Awong, Marcia, 99
Aycock, Joseph, 75

Backus, Helen, 4
Baetjar, Anna, 51
Baetjar, J., 51
Baetjar, Ruth, 51
Bagby, Richard, 84
Bagby, William, 84
Baggerly, Nancy, 61
Baile, Gertrude, 54
Baile, Nathan, 54
Bailey, Geneva, 98
Bailey, Margaret, 20
Baker, Alice, 41
Baker, Charles, 9
Baker, George, 9
Baker, M., 81
Baker, Mary, 44
Baker, Patricia, 65
Baker, Thelma, 26
Ball, William, 7

Ballenger, Ernest, 17
Ballew, Lee, 85
Bankerd, Adelia, 51
Barber, Charles, 75
Barber, James, 75
Barber, Julia, 75
Barber, Monroe, 75
Barnes, Ida, 36
Barnesville, 10, 24
Barnett, Elizabeth, 64
Barnett, Judith, 64
Barnett, Leigh, 64
Barnett, Rainey, 64
Barnett, Ray, 64
Barnett, Rob, 64
Barrett, Susannah, 81
Barrick, Charles, 79
Barrick, Hattie, 80
Barron, Oliver, 104
Bartlett, Rebecca, 123
Bartlett, Sarah, 124
Barton, Gladys, 22
Basford, Alice, 20
Bassford, Oliver, 101
Bateman, Sarah, 69
Bates, Lisa, 64
Baynes, John, 104
Baze, Darren, 98
"Bazingthorp Hall", 88
Beach, Clfford, 21
Bealer, Ernestine, 64
Bealer, Pierre, 64
Beall, Aaron, 104
Beall, Alley, 105
Beall, Altha, 106
Beall, Andrew, 85, 104
Beall, Ann, 57, 104, 106
Beall, Barbara, 46
Beall, Benjamin, 104
Beall, Betty, 101
Beall, Bob, 27
Beall, Brice, 8

Beall, Brooke, 105
Beall, Catherine, 99, 104
Beall, Christi, 85
Beall, Dallas, 85
Beall, Della, 85
Beall, E. Eileen, 85
Beall, Eleanor, 104, 105
Beall, Elizabeth, 104, 105
Beall, Emmerline, 105
Beall, Esther, 85
Beall, Eutha, 106
Beall, Fanny, 106
Beall, George, 104, 105
Beall, Gideon, 85
Beall, Hettie, 101
Beall, James, 70, 104, 106
Beall, Jerry, 85
Beall, John, 27, 70, 86, 104, 105
Beall, Joseph, 70
Beall, Leathe, 104
Beall, Leathy, 104
Beall, Lee, 98, 99, 100, 101
Beall, Linda, 85
Beall, Lucinda, 83
Beall, Luther, 85
Beall, Margaret, 5, 6
Beall, Margery, 104
Beall, Marshall, 85
Beall, Martha, 85, 104
Beall, Maria, 105
Beall, Mary, 65, 70, 85, 104, 105
Beall, Matthias, 105
Beall, Naomi, 104
Beall, Nathan, 104
Beall, Nathaniel, 70
Beall, Nettie, 59, 99, 101
Beall, Ninian, 2, 104
Beall, Owen, 105
Beall, Ralph, 85
Beall, Raymond, 85

Beall, Rezin, 105
Beall, Richard, 2, 104
Beall, Ruth, 85
Beall, Sarah, 2, 70
Beall, Susie, 85
Beall, Teressa, 104
Beall, Theodore, 99, 100, 101, 104, 105, 106
Beall, Thomas, 104
Beall, William, 71, 105
Beall, Willis, 86
Beall, Zachariah, 105
Beall, Zadock, 104
Beall, Zephaniah, 70
Beall, Zeriah, 83
Beallsville, 8, 20, 25
Beane, Forrest, 76
Beanes, William, 104
Becker, Ruby, 51
Becraft, Herbert, 26
Beeser, Mr., 84
Behr, Carrie, 51
Belt, Benjamin, 1
Belt, Elizabeth, 6
Beiser, Daniel, 11
Bell, Alexander, 70
Bell, Andrew, 70
Bell, James, 70
Bell, Robert, 70
Bell, William, 70
Belt, Isabel, 6
Bennett, Bessie, 14
Bennett, Charles, 14
Bennett, Clifton, 14
Bennett, James, 14
Bennett, Louis, 53
Bennett, Lula, 14
Bennett, Mabel, 14
Bennett, Margaret, 53
Bennett, Margit, 98
Bennett, Matilda, 76
Bennett, Robert, 98
Bennett, Russell, 14

Bennett, Sarah, 15
Bennett, Thomas, 14
Bennett, William, 14
Benson, Cephas, 61
Benson, Jane, 61
Benson, Jonathan, 27
Benson, Richie, 23, 27
Benson, William, 27
Benton, Rachel, 84
Benton, Theodore, 57
Berger, John, 33
Bergh, Chauncey, 49
Bingham, Martha, 42
Bishop, Edwin, 49
Bishop, Virginia, 98, 99
Blackburn, Laura, 48
Blackmar, Alzina, 122
Blackmar, Charles, 122
Bladensburg, 1, 21, 41
Blood, Abel, 121
Blood, Amy, 120
Blood, Charles, 122
Blood, Deborah, 121
Blood, Eleanor, 120
Blood, Elizabeth, 120
Blood, Eunice, 120, 122
Blood, Ezra, 121, 122
Blood, Hannah, 120
Blood, Isabel, 120
Blood, James, 120
Blood, John, 120
Blood, Joseph, 120
Blood, Josiah, 120
Blood, Lemuel, 121
Blood, Leroy, 122
Blood, Lois, 120
Blood, Martha, 120
Blood, Mary, 120, 121, 122
Blood, May, 115, 122
Blood, Nathaniel, 120
Blood, Orville, 122
Blood, Richard, 120

Blood, Sampson, 120
Blood, Sarah, 120
Blood, Silas, 120
Blood, Simeon, 120, 121
Blood, Simon, 120
Blood, Solomon, 120
Blood, Wilbur, 122
Blood, William, 122
Bluege, Carol, 22
Bluege, Lynn, 22
Bluege, Ozzie, 22
Bluege, Wilor, 22
Blumanauer, Edith, 36
Blumenaur, Margaret, 12
Bode, Carolena, 42
Boldac, Lillian, 97
Bolgiano, Charles, 80
Bolgiano, Frank, 80
Bolt, D., 82
Bostic, Lucinda, 24
Bowen, Edith, 84
Bowen, Ella, 74
Bowers, Nathaniel, 120
Bowie, William, 105
Bowman, Mary, 72
Bowman, William, 4, 74
Bowyer, Cheryl, 36
Bowyer, Christopher, 36
Bowyer, Robert, 36
Boyer, Annie, 44
Boyer, Brian, 44
Boyer, Charles, 43
Boyer, Cynthia, 44
Boyer, Donna, 44
Boyer, Elizabeth, 43
Boyer, George, 43
Boyer, Helen, 43
Boyer, Jennifer, 43
Boyer, JoAnn, 43
Boyer, Katherine, 43
Boyer, Laura, 45
Boyer, Lester, 43
Boyer, Marion, 44

Boyer, Mark, 44
Boyer, Martha, 78
Boyer, Mary, 78
Boyer, Mildred, 78
Boyer, Peggy, 43
Boyer, Ruth, 43
Boyer, Samuel, 43, 44
Boyer, Sarah, 39, 41
Boyer, Steven, 44
Boyer, Timothy, 44
Boyer, Todd, 44
Bradford, Abigail, 124
Bradford, Alice, 123
Bradford, Anna, 124
Bradford, Benjamin, 124
Bradford, Beulah, 124
Bradford, David, 124
Bradford, Dorothy, 123
Bradford, Ebenezer, 124
Bradford, Edith, 124
Bradford, Elizabeth, 123
Bradford, Ephraim, 124
Bradford, Hannah, 123
Bradford, Hezekiah, 124
Bradford, Israel, 124
Bradford, James, 124
Bradford, Jerusha, 124
Bradford, John, 123
Bradford, Joseph, 123, 124
Bradford, Joshua, 124
Bradford, Josiah, 124
Bradford, Keziah, 124
Bradford, Lydia, 124
Bradford, Margaret, 123
Bradford, Mary, 123, 124
Bradford, Melatiah, 123
Bradford, Mercy, 123
Bradford, Moses, 124
Bradford, Olive, 124
Bradford, Robert, 123
Bradford, Roger, 123
Bradford, Samuel, 123, 124

Bradford, Sarah, 123, 124
Bradford, Thomas, 123, 124
Bradford, William, 123, 124
Bradford, Zerviah, 124
Bradfuth, Robert, 123
Bradley, Emma, 6
Brady, Sallie, 61
Bragg, Ada, 110
Bragg, Charles, 110
Bragg, James, 108
Bragg, Robert, 110
Braley, Charlotte, 3
Brandenburg, George, 15
Brandenburg, Jeremiah, 78
Brandenburg, W., 100
Brannan, Elenia, 61
Branson, Evan, 105
Branson, Mary, 105
Brashear, Elizabeth, 33
Brashears, Rebecca, 46
Breide, Anna, 31
Brengle, Caroline, 45
Brengle, Ezra, 48
Brengle, Laura, 48
Brengle, Lydia, 47
Brewer, Mary, 3
Brewster, Elizabeth, 124
Brosius, Bernard, 3
Brown, Doris, 76
Brown, Filmore, 76
Brown, Francis, 76
Brown, J., 121
Brown, John, 120
Brown, Joseph, 120
Brown, Julian, 76
Brown, Lithe, 104
Brown, Nora, 85
Brown, Roby, 85
Brown, Ruth, 76
Brown, Zacharieh, 104
Bruce, Debra, 24

Brunner, Cora, 39
Bryan, Mary, 106
Bryant, Pauline, 27
Buckingham, Louise, 21
Buckey, Herman, 45
Buckey, Mildred, 45
Buckey, William, 45
Buckeystown, 11
Buker, Barbara, 109
Buker, Joyce, 109
Buker, Kenneth, 109
Buker, Mary, 109
Buker, Ruth, 109
Burbank, Deborah, 65
Burbank, Jared, 65
Burch, Edgar, 20
Burch, Francis, 20
Burch, Henrietta, 20
Burch, John, 20
Burch, Marcia, 20
Burch, Patricia, 20
Burch, Russell, 20
Burdette, Caleb, 86
Burdette, Claude, 86
Burdette, Clifford, 86
Burdette, Donald, 86
Burdette, Grace, 86
Burdette, James, 17
Burdette, Judith, 17
Burdette, Martha, 78
Burdette, Sophronia, 86
Burdette, Virginia, 86
Burdette, William, 17
Burger, Charlotte, 44
Burgee, Ann, 57
Burgee, Martha, 73, 76
Burgee, Miel, 71
Burgee, Osie, 74
Burgess, Leigh, 27
Burgess, Nolan, 27
Burgess, Scott, 27
Burgoon, Edward, 109
Burnam, Dorothy, 113

Burns, Emily, 84
Burnside, Ann, 9
Burton, Joseph, 69
Burton, Sarah, 69
Burucker, George, 34
Burucker, John, 33
Burucker, Oscar, 34
Buss, Roger, 40
Buss, Russell, 39
Butcher, Howard, 40
Butt, Elizabeth, 19
Butterwick, Mary, 76
Butterwick, Ralph, 76
Butterworth, Mercy, 120
Buttion, Glenn, 21
Buttion, Melvin, 21
Buxton, Betty, 84

Callan, Andrew, 108
Callaway, Edda, 108
Callaway, Levi, 108
Campbell, Alexander, 56
Campbell, Delcy, 110
Campbell, Muriel, 110
Campbell, Syvia, 110
Cannon, Edith, 115
Cannon, George, 42
Cantwell, Howard, 43
Caplan, Maxwell, 106
Carbaugh, Dorothy, 40
Carbaugh, Robert, 40
Carlan, Cab, 64
Carlisle, E. Dorothy, 27
Carlisle, Mary, 77
Carr, Samuel, 8
Carr, Sarah, 6
Carraway, Thelma, 117
Carter, Betty, 41
Carter, Lydia, 91
Carter, Nora, 27
Carty, C., 34
Caruthers, Bertie, 18
Carver, Charles, 10

Carver, Dorothy, 10
Carver, Josephine, 10
Cash, Richard, 8
Cashell, Amanda, 19
Cashell, Andrew, 19
Cashell, Douglas, 18
Cashell, Edna, 18
Cashell, Elizabeth, 19
Cashell, Emily, 18
Cashell, George, 19
Cashell, Hanson, 18
Cashell, Hazel, 19
Cashell, Henrietta, 18, 19
Cashell, James, 19
Cashell, Kelly, 18
Cashell, Lois, 18
Cashell, Malvinia, 19
Cashell, Mary, 18
Cashell, Nellie, 18
Cashell, Richard, 19
Cashell, Samuel, 19
Cashell, Thomas, 18, 19
Cashell, William, 19
Castle, Eva, 38
Cecil, Adam, 24
Cecil, Alice, 16, 20, 21, 22, 23
Cecil, Anice, 23
Cecil, Ann, 1, 6, 8, 9, 25, 104
Cecil, Anna, 14
Cecil, Annie, 13, 16, 20
Cecil, Amanda, 9
Cecil, Amy, 24
Cecil, Arabella, 14
Cecil, Archibald, 7, 8, 9, 12
Cecil, Arthur, 17, 22
Cecil, Barbara, 11
Cecil, Benjamin, 6, 7, 8
Cecil, Bessie, 8
Cecil, Byron, 6, 7
Cecil, Carol, 6

Cecil, Catherine, 2, 9, 13, 24
Cecil, Charles, 6, 11, 14, 16, 20, 23
Cecil, Charlotte, 9, 20
Cecil, Chris, 24
Cecil, Christopher, 14
Cecil, Clara, 14, 15, 25
Cecil, Clinton, 6
Cecil, Cora, 16, 18, 19
Cecil, Daisy, 16, 22
Cecil, Daniel, 24
Cecil, Donna, 22
Cecil, Dorothy, 20, 21
Cecil, Edith, 17
Cecil, Edward, 6, 10, 15
Cecil, Eleanor, 1, 2
Cecil, Elizabeth, 1, 2, 6, 7, 8, 13
Cecil, Ellen, 14, 16
Cecil, Ellie, 22
Cecil, Elmer, 25
Cecil, Elsie, 11
Cecil, Emily, 13
Cecil, Emma, 11, 14
Cecil, Emory, 15
Cecil, Ethel, 17
Cecil, Eugene, 8
Cecil, Evelyn, 20, 21
Cecil, Everett, 15, 25
Cecil, Evonne, 11
Cecil, Florence, 11, 14
Cecil, Frances, 14
Cecil, Frank, 20
Cecil, Frederick, 6
Cecil, George, 6, 7, 11, 12, 13, 15, 16, 20, 21, 22, 34
Cecil, Georgia, 25
Cecil, Greenberry, 12
Cecil, Hammondatha, 9, 13
Cecil, Harry, 25
Cecil, Helen, 20
Cecil, Henry, 6
Cecil, Holly, 24
Cecil, Ida, 10, 11, 13
Cecil, Ira, 11, 16
Cecil, Isabel, 6
Cecil, James, 6, 11, 14, 22
Cecil, Jane, 1
Cecil, Jennie, 14
Cecil, John, 1, 7, 8, 11, 12, 13
Cecil, Jonas, 12
Cecil, Joseph, 2
Cecil, Joshua, 1
Cecil, Kathy, 11
Cecil, Kenneth, 11
Cecil, Larry, 23
Cecil, Laura, 25
Cecil, Laurence, 24
Cecil, Laurette, 11
Cecil, Lawrence, 17, 23, 27
Cecil, Leslie, 22
Cecil, Levin, 9, 10
Cecil, Lillian, 16, 17, 59
Cecil, Luther, 15, 22, 25
Cecil, Mamie, 10
Cecil, Margaret, 11
Cecil, Marian, 17
Cecil, Marie, 6
Cecil, Martha, 2
Cecil, Maurice, 26
Cecil, Mary, 1, 6, 7, 8, 9, 10, 15, 25
Cecil, Matthew, 24
Cecil, Medora, 24
Cecil, Melvin, 26
Cecil, Mildred, 20
Cecil, Millard, 25
Cecil, Milton, 6
Cecil, Minnie, 15
Cecil, Minor, 59
Cecil, Morgan, 14
Cecil, Mort, 23
Cecil, Munroe, 14
Cecil, Murrell, 25
Cecil, Myrtle, 25
Cecil, Nellie, 25
Cecil, Nettie, 15
Cecil, Noah, 24
Cecil, Oda, 11
Cecil, Osborn, 6
Cecil, Oscra, 25
Cecil, Otho, 8, 10, 13, 16
Cecil, Peter, 24
Cecil, Philip, 1, 2, 6, 7, 8
Cecil, Priscilla, 8
Cecil, Rebecca, 6
Cecil, Reginald, 25
Cecil, Rhoda, 9
Cecil, Richard, 2, 11
Cecil, Robin, 24
Cecil, Roger, 26
Cecil, Ruby, 11
Cecil, Ruth, 13, 24
Cecil, Sabert, 1
Cecil, Sadie, 11
Cecil, Sallie, 6
Cecil, Samuel, 1, 2, 6, 8, 9, 10, 11, 13, 15
Cecil, Sarah, 2, 6, 8, 13, 24, 34, 42
Cecil, Selma, 25
Cecil, Simon, 24
Cecil, Susan, 12, 24
Cecil, Susannah, 1, 7
Cecil, Susie, 6
Cecil, Talmadge, 11
Cecil, Thomas, 2, 6, 7, 11, 25
Cecil, Verlinda, 1
Cecil, Virginia, 14
Cecil, Walter, 11, 13
Cecil, Wilbur, 6, 10, 11
Cecil, William, 1, 2, 6, 7, 8, 9, 11, 15, 16, 17, 25
Cecil, Wilson, 9, 13, 15, 24, 25

Cecil, Zephaniah, 1, 2, 6
Champ, Eleanor, 39
Chandler, Mary, 124
"Chance", 7, 8
Chase, Daniel, 40
Chase, Jeanette, 40
Chase, Jeanine, 40
Chase, Larry, 40
Chase, Neil, 40
Chew, Anna, 45
Chew, B. Frank, 45
Chew, Christina, 34
Chew, Frank, 34
Chew, Mary, 45
Chew, William, 45
Childs, Joseph, 6
Childs, William, 6
Chiswell, Dorothy, 61
Chiswell, Elizabeth, 71, 80
Chiswell, Hester, 3
Chiswell, Joseph, 71, 80
Chiswell, Margaret, 4
Chiswell, Sarah, 5
Chitry, Margaret, 116, 117
Church, Clara, 72
Cissel, Ada, 2
Cissel, Albert, 5
Cissel, Charles, 5
Cissel, Cora, 6, 7
Cissel, David, 2
Cissel, Edward, 3, 7
Cissel, Elizabeth, 2, 4, 7
Cissel, Ella, 7
Cissel, Elmo, 5
Cissel, Eugene, 3, 4, 5
Cissel, George, 5
Cissel, Hardy, 7
Cissel, Humphrey, 5
Cissel, James, 7
Cissel, John, 7
Cissel, Lawrence, 5
Cissel, Lisa, 5
Cissel, Margaret, 7

Cissel, Martha, 2, 4
Cissel, Mary, 4, 5, 6, 7
Cissel, Philip, 2
Cissel, Richard, 5, 7
Cissel, Ruth, 5
Cissel, Samuel, 5, 7
Cissel, Sarah, 4, 5
Cissel, Theodore, 7
Cissel, Wilburfisk, 5
Cissel, William, 2, 4, 5, 7
Clagett, Mary, 70
Clapp, Susan, 24
Clark, Neale, 88
Clarksburg, 9, 14, 17, 18
Clarke, Martha, 20
Clay, Henry, 122
Cleek, Karla, 62
Cleveland, Mary, 124
Clifford, Gertie, 59
Cockrell, Nettie, 11
Cole, Charles, 59, 101
Collins, Emma, 23
Collins, Franklin, 23,
Collins, Isabel, 22, 23
Collins, James, 23
Collins, Jeanette, 23
Collins, Katherine, 23
Collins, William, 22
Collinson, Sarah, 3
Comus, 9, 13, 16, 18, 21
    23, 27, 34, 58, 59, 66,
    76, 59, 76
Conklin, Frances, 122
Conkling, Hudson, 122
Conkling, Samuel, 122
Conrad, Della, 98
Conrad, Louis, 83
Cook, Benjamin, 50
Cook, Clara, 50
Cook, J., 46
Cooper, James, 122
Corbin, Carol, 40
Corbin, Daryll, 40

Corbin, Patricia, 63
Corbin, Rosa, 40
Corbin, William, 40
Corbin, Woodrow, 40
Cordell, Carrie, 13
Corvin, Julia, 122
Cosgrove, Nelle, 76
Cotton, Grace, 23
Covington, Annie, 3
Coyle, Jenny, 72
Crampton, Joseph, 37
Crane, Sarah, 116
Craven, Sophia, 2
Crawford, Gweneth, 98
Crawford, Mary, 14
Crawford, Sarah, 74
Crawford, Thomas, 14
Creaser, Mary, 61
Creasy, Maude, 109
Crist, Richard, 11
Crompton, R., 101
Cross, Thomas, 59
Crum, Alton, 52
Crum, Arthur, 52
Crum, Evelyn, 52
Crum, Frances, 52
Crum, Harold, 52
Crum, Jesse, 52
Crum, Mary, 52
Crum, Pauline, 52
Crum, Vinona, 52
Cullen, Austin, 62
Cumming, Jane, 79
Curfew, Ruth, 53
Curreri, Andrew, 51
Cutsail, Lucille, 40
Cutsail, James, 44
Cutsail, Roy, 40
Cutsail, Susan, 44
Cutsail, Walter, 44

Dalfuss, Marie, 31
Daly, Alexander, 101

Daly, David, 101
Daly, Donald, 101
Daly, John, 101
Damascus, 88
Dancy, Allen, 23
Dancy, Linda, 23
Darby, R. Clifton, 17
Darner, Anna, 40
Darner, Carl, 40
Darner, Edna, 40
Darner, Helen, 40, 41
Darner, Laura, 41
Darner, Lloyd, 41
Darner, Louis, 40
Darner, Louise, 40
Darner, Margaret, 40
Darner, Sally, 40
Darner, Stephen, 40
Darner, Timothy, 40
David, Jenkin, 81
David, Martha, 91
Davies, David, 91
Davies, Evan, 91
Davies, Isaac, 91
Davies, Jaen, 91
Davies, Jenkin, 91
Davies, John, 91
Davies, Martha, 91
Davies, Richard, 91
Davies, Sarah, 91
Davies, Thamar, 91
Davis, Bessie, 74
Davis, Betty, 76
Davis, Carrie, 71
Davis, Catherine, 91, 92
Davis, Clarence, 77
Davis, Edgar, 75, 76
Davis, Edith, 74
Davis, Eli, 92
Davis, Elbert, 58
Davis, G., 76
Davis, George, 57, 82, 89, 92

Davis, Hannah, 82
Davis, Howard, 119
Davis, Isaac, 10, 91, 92
Davis, James, 58, 76
Davis, Jane, 44
Davis, Jonathan, 92
Davis, Joseph, 39
Davis, Julia, 75, 92
Davis, Katie, 92
Davis, Laura, 75
Davis, Leona, 72
Davis, Lois, 77
Davis, Louise, 76
Davis, Mary, 10, 57, 71, 92
Davis, Nicetas, 58
Davis, Rachel, 82
Davis, Rees, 91
Davis, Richard, 92, 95
Davis, Samuel, 82
Davis, Sarah, 91, 92
Davis, Thomas, 71
Davis, Verna, 74
Davis, Warren, 74
Davis, William, 58, 74, 85, 92
Davis, Zachariah, 89
Davis, Zaccheus, 91
Dawson, Annie, 5
Day, Barbara, 86
Day, Carmye, 83
Day, Dorothy, 86
Day, Eunice, 57
Day, Raymond, 86
Day, Sarah, 57
Deangelis, Amelia, 43
Deason, DeAnn, 43
Decker, Melvin, 53
DeLaughter, Elias, 43
DeLaughter, Helen, 43
DeLaughter, Rebecca, 43
DeMoreland, Donald, 116
DeMoreland, Douglas, 116
DeMoreland, Grace, 116

DeMoreland, Robert, 116
DeMoreland, Sean, 116
DeMoreland, Stephen, 116
Dentzer, Anna, 93
Dentzer, Maria, 93
Dentzer, Othmar, 93
Derr, Ann, 36
Derr, David, 36
Derr, Dorothy, 36
Derr, Frances, 36
Derr, Francis, 36
Derr, Richard, 36
Derr, Ruth, 36
Derr, Sue, 36
Derr, Willis, 36
Dertzbaugh, Mary, 54
Deunger, Ida, 51
Dicke, Pamela, 43
Dickerson, 11
Dickerson, Sarah, 44
Diehl, Laura, 48
Diekman, Elisabeth, 25
Dilahay, Wilfred, 8
Diller, Leonard, 95
Dinterman, Ruth, 53
Dixon, Clinton, 38
Dixon, Dallas, 83
Dixon, Dewitt, 38
Dixon, Dorothy, 39
Dixon, Elizabeth, 39
Dixon, Eugene, 38
Dixon, George, 39
Dixon, Howard, 38
Dixon, Lottie, 83
Dixon, Lynn, 39
Dixon, Margaret, 39
Dixon, Mary, 39
Dixon, Nancy, 38
Dixon, Penny, 38
Dixon, Stephen, 39
Dixon, William, 39
Doan, Larry, 99
Dodson, Hezekiah, 100

Doering, Alvin, 54
Doering, Cynthia, 54
Doll, Charles, 11, 12
Doll, Martha, 11
Donaldson, Joseph, 74
Doolin, Gideon, 85
Doolin, Esther, 85
Doolin, Martha, 85
Doolin, Ruth, 85
Dorman, David, 35
Dorman, Mary, 35
Dorman, Michael, 35
Dorman, Steven, 35
Dorsey, Helen, 39
Dorsey, Henrietta, 58
Dorsey, James, 39
Dorsey, Rachel, 3, 79
Dorsey, William, 14
Doty, Louise, 36
Doty, Robert, 36
Doub, Alice, 40
Doub, Ernest, 40
Dougherty, Melba, 99
Doulong, Fred, 21
Doulang, Jean, 21
Dove, James, 98
Dove, Judith, 98
Dove, Rebecca, 98
Drescher, Jack, 106
Dreyer, Maria, 46
Dronenberg, Gertrude, 74
Dryer, C., 14
Duckett, Sophronia, 61
Duffield, Peggy, 4
Duke, Catherine, 2
Durkee, Martha, 113
Dutrow, John, 72, 80
Dutrow, Rachel, 71, 72
Dutrow, William, 27, 58
Dutterer, Andrew, 64
Dutterer, Dennis, 64
Dutterer, Emily, 64
Duvall, Leone, 36

Duvall, Louise, 61
Duvall, Mareen, 1
Duvall, Polly, 108
Duvall, Thomas, 90
Duvall, William, 92
Dyker, Brian, 10

Eade, Michael, 24
Eagle, Charles, 39, 41
Eagle, Katie, 41
Eagle, Margaret, 39
Eby, Elton, 91
Edwards, Ann, 114
Edwards, Elizabeth, 95
Edwards, Emory, 86
Edwards, James, 114
Edwards, John, 91
Edward, Mary, 114
Eichelberger, Elise, 47
Eller, Sarah, 58
Elliott, Louis, 27
Elliot, William, 109
"Elverton Hall", 105
Embrey, Donald, 20
Embrey, Elaine, 20
Embrey, William, 20
Emanuel, Steve, 20
Engle, Anne, 109
Erb, Fred, 63
Evans, Musgrover, 121

Facer, Georgia, 99
Faubel, Alice, 32
Faubel, David, 32
Feather, Margaret, 38
Feaster, Catherina, 12, 13
Feaster, Henry, 11
Feaster, Lydia, 11
Fellers, Mary, 64
Fenton, M., 101
Ferguson, Robert, 56
Ferry, Olive, 116
Fetch, James, 123

Filler, Elizabeth, 37
Filler, James, 37
Filler, Janet, 37
Filler, Martha, 37
Finney, Elizabeth, 124
Fischbach, Margaret, 23
Fisher, Ann, 7
Fisher, Hugh, 45
Fisher, J. Roger, 45
Fisher, Mary, 34
Fisher, Moses, 34, 45
Fisher, William, 39
Fitzgerald, Henry, 8
Flack, Augustus, 58
Flack, Bruce, 58
Flack, Lawrence, 58
Flack, Valerie, 58
Flair, Glenrose, 76
Flanagan, Somer, 63
Flanangan, Timothy, 63
Fleming, Elizabeth, 24
Flynn, William, 85
Fogle, Edith, 11
Fogle, Ethel, 35
Ford, Charles, 36
Ford, Dorothy, 43
Ford, Helen, 43
Ford, Miriam, 43
Ford, Raymond, 43
Foster, Sarah, 120
Foushee, John, 109
Foust, James, 97
Foust, Mary, 97
Foust, Rosabell, 97
Foust, Thomas, 97
Fowler, William, 89
Flager, Lucy, 4
Francis, Milcah, 69
Frank, Donna-Lee, 22
Free, Catherine, 104
French, Jacob, 97
French, Priscilla, 97
French, Rebecca, 61, 97

Frick, Dean, 40
Frost, Laurence, 23
Frye, Dallas, 63
Frye, Frank, 62
Frye, Michael, 63
Frye, Patricia, 63
Frye, Paula, 63
Frye, Peter, 63
Frye, Rhonda, 63
Frye, Shannon, 63
Frye, Thomas, 63
Fulks, Charles, 15
Funk, Ann, 34
Funk, Christian, 44
Funk, Edgar, 44
Funk Eleanor, 44
Funk, George, 44
Funk, Jessie, 44
Funk, Julia, 44
Funk, Julian, 44
Funk, Wilbur, 44
Funk, William, 34, 43, 44

Gagnon, Lucille, 117
Gaither, Francis, 41
Galbraith, Margaret, 99
Galliher, Sophronia, 72
Gardner, Edward, 84
Gardner, Ella, 84
Gardner, John, 84
Gardner, Minnie, 84
Gardner, Verna, 83
Garnett, Richard, 74
Garrott, Hannah, 71, 76
Garrott, Julia, 71, 73
Garrott, Nicholas, 73, 76
Garthright, Hester, 110
Gartrell, William, 82
Geiger, Valentin, 94
Gershon, Yvette, 115
Getzendanner, John, 33
Getzendanner, Mary, 33
Gibbs, David, 39

Gibson, John, 26
Gibson, R. Frank, 25
Gibson, Selma, 25
Gilbert, Bernard, 41
Gilbertson, Jean, 81
Gilbertson, Linda, 81
Gilbertson, Robert, 81
Gilliam, Anna, 49
Gilson, Sarah, 120
Gingell, Bernard, 76
Gipple, Evelyn, 64
Gittings, Elizabeth, 1
Gittings, Maria, 61
Gittings, Thomas, 1
Gladhill, Flora, 48
Gladhill, Helen, 49
Gladhill, Upton, 48
Glancy, Louise, 22
Glascock, J., 101
Glaze, Basil, 82
Glaze, Sarah, 82
Glaze, William, 82
Goetzinger, Susannah, 95
Goswell, Barbara, 61
Gott, Ann, 3, 4
Gott, Benjamin, 3
Gott, Dorothy, 3
Gott, Eleanor, 4
Gott, Elizabeth, 4
Gott, James, 3
Gott, Lillian, 3, 4
Gott, Louise, 4
Gott, Lucille, 3
Gott, Lulu, 3
Gott, Mabel, 3
Gott, Mary, 3
Gott, Muriel, 4
Gott, Nathan, 3
Gott, Rachel, 3
Gott, Richard, 3
Gott, William, 3
Graham, James, 46
Grant, Edwina, 117

Grant, Roscoe, 117
Gravier, Maryelle, 62
Gray, Caroline, 122
Green, Charles, 77
Green, Harvey, 76
Green, Kathie, 81
Green, Kevin, 77
Green, Rita, 77
Greene, Britnie, 85
Greene, Christopher, 85
Greene, Larry, 84
Greenfield Mills, 9
Greenlee, Sue, 40
Greenstone, S., 109
Greentree, Ezra, 92
Greenwood, Agnes, 23
Griffith, Greenberry, 79
Griffith, Ignatius, 79
Griffith, Julia, 5
Griffith, Lydia, 79
Griffith, Thomas, 5
Grimes, Elinor, 38
Grimes, Ida, 74
Grimes, Mary, 84
Groomes, Caroline, 19
Groomes, Christiannia, 19
Groomes, Ellen, 19
Groomes, Emily, 19
Groomes, Hanson, 19
Groomes, Mary, 19
Grove, John, 47
Grubbs, Charles, 58
Gruber, Mary, 108
Gue, Ethel, 75
Gugle, Nancy, 39

Hadley, Linda, 64
Hagan, Calvert, 54
Hagan, Carl, 54
Hagan, Catherine, 54
Hagan, John, 54
Hagan, Marshall, 54
Hahn, Alice, 51

Hahn, Clara, 51
Hahn, Edgar, 50
Hahn, Irvin, 51
Hahn, Irving, 51
Hahn, Jessie, 51
Hahn, John, 51
Hahn, Joseph, 50, 51
Hahn, Katherine, 51
Hahn, Mildred, 50, 51
Hahn, Philip, 51
Haines, Walter, 86
Hale, Hannah, 121
Hale, Joseph, 121
Hale, Lucy, 121
Hall, John, 105
Hall, Norma, 39
Haller, Anna, 35
Haller, David, 34
Haller, Elizabeth, 35
Haller, George, 35
Haller Grover, 35
Haller, Mary, 35
Haller, Nicholas, 52
Haller, Thomas, 33
Hammond, Ariana, 79
Hammond, Barbara, 79
Hammond, Philip, 79
Hammond, Rachel, 79
Hammond, William, 84
Hampe, William, 49
Handley, Clara, 45
Haney, Forrest, 84
Haney, M. Eloise, 84
Haney, Mickey, 84
Haney, Rickey, 85
Haney, Ritchie, 84
Hanshew, Lucy, 43
Hanson, Ardis, 86
Hanson, Todd, 116
"Hard Struggle", 56
Hardesty, Francis, 69
Hardy, Betty, 38
Harris, Charles, 81

Harris, David, 47
Harris, Eberle, 81
Harris, Eliza, 80, 83
Harris, Ellen, 64
Harris, Ernest, 27
Harris, Karen, 64
Harris, Lee, 64
Harris, Leroy, 64
Harris, Margaret, 81
Harris, Susan, 64
Harrison, George, 106
Harrison, Helen, 117
Harry, Alice, 62
Harry, Daniel, 62
Harry, David, 62
Harry, Drew, 62
Harry, Dylan, 62
Harry, Edward, 61, 62
Harry, G., 62
Harry, Hannah, 62
Harry, Helen, 62
Harry, Hope, 62
Harry, Ida, 62
Harry, Janet, 62
Harry, Jason, 62
Harry, Jennifer, 62
Harry, John, 61, 62
Harry, Lane, 62
Harry, Lawrence, 62
Harry, Lillian, 62
Harry, Mary, 62
Harry, Sabra, 62
Harry, Sally, 62
Hart, Brian, 27
Harvey, Amelia, 106
Harvey, Annie, 61
Harvey, Florence, 106
Harvey, Frederick, 106
Harvey, Harry, 106
Harvey, Lena, 106
Harvey, Nellie, 106
Harvey, Nelson, 106
Harvey, Norval, 106

Harvey, Thomas, 106
Harwood, Ford, 37
Harwood, Mary, 37
Haskins, Dana, 116
Haskins, Dawn, 116
Haskins, Denise, 116
Haskins, Larry, 116
Hauer, Anna, 45
Havanner, Margaret, 19
Hawkins, Louise, 99
Hawkins, Mary, 24
Hawkins, Peter, 9
Hawkins, Sarah, 12, 25
Hayes, Amelia, 104
Heavner, Cleo, 43
Hebbard, Alonzo, 116, 117
Hebbard, Andrew, 113
Hebbard, Annice, 113
Hebbard, Araunah, 113
Hebbard, Betsie, 116
Hebbard, Carl, 115
Hebbard, Carrie, 117
Hebbard, Dorothy, 113
Hebbard, Ebenezer, 113, 114
Hebbard, Edgar, 116
Hebbard, Edna, 117
Hebbard, Elisha, 116, 117
Hebbard, Ella, 117
Hebbard, Franklin, 117
Hebbard, Gertrude, 117
Hebbard, Harriet, 116
Hebbard, Harriett, 114
Hebbard, Harrison, 117
Hebbard, Henry, 114, 116
Hebbard, Hezekiah, 113
Hebbard, Hiram, 116
Hebbard, Horace, 116
Hebbard, Jack, 116
Hebbard, Jane, 116
Hebbard, Jean, 117
Hebbard, Jennie, 117
Hebbard, Jeptha, 113

Hebbard, Joseph, 113
Hebbard, Josephine, 117
Hebbard, LeRoy, 117
Hebbard, Lester, 60, 109, 115
Hebbard, Louise, 60, 117
Hebbard, Lucy, 113
Hebbard, Lydia, 113
Hebbard, Maria, 114
Hebbard, Marguerite, 117
Hebbard, Mary, 113, 114, 116, 117
Hebbard, May, 117
Hebbard, Moses, 113
Hebbard, Myrtle, 116
Hebbard, Nathaniel, 116
Hebbard, Oliva, 117
Hebbard, Olive, 113
Hebbard, Paul, 116
Hebbard, Peggy, 60
Hebbard, Ralph, 109, 115
Hebbard, Richard, 117
Hebbard, Rufus, 113, 124
Hebbard, Russell, 115, 117
Hebbard, Susan, 114
Hebbard, Thomas, 114
Hebbard, William, 113, 114, 115, 116, 117
Heinecke, C., 100
Heller, Edward, 99
Hellwig, Jean, 20
Helvin, Luella, 20
Hemp, Clarence, 41
Henckel, Anna, 94
Henckel, Anthony, 93, 94
Henckel, Benigna, 94
Henckel, Casper, 93
Henckel, Elizabeth, 93
Henckel, George, 93, 94
Henckel, Jacob, 93, 94
Henckel, Johann, 93, 94
Henckel, Johanna, 94
Henckel, Johannes, 93
Henckel, John, 94
Henckel, Maria, 94
Henckel, Matthias, 93
Henckel, Philip, 93
Henckel, Susannah, 94
Hendricks, Landon, 48
Hendry, Sarah, 73
Hermann, Carrie, 50
Herndon, Frances, 110
Herndon, John, 110
Herndon, Malcolm, 110
Herrold, Howard, 53
Hetrick, Jerilyn, 116
Hewitt, Mary, 11
Hibbard, Abigail, 112
Hibbard, Anna, 113
Hibbard, Daniel, 113
Hibbard, David, 112
Hibbard, Ebenezer, 112, 113
Hibbard, Elizabeth, 112, 113
Hibbard, Jedediah, 113
Hibbard, Joanna, 112
Hibbard, John, 112, 113
Hibbard, Josiah, 112
Hibbard, Joseph, 112
Hibbard, Joshua, 112
Hibbard, Lemuel, 113
Hibbard, Lydia, 112
Hibbard, Martha, 112, 113
Hibbard, Mary, 112, 113
Hibbard, Nathaniel, 112, 116
Hibbard, Robert, 112, 123
Hibbard, Samuel, 112
Hibbard, Sarah, 112, 113
Hibbard, Seth, 113
Hibbard, William, 113
Hickman, Mary, 71
Hicks, Linda, 25
Hicks, Ralph, 41
Hicks, Samuel, 41
Hightman, George, 42
Hightman, Helen, 37
Hightman, John, 42
Hightman, Maude, 42
Hilderbridle, Viola, 11
Hill, Anna, 82
Hill, Charles, 105
Hill, Emily, 105
Hill, F., 105
Hilton, William, 10, 17, 58
Himbury, Alice, 46, 51
Himbury, John, 51
Hinkle, Anna, 95
Hinkle, Catherine, 91, 92, 95
Hinkle, George, 91, 94, 95
Hinkle, Henry, 95
Hinkle, John, 95
Hinkle, Jonathan, 95
Hinkle, Mary, 95
Hinkle, Samuel, 95
Hinkle, Susannah, 95
Hinton, Mr., 89
Hipkins, Rufus, 83
Hirsch, Charles, 13
Hirsch, George, 13, 15
Hobbs, Anna, 46
Hobbs, Asbury, 16
Hobbs, Bunk, 46
Hobbs, Clara, 45
Hobbs, Gregory, 45
Hobbs, James, 13, 45
Hobbs, Kay, 46
Hobbs, Mary, 13
Hobbs, Mehrl, 45
Hobbs, Pamela, 45
Hobbs, Paul, 45, 46
Hobbs, Philip, 45
Hobbs, Robert, 46
Hobbs, Samuel, 9, 10
Hobbs, Shayne, 45
Hobbs, Susannah, 88, 89
Hobbs, Wanda, 46

Hodge, Mary, 60
Hodges, Elizabeth, 61
Hodges, Mary, 76
Hodges, Thomas, 76
Hoke, Grace, 53
Holderead, Jerome, 40
Holins, Eleanor, 37
Holland, Emily, 9
Holland, James, 9
Holland, Mary, 27
Holland, Rhoda, 13
Holmes, Mary, 123
Hood, Clarence, 85
Hood, Dennis, 85
Hood, Dixie, 84
Hood, Glenn, 84
Hooper, Anna, 43
Hooper, Donald, 43
Hooper, Julia, 51
Hooper, Marshall, 43
Hooper, Sarah, 43
Hooper, Susan, 43
Hooper, Walter, 43
Hopfengartner, John, 117
Hopkins, G., 13
Howard, Charlotte, 13
Howard, Dowell, 4
Howard, Glynda, 63
Howard, Henry, 4
Howard, Marianna, 4
Howard, Ralph, 53
Howes, Ann, 97
Howes, Elisha, 97
Howes, Emily, 97
Howes, Mary, 97
House, Ann, 83
House, George, 9, 10
House, John, 83
House, Martha, 9
House, Peregrine, 9
House, Rebecca, 9
House, William, 9
Hoyle, Ann, 86
Hoyle, Donald, 86
Hoyle, Ernest, 86
Hoyle, Kenneth, 86
Hoyle, Richard, 86
Huett, Elizabeth, 44
Huett, Harry, 44
Huett, Roger, 44
Hunt, William, 123
Huntington, Archer, 88
Hurd, Etta, 117
Hurley, Eliza, 83
Huseman, F., 15
Hutchins, Mary, 121
Hyatt, Abednego, 88, 89
Hyatt, Alice, 88
Hyatt, Alpheus, 88
Hyatt, Anna, 88
Hyatt, Asa, 89
Hyatt, Avarilla, 88
Hyatt, Caroline, 57
Hyatt, Catherine, 89
Hyatt, Charles, 88
Hyatt, Charlotte, 89, 90
Hyatt, Edna, 78
Hyatt, Eli, 89
Hyatt, Elisha, 89
Hyatt, Elizabeth, 88, 89, 92
Hyatt, Ezra, 89
Hyatt, Hannah, 88
Hyatt, Hilda, 75
Hyatt, Isabella, 89
Hyatt, Jesse, 57, 89
Hyatt, John, 89
Hyatt, Joseph, 89
Hyatt, Laura, 57
Hyatt, Lavinia, 56, 57, 89, 90
Hyatt, Leah, 89
Hyatt, Lloyd, 89
Hyatt, Luther, 57
Hyatt, Mary, 89
Hyatt, Meshach, 88, 89, 90
Hyatt, Meshack, 89
Hyatt, Penelope, 88
Hyatt, Peter, 88
Hyatt, Polly, 89
Hyatt, Samuel, 89
Hyatt, Sarah, 89
Hyatt, Seth, 88
Hyatt, Shadrach, 89
Hyatt, Shadrack, 88
Hyatt, Sophia, 89
Hyatt, Susan, 89, 90
Hyatt, Susana, 89
Hyatt, Susannah, 88
Hyatt, Theophilus
Hyatt, Verill, 88
Hyatt, William, 78, 88, 89, 90
Hyatt, Willson, 89
Hyattstowm, 7, 8, 10, 56, 57, 59, 71, 73, 89, 90

Iglehart, William, 75
Ingalls, Isabella, 22
Ingram, Betty, 51
Ingram, Judy, 51
Ingram, Marion, 50
Ingram, Sois, 46
"Ivey Reach", 56

Jackson, Richard, 104
Jacoby, Ezra, 41
Jaggers, Frank, 23
Jakeway, Eliza, 18
James, Lois, 36
Jarvis, Betty, 60
Jefferson, 9
Jefferson, Esther, 19
Jewell, Edgar, 77
Jewell, Olivia, 77
Jewell, Thomas, 120
Johnson, Annie, 9
Johnson, Benjamin, 9, 10
Johnson, Druscilla, 11
Johnson, Edward, 25

Johnson, Eliza, 9
Johnson, Jacob, 9
Johnson, James, 25
Johnson, Julia, 25
Johnson, Kathryn, 25
Johnson, Kenneth, 63
Johnson, Margaret, 25
Johnson, Martha, 9
Johnson, Marscilla, 9
Johnson, Mary, 25
Johnson, Patricia, 25
Johnson, Roger, 10
Johnson, Walter, 5
Jones, Alice, 79
Jones, Andrew, 4
Jones, Catherine, 2, 105, 106
Jones, Edward, 106
Jones, George, 106
Jones, Grace, 22, 74
Jones, Harriet, 19
Jones, James, 106
Jones, Jemima, 88
Jones, John, 5
Jones, Louise, 4
Jones, Mary, 4, 106
Jones, Maxine, 22
Jones, Pauline, 5
Jones, Rachel, 2
Jones, Richard, 106
Jones, Sarah, 106
Jones, Verla, 86
Jones, Walter, 106
Jordan, Mary, 52
Jordan, Nancy, 108

Kanode, Lydia, 44
Kanode, Robert, 14
Karn, Verna, 41
Kasting, Edward, 49
Keefer, Margaret, 11
Keller, Arnold, 41
Kelley, John, 83

Kemp, Abigail, 120
Kemp, Ralph, 86
Kemp, Samuel, 120
Kempson, Elizabeth, 83
Kennedy, Henry, 58
Kepler, Elizabeth, 41
Kerr, John, 114
Keyes, Linda, 21
Keyes, T., 21
Kidd, Charles, 14
Kindig, Kelley, 39
King, Annie, 45
King, Bertie, 82
King, Carrie, 74
King, Charles, 36
King, Elias, 85
King, Elizabeth, 25
King, Franklin, 75
King, George, 45
King, Gloria, 85
King, Ira, 75
King, John, 73, 74, 84
King, Julia, 74
King, Kenneth, 77
King, Lillian, 85
King, Luther, 75
King, M. Esther, 84
King, Maude, 75
King, Mary, 45, 75
King, Merhle, 84
King, Myrtle, 75
King, Oliver, 85
King, Ora, 85
King, Reginald, 74
King, roberta, 86
King, Walden, 84
Kinna, David, 17
Kinna, Edith, 17
Kinna, Etta, 17
Kinna, John, 17
Kinna, Luella, 17
Kinna, Margaret, 17
Kinna, May, 17

Kinna, Peggy, 89
Kinna, Nathan, 17
Kinna, Rena, 17
Kinna, Samson, 17
Kinna, Sarah, 17
Kinnear, Lori, 109
Kinsella, Briana, 98
Kinsella, David, 98
Kinsella, Holly, 98
Kinsella, Kristoffer, 98
Kinsella, Samantha, 98
Kinsella, Thomas, 98
Kinsey, Allen, 43
Kirk, William, 7
Kirtland, Townsend, 57
Kitchenmaster, JoAnn, 40
Kitchenmaster, LeRoy, 40
Kitchenmaster, Ronald, 40
Kittera, Jospeh, 91
Kleinard, Mary, 32
Kline, Sherman, 78
Kinght, James, 49
Klocksiem, Henry, 115
Knott, Arthur, 15
Knott, Cecilia, 15
Knott, Frances, 15
Knott, Francis, 15
Knott, Harry, 15
Knott, Joseph, 15
Knott, Mary, 15
Knox, George, 101
Koester, Anna, 33
Koester, John, 32
Koester, Lewis, 32
Koester, Martha, 33
Koester, Mary, 33
Koester, Sophia, 32
Koester, William, 33
Kolb, Ada, 45
Kolb, Bettie, 34
Kolb, Daniel, 45
Kolb, Lewis, 45
Kolb, Nettie, 36

Krieger, William, 43
Krow, Lela, 76
Kurtz, Suzanne, 20
Kurtz, Thomas, 20
Kyle, Barbara, 63
"Labrynth", 9, 10, 15, 21
Lafferty, Bret, 27
Lafferty, Joseph, 27
Lafferty, Lane, 27
Lampson, Jonathan, 120
"Land Above", 1
Landrum, C., 25
Landwehr, Mary, 82
Lane, Bessie, 53
Lange, Constantin, 33
Lawrence, Robert, 117
Lawson, Caleb, 78
Lawson, Hester, 58, 77, 86
Lawson, Ivan, 78
Lawson, James, 86
Layton, Frances, 77
Layton, Grace, 77
Layton, Harry, 77
Layton, Lenora, 77
Layton, Lycurgus, 77
Layton, Raymond, 77
Layton, Sarah, 77
Laytonsville, 88
Leach, Becky, 20
Lee, Sandra, 20
Leek, Mary, 79
Leister, Alice, 37
Leister, David, 21
Leister, Glenice, 37
Leister, Nina, 37
Leister, Thurlow, 21
Leister, William, 37
Lemon, Martha, 2
Lenard, Thomas, 81
Lester, William, 61
Lewis, Mary, 76, 82
Lewis, Thomas, 73

Lightner, Ann, 95
Linthicum, Alverda, 77
Linthicum, Amanda, 43
Linthicum, Ann, 69, 70, 71
Linthicum, Anna, 58, 73
Linthicum, Anne, 73
Linthicum, Annie, 74, 76
Linthicum, Aseal, 70
Linthicum, Assaiel, 69
Linthicum, Bernard, 43, 72, 78
Linthicum, Bertha, 76
Linthicum, Bradley, 76
Linthicum, Burton, 69
Linthicum, Burwell, 74
Linthicum, Carrie, 71
Linthicum, Cassidy, 71, 72, 80
Linthicum, Charles, 71, 72, 73, 74, 76, 81
Linthicum, Cora, 72
Linthicum, Daisy, 76
Linthicum, Debora, 78
Linthicum, Deborah, 69, 70
Linthicum, Donald, 73
Linthicum, Dorcas, 69
Linthicum, Earl, 78
Linthicum, Edmund, 69
Linthicum, Edward, 71, 72, 74
Linthicum, Edwin, 72, 78
Linthicum, Eleanor, 71, 72, 78
Linthicum, Eliza, 72
Linthicum, Elizabeth, 69, 71
Linthicum, Elmer, 74
Linthicum, Elsie, 72
Linthicum, Ethan, 43
Linthicum, Erma, 48
Linthicum, Ethel, 78
Linthicum, Fitzhue, 77

Linthicum, Florence, 77
Linthicum, Francis, 71
Linthicum, Frank, 72, 73
Linthicum, Fred, 77
Linthicum, Frederick, 71, 73, 76, 77, 79
Linthicum, Garrott, 74, 76, 77
Linthicum, Genevieve, 72
Linthicum, George, 58, 71, 77, 78
Linthicum, Gideon, 69
Linthicum, Grover, 77
Linthicum, Guy, 75, 77
Linthicum, Hamilton, 72
Linthicum, Hannah, 73
Linthicum, Harvey, 76
Linthicum, Hattie, 76
Linthicum, Henry, 70
Linthicum, Herbert, 74
Linthicum, Hezekiah, 69, 70, 71
Linthicum, James, 73, 74
Linthicum, Jane, 69, 70
Linthicum, John, 69, 71, 72, 73, 74
Linthicum, Joseph, 70, 72, 78
Linthicum, Julia, 73, 75
Linthicum, Katherine, 72
Linthicum, Laura, 73
Linthicum, Lelia, 72
Linthicum, Leona, 72
Linthicum, Leonard, 69, 72
Linthicum, Louise, 73
Linthicum, Lydia, 71
Linthicum, Mabel, 77
Linthicum, Madeline, 72
Linthicum, Margaret, 72, 73
Linthicum, Margo, 72
Linthicum, Martha, 73, 74

Linthicum, Mary, 69, 71, 72, 74, 75, 78
Linthicum, Mattie, 74
Linthicum, Miel, 43, 78
Linthicum, Myrtle, 76
Linthicum, Nellie, 76
Linthicum, Nettie, 76
Linthiucm, Nicholas, 73
Linthicum, Olivia, 77
Linthicum, Ollie, 74
Linthicum, Otho, 71, 77, 78
Linthicum, Paul, 73, 78
Linthicum, Purdum, 78
Linthicum, Philip, 71, 72, 73
Linthicum, Rachel, 72
Linthicum, Richard, 69
Linthicum, Rignall, 70
Linthicum, Rosia, 78
Linthicum, Roy, 72
Linthicum, Ruth, 69
Linthicum, Samuel, 77
Linthicum, Sarah, 70, 71, 77, 79
Linthicum, Shirley, 78
Linthicum, Smith, 77
Linthicum, Stannie, 74
Linthicum, Thomas, 69, 70, 71, 74
Linthicum, Walker, 78
Linthicum, Warren, 74
Linthicum, Wesley, 74
Linthicum, Wilbur, 74
Linthicum, William, 72, 73, 74, 78
Linthicum, Zacharieh, 70, 73
Linton, Mary, 7
Llorens, Alfred, 99
Llorens, Jean, 99
Llorens, John, 99
Llorens, Mary, 99

Llorens, William, 99
Loffel, Joanna, 112
Longley, Elizabeth, 120
Loomis, Lynn, 65
Lothrop, Zerviah, 124
Lovett, Herman, 97
Lovett, James, 97
Lovett, Rose, 97
Lovewell, Hannah, 121
Luhn, Esther, 75
Lumley, Robert, 26
Lupton, Ellis, 72
Lusby, Susannah, 80
Lydanne, Margaret, 24
Lyle, Travis, 72
Lynch, Roland, 51

MacLaury, Melvin, 117
McBee, Alexander, 104
McCaslin, Jamie, 62
McClure, Chlesea, 63
McClure, Jack, 63
McClure, Kenneth, 63
McClure, Ryan, 63
McClure, Vicki, 63
McCormick, George, 11
McDonough, Bettie, 76
McDonough, Beulah, 9
McDonough, Carrie, 17
McDonough, Jacqueline, 14
McDonough, Joyce, 14
McDonough, Kenneth, 76
McDonough, Louis, 14
McDonough, Luther, 76
McDonough, Mary, 76
McDonough, Randy, 14
McElfresh, Abner, 81
McElfresh, Alice, 82
McElfresh, Ann, 86
McElfresh, Anna, 79, 82
McElfresh, Annie, 81, 86
McElfresh, Ariana, 79

McElfresh, B., 82
McElfresh, Bessie, 80
McElfresh, Betsy, 71
McElfresh, Caleb, 79
McElfresh, Carrie, 81
McElfresh, Casper, 79, 82
McElfresh, Charles, 71, 80, 81, 82, 83
McElfresh, Colvin, 86
McElfresh, Cora, 87
McElfresh, Corilla, 79
McElfresh, David, 79
McElfresh, Edmund, 82, 83
McElfresh, Eleanora, 82
McElfresh, Ellen, 80
McElfresh, Elizabeth, 72, 80, 82
McElfresh, Evelyn, 86
McElfresh, Fannie, 86
McElfresh, Frances, 87
McElfresh, Francis, 79
McElfresh, Fuller, 82
McElfresh, George, 81
McElfresh, Gertrude, 81
McElfresh, Hannah, 82
McElfresh, Henry, 79
McElfresh, Ignatius, 82
McElfresh, James, 80, 82
McElfresh, Jeanette, 82
McElfresh, Joann, 81
McElfresh, John, 79, 80, 81, 82, 86, 87
McElfresh, Joseph, 80
McElfresh, Joyce, 87
McElfresh, Katie, 80
McElfresh, Kenneth, 86
McElfresh, Laura, 57, 83
McElfresh, Lenora, 82
McElfresh, Linda, 86
McElfresh, Lindsey, 86
McElfresh, Lucy, 82, 83

McElfresh, Margaret, 71, 81, 82, 83, 86
McElfresh, Marjorie, 86
McElfresh, Mary, 71, 80, 81, 82, 83, 86
McElfresh, Nigel, 83
McElfresh, Philemon, 71, 80
McElfresh, Philip, 79
McElfresh, Rachel, 71, 79, 80, 82, 83
McElfresh, Rhoderick, 79
McElfresh, Robert, 82
McElfresh, Rosetta, 84
McElfresh, Ruth, 79
McElfresh, Samuel, 82
McElfresh, Sarah, 79, 82
McElfresh, Somerset, 82
McElfresh, Susannah, 82
McElfresh, Terrence, 87
McElfresh, Thomas, 79, 83
McElfresh, William, 79, 82, 83
McElfresh, Zeruiah, 84
McGrath, J., 114
McKay, C., 101
McKinsey, Susan, 101
McNitt, Lawrence, 41

Mackelfreishe, John, 79
Mackelfresh, David, 79
Mackelfresh, William, 71
Madrid, Ana, 81
Magaha, Evelyn, 52
Magaha, Jessie, 40
Magruder, James, 71
Magruder, John, 71
Mahn, Eliss, 12
Mahone, Ashby, 109, 110
Mahone, Charles, 108, 109, 110
Mahone, Chiswell, 108
Mahone, Connie, 110

Mahone, Cora, 108, 109
Mahone, Daniel, 108
Mahone, E., 108
Mahone, Edith, 110
Mahone, Elaine, 109, 115
Mahone, Elizabeth, 110
Mahone, Florence, 108, 110
Mahone, Francis, 110
Mahone, Gay, 110
Mahone, Gayle, 110
Mahone, Gertrude, 108, 109
Mahone, J., 109
Mahone, James, 108
Mahone, Jerry, 110
Mahone, John, 108
Mahone, Kathy, 110
Mahone, L., 108
Mahone, Lanney, 110
Mahone, Lenny, 110
Mahone, Lester, 110
Mahone, Major, 108
Mahone, Martha, 108
Mahone, Mickey, 110
Mahone, Nancy, 108
Mahone, Patsy, 108
Mahone, Pearl, 109
Mahone, Robert, 110
Mahone, Sally, 108
Mahone, Sarah, 108
Mahone, Thomas, 108
Mahone, Viola, 110
Mahone, William, 108
Mahone, Willis, 108
Mahoney, Elsie, 48
Mahoney, Isabel, 48
Mahoney, Jan, 48
Mahoney, Jay, 48
Mahoney, Joseph, 48
Mahoney, Karen, 48
Mahoney, Melissa, 48
Mahoney, Monaca, 48

Mahoney, Stephanie, 48
"Maiden's Fancy", 88
Maier, Jeanette, 44
Main, Charles, 40
Main, Emogene, 36
Malone, Anthony, 97
Malone, Elizabeth, 99
Malone, Herbert, 98
Malone, Hettie, 98
Malone, John, 99
Malone, June, 99
Malone, Mary, 98
Malone, Robert, 99
Malone, Rosabelle, 98
Malone, Virginia, 99
Malone, William, 98, 99
Manakee, Edna, 5
Mannakee, Eliza, 26
Mantz, Theresa, 79
Marken, Jean, 41
Marsh, Francis, 117
Martin, Cynthia, 76
Martin, Delores, 76
Martin, Guy, 76
Martin, Ida, 21
Martin, Roland, 76
Martrell, Helen, 10
Martufi, Manuel, 99
Martz, Alma, 43
Martz, Hilda, 43
Mason, John, 124
Mason, Priscilla, 124
Massino, Marguerite, 21
Masters, Kelsey, 22
Masters, Kenneth, 22
Mastin, S., 101
Mattingly, Ashton, 98
Mattingly, Cezar, 97
Mattingly, Elizabeth, 97
Mattingly, Eva, 97
Mattingly, Evelyn, 99
Mattingly, Hettie, 98, 99, 106

Mattingly, John, 97
Mattingly, Joseph, 97
Mattingly, Judith, 97
Mattingly, Margaret, 99
Mattingly, Mary, 97, 98
Mattingly, Robert, 98
Mattingly, Rosa, 97
Mattingly, Sallie, 97
Mattingly, Thomas, 97
"Mavron Hills", 88
Maxwell, George, 22
Maxwell, Jay, 22
Maxwell, Robert, 22
Maxwell, Wilor, 22
May, Dorothy, 123
Mayerle, Raymond, 63
Maylan, Daniel, 74
Maynard, Rachel, 79
Measell, Elizabeth, 47
Meisinger, David, 32
Melvin, Larry, 24
Mentzer, Albert, 35
Mercer, Mary, 35
Merchant, Carrie, 117
Mermel, Marilyn, 63
Merz, Louise, 15
Metcalf, Julia, 47
Metzger, William, 19
Meyer, Catherine, 95
Meyerson, Amy, 62
Miles, Annie, 73
Miles, Catherine, 92
Miles, Edward, 17
Miles, Elizabeth, 17
Miles, Samuel, 17
Miller, Edna, 53
Miller, Jacob, 19
Miller, Marian, 45
Miller, Stephanie, 45
Minnick, Joy, 38
Mix, Charlotte, 52
Moberly, Arthur, 53
Moberly, Charles, 52

Moberly, Florence, 53
Moberly, George, 53
Moberly, Gerald, 53
Moberly, Lorraine, 18
Molesworth, Carol, 54
Molesworth, David, 54
Molesworth, John, 54
Molesworth, Margaret, 14
Moore, Mary, 25
Moore, Russell, 76
Morgan, Joanna, 91
Morrison, Earl, 25
Morsel, Rachel, 92
Morton, William, 41
Mountfort, Michajah, 108
Moxley, Caleb, 57
Mullican, Ernest, 17
Mullican, William, 104
Mullinix, Edward, 86
Mullinix, Vertie, 75
Mumford, Catherine, 46, 50
Murkhardt, Anna, 51
Murkhardt, Charles, 51
Murkhardt, Clara, 51
Murkhardt, Conrad, 51
Murkhardt, Emma, 51
Murkhardt, Ernestine, 51
Murkhardt, James, 51
Murkhardt, Mary, 51
Murphy, Adelia, 117
Murphy, Anice, 23, 27
Murphy, Annie, 26
Murphy, Charles, 23, 26, 27
Murphy, Cornelius, 27
Murphy, Daisy, 26
Murphy, Elizabeth, 27
Murphy, Elsie, 26
Murphy, Eugene, 27
Murphy, Florence, 26
Murphy, Frances, 26

Murphy, George, 26, 27, 28
Murphy, Gertrude, 23
Murphy, Harry, 27
Murphy, Helen, 26
Murphy, Horace, 12
Murphy, James, 27
Murphy, John, 26, 27
Murphy, Julia, 27
Murphy, Leonard, 63
Murphy, Lily, 26
Murphy, Louis, 27
Murphy, Lucinda, 27
Murphy, Margaret, 27
Murphy, Marian, 27
Murphy, Mary, 26
Murphy, Minnie, 27
Murphy, Randolph, 26
Murphy, Robert, 27
Murphy, Sherwood, 26
Murphy, Vernon, 26
Murphy, Violet, 27
Murray, Brian, 64
Myers, Edwin, 49
Myers, Ella, 47
Myers, Lew, 49
Myers, Margaret, 49

Nagengast, Barbara, 109
Nagengast, John, 109
Nagengast, Katie, 109
Nagengast, Mary, 109
Nagengast, Ursula, 109
Nally, John, 106
Nance, James, 24
Neat, Linda, 65
Neilson, Otto, 99
Neilson, Patricia, 99
Nelison, Ralph, 99
Nichols, Carol, 117
Nichols, Sarah, 10
Nicholson, Anna, 14
Nicholson, Margaret, 19

Nicodemus, Allen, 35
Nicodemus, Emma, 35
Nicodemus, Mary, 35
Nicodemus, Ruth, 35
Nicodemus, Vernon, 35
Niemeyer, Elisabeth, 31
Niemeyer, Johann, 31
Nixdorff, Henry, 32
Noll, Adam, 97
"None Left", 9
Norfolk, David, 116
Norris, Ann, 9
Norris, John, 79
Novak, Frank, 25
Norfleet, Eleanor, 38
Norwood, Alice, 78
Norwood, Cecile, 10
Norwood, Charles, 10
Norwood, Edward, 83
Norwood, Jeremiah, 10
Norwood, Katherine, 10
Norwood, Mamie, 10
Norwood, Mary, 10
Norwood, Ralph, 89
Norwood, Roxye, 83
Nusbaum, Margaret, 45
Nutter, James, 66
Nutter, Mary, 66
Nutter, Richard, 66
Nutting, Katherine, 120

Oagle, Ada, 78
Odell, Rachel, 70
O'Donoghue, 101
Ogle, Christian, 11
O'Hugas, Rev., 89
O'Keefe, William, 83
O'Rioridan, Stella, 24
Orndorff, Virginia, 54
Osborn, Elizabeth, 116
Owings, Florence, 82

Paddison, E., 21

Padgett, Dora, 57
Padgett, William, 108
Parker, Abraham, 120
Parker, Hannah, 120
Parker, John, 11
Parker, Joseph, 120
Parrish, Kristy, 63
Parrish, Shannon, 64
Parrish, Stephan, 64
Parsons, A., 100
"Paschaham", 8, 9, 10
Patti, Angela, 116
Payne, Betty, 62
Payne, Earl, 27
Payne, Mary Ann, 27
Pearce, Helen, 84
Penn, Elizabeth, 92
Penn, Samuel, 92
Perks, Doris, 63
Perry, Samuel, 2
Pfarr, William, 72
Phelps, Charlotte, 8
Phelps, Martha, 79
Phillips, Evelyn, 38
Phillips, John, 89
Phillips, Mary, 89
Phillips, Sarah, 57
Phipps, T., 101
Pickens, Jane, 17
Pierce, Sarah, 70
Pippen, Sarah, 21
Pittman, Benjamin, 108
Pitts, Elizabeth, 80
Pitts, Thomas, 80
"Plummer's Delight", 7
Plunkett, Peter, 104
Pope, Robert, 61
Pope, Zach, 61
Pope, Zeb, 61
Popovic, Neven, 47
Poole, Dorothy, 73
Prather, John, 70, 88
Prather, Sarah, 70

Prebish, Pauline, 40
Price, Bessie, 84
Price, Cada, 84
Price, Charles, 57, 84
Price, Daisy, 84
Price, Daniel, 57
Price, Dean, 17
Price, Elijah, 57, 84
Price, Elizabeth, 57
Price, Ernest, 84
Price, George, 57
Price, Hannah, 57
Price, Joseph, 17
Price, Laura, 84
Price, Levi, 25, 57, 83, 84
Price, Minnie, 83
Price, Nina, 17
Price, Perry, 10
Price, Robert, 26
Price, Sadie, 84
Price, Thomas, 57
Price, Virgie, 85
Price, William, 57
Price, Willie, 17
Prince George's Co., 1, 41, 57, 68, 70, 89, 101, 104, 105, 125
Prowse, Sarah, 81
Pumphrey, Kevin, 84
Purdom, Reverdy, 74
Purdum, Flora, 78
Purdum, James, 75
Purdum, Jemima, 85
Purdum, John, 75
Purdum, Joshua, 78
Purdum, Mary, 76, 78, 89
Purdum, Nora, 75
Purdum, Rachel, 78
Pyle, Anna, 81
Pyle, Eleanor, 81
Pyle, Henry, 81
Pyle, Thomas, 81

Quinn, Joseph, 116

Raley, Caron, 20
Ramsburg, Charlotte, 85
Ramsburg, Dennis, 47
Ramsburg, Earl, 47
Ramsburg, Ethel, 47
Ramsburg, Guy, 47
Ramsburg, Harvey, 47
Ramsburg, Jacob, 47
Ramsburg, Laura, 47
Ramsburg, Martha, 47
Ramsburg, Mary, 47
Ramsburg, Merhl, 35
Ramsburg, Richard, 47
Ramsburg, Ruth, 35
Ramsburg, Sarah, 35
Ramsey, Margaret, 70
Raup, Joseph, 20
Rawlings, Elizabeth, 80
Redland, 18
Reed, Eleanor, 39
Reed, Mary, 112
Reedy, David, 108
Reedy, Levi, 108
Reedy, Rebecca, 108
Reedy, Solomon, 108
Reehling, Millard, 44
Reese, Edna, 42
Reese, George, 42
Reese, John, 42
Reichert, Charlotte, 37
Reichert, Susan, 37
Reichert, Warren, 37
Reichert, William, 37
Remick, Mary, 76
Remsburg, Dorothy, 36
Remsburg, Emory, 36
Remsburg, Kathleen, 36
Remsburg, Marianna, 36
Remsburg, Paul, 36
Remsburg, Rachel, 36
Remsburg, Robert, 36
Remsburg, Willis, 36
Renn, Martha, 36
Renneberger, R., 14
Reynolds, Oscar, 116
Rhinecker, Merton, 76
"Rhoades Best", 9
Rhoades, Honora, 9
Rhoades, Mary, 9
Rhodes, George, 9
Rhodes, John, 9
Rhodes, Nicholas, 9
Rice, Annie, 9
Rice, Eleanor, 122
Richards, Alice, 123
Richards, Carl, 27
Richards, Charlotte, 56
Richards, Hazel, 27
Richards, Jacob, 26, 27
Richards, William, 27, 56, 89
Richardson, Elsie, 25
Richardson, Julia, 26
Richardson, Mary, 26
Rickerd, Susan, 52
Ridgley, Henry, 70
Ridgely, Sarah, 70
Rippeon, 86
Riggs, Ann, 57, 89
Riggs, Nancy, 89
Riggs, Ruth, 79
Ritter, Andrew, 37
Ritter, John, 37
Ritter, Leo, 37
Ritter, Martha, 37
Roberson, Ellis, 14
Roberson, Gwenda, 14
Roberson, James, 14
Roberson, Kevin, 14
Roberson, Larry, 14
Robertson, Thomas, 26
Robeson, Diane, 65
Robinette, B. Dean, 23
Robinson, C., 100
Robinson, L., 100
Robinson, Sarah, 8
Rodner, Barry, 51
Roelke, Ann, 34, 42, 44
Roelke, Anna, 31
Roelke, Augustus, 42
Roelke, Bettie, 34, 45
Roelke, Blanche, 44
Roelke, Carol, 39
Roelke, Caroline, 42
Roelke, Christian, 32, 34, 45
Roelke, Christina, 34, 45
Roelke, Christine, 32, 33
Roelke, Clara, 34
Roelke, Clementine, 42
Roelke, Dorothee, 32
Roelke, Dorothy, 40
Roelke, Edna, 41
Roelke, Edward, 33
Roelke, Eleanor, 33
Roelke, Eli, 33
Roelke, Frederick, 33
Roelke, Georg, 31, 32, 33
Roelke, George, 31, 33
Roelke, Harmon, 42
Roelke, Helen, 41
Roelke, Henry, 39
Roelke, Henrich, 31, 32, 42
Roelke, Henrietta, 42
Roelke, James, 39, 42
Roelke, Johann, 31, 32, 34
Roelke, Johannes, 31, 32
Roelke, John, 34, 39, 42, 44
Roelke, Judith, 39
Roelke, Kathryn, 39
Roelke, Laura, 38
Roelke, Lawrence, 42
Roelke, Lloyd, 39, 41
Roelke, Margaret, 33, 41
Roelke, Maria, 31
Roelke, Marie, 31, 32, 34

Roelke, Mary, 34, 40, 44
Roelke, Milburn, 39
Roelke, Monroe, 33
Roelke, Norman, 39
Roelke, Olivia, 40
Roelke, Paul, 39
Roelke, Richard, 33
Roelke, Robert, 42
Roelke, Roy, 39
Roelke, Robert, 33, 39
Roelke, Samuel, 33
Roelke, Sarah, 16, 34, 42
Roelke, Sophie, 42
Roelke, Virginia, 39
Roelke, Wilhelmina, 32, 42
Roelke, William, 33
Roelkey, Albert, 38, 53
Roelkey, Allen, 53
Roelkey, Almeria, 47
Roelkey, Anna, 35
Roelkey, Arthur, 53, 54
Roelkey, Betty, 52
Roelkey, Blaine, 52
Roelkey, Blanche, 38
Roelkey, Caroline, 46, 49
Roelkey, Carolyn, 53
Roelkey, Carrie, 46
Roelkey, Catherine, 53
Roelkey, Celeste, 49
Roelkey, Charles, 38, 46, 48, 52
Roelkey, Christian, 46, 50
Roelkey, Christina, 46, 50
Roelkey, Clara, 52
Roelkey, Clarence, 46
Roelkey, Clementina, 47
Roelkey, David, 36, 37, 38, 54
Roelkey, Dorcas, 46
Roelkey, Dorothee, 46
Roelkey, Dorothy, 53
Roelkey, Edna, 53

Roelkey, Edward, 46, 51
Roelkey, Elinor, 38
Roelkey, Elroy, 48
Roelkey, Emma, 35
Roelkey, Eugene, 52
Roelkey, Fanny, 47
Roelkey, Florence, 53
Roelkey, Franklin, 52
Roelkey, Georg, 50
Roelkey, George, 46, 52, 53
Roelkey, Gertrude, 48, 54
Roelkey, Harry, 53
Roelkey, Heinrich, 35, 51
Roelkey, Helen, 37, 53
Roelkey, Henry, 50
Roelkey, Hjalmar, 54
Roelkey, Ida, 36
Roelkey, James, 50
Roelkey, Jerry, 52
Roelkey, Jesse, 52
Roelkey, Johann, 46, 50
Roelkey, John, 38, 46, 47
Roelkey, Johnny, 37
Roelkey, Joseph, 49
Roelkey, Joyce, 38
Roelkey, Julia, 49
Roelkey, Karen, 38
Roelkey, Laura, 52
Roelkey, Lawrence, 53
Roelkey, Lee, 53
Roelkey, Lew, 48
Roelkey, Lewis, 52
Roelkey, Lillian, 37, 38
Roelkey, Lisa, 38
Roelkey, Lougene, 53
Roelkey, Lucy, 53
Roelkey, Ludwig, 52
Roelkey, Margaret, 48
Roelkey, Marian, 53
Roelkey, Maria, 55
Roelkey, Martha, 37

Roelkey, Mary, 36, 38, 50, 52, 53, 54
Roelkey, Michael, 38
Roelkey, Nancy, 53
Roelkey, Nina, 37
Roelkey, Oliver, 38
Roelkey, Patricia, 38
Roelkey, Paul, 53
Roelkey, Pauline, 52
Roelkey, Philip, 52
Roelkey, Robert, 38, 52
Roelkey, Roberta, 49
Roelkey, Sarah, 36
Roelkey, Sophia, 51
Roelkey, Viola, 53
Roelkey, Warren, 38
Roelkey, Wilhelmina, 46
Roelkey, William, 38
Roelkey, Winifred, 54
Rogers, Charles, 41
Rogers, Hannah, 123
Rogers, Katherine, 63
Rolcke, Johann, 31
Rolicke, Johann, 31
Rolke, Johann, 31
Roschen, Hermine, 51
Rosenmarkle, Margaret, 53
Rotramel, Joyce, 64
Rowland, Barbara, 94
Rowland, Jacob, 94
Russell, Betty Lou, 27
Russell, Brian, 109
Russell, Craig, 109
Russell, Patricia, 27
Russell, Samuel, 27
Russell, Shannon, 109
Russell, Sharon, 27
Russell, Thomas, 27
Rutland, Thomas, 69
Ryan, Charles, 57
Ryan, Clarence, 37
Ryan, Doris, 37
Ryan, Edith, 37

Ryan, Helen, 37
Ryan, James, 57
Ryan, Judith, 37
Ryan, Mary, 57
Ryon, Mary, 105
Saffold, J., 77
Salmon, William, 92
Salser, Thomas, 13
Sanford, Caline, 62
Sanford, Cameron, 62
Sanford, John, 62
Sanford, Peter, 62
Sanford, Valarie, 62
Saunders, G., 10
Savage, Lucy, 85
Savilla, Helen, 21
Schachtebeck, Sophie, 46
Schaefer, John, 25
Schaeffer, D., 32
Scott, Joseph, 121
Scott, Mary, 108
Schramm, Donald, 64
Schramm, Fred, 64
Schramm, Gary, 64
Schroeder, Frances, 41
Schroder, Margaret, 41
Schroeder, Nancy, 41
Schroeder, Roy, 41
Schultz, Violet, 43
Schutzman, Fanny, 52
Schwartz, Donald, 36
Schwed, Mary, 24
Sears, Ann, 10
Sears, Thomas, 10
"Self Defence", 9
Selkirk, N. Jean, 23
Sellman, Martha, 79
Settle, Virgil, 101
Seward, Pete, 99
Shafer, Edgar, 36
Shafer, Edna, 36
Shafer, Evelyn, 36

Shattucks, John, 120
Shattucks, Samuel, 120
Shaw, James, 104, 105
Shawbaker, Anna, 35
Shawbaker, George, 35
Shawbaker, Jacob, 35
Shawbaker, Jessie, 35
Shawbaker, Nettie, 35
Shawbaker, Ruth, 35
Shea, Carlton, 36
Sheaffer, Terri, 62
Sheckles, Anna, 84
Sheckles, Cora, 84
Sheckles, Nancy, 47
Sheckles, Nathan, 84
Sherwood, Abigail, 116
Shifler, Seibert
Shifter, Sheri, 24
Shipley, Carroll, 85
Shipley, Donald, 85
Shipley, E., 79
Shipley, Edward, 84
Shipley, Franklin, 84
Shipley, Fred, 85
Shipley, John, 84
Shipley, Kenneth, 84
Shipley, Maurice, 85
Shipley, Mary, 85
Shipley, Norita, 85
Shipley, Robey, 85
Shipley, Samuel, 84
Shipley, Thelma, 84
Shipley, Violena, 84
Shipley, Walker, 84
Shipley, Zerah, 85
Shoemaker, Jeanette, 20
Showacre, Gidonia, 82
Shriner, Julia, 26
Shriver, Earl, 48
Shry, Carroll, 17
Sier, Sarah, 34
Simmons, Alfred, 49
Simmons, Bessie, 80

Simmons, Ellen, 21
Simmons, Grace, 21
Simmons, Harry, 21
Simmons, Jane, 83
Simmons, Jefferson, 21
Simmons, Jessie, 21
Simmons, John, 21
Simmons, Malynda, 21
Simmons, Nancy, 21
Simmons, Peggy, 21
Simmons, Robert, 21
Simmons, Samuel, 21
Simmons, Vaughan, 21
Simmons, Viola, 20, 21
Simmons, William, 80, 83
Simpson, Jack, 38
Simpson, Kathryn, 38
Simpson, Roy, 38
Simpson, Selva, 38
Sinyard, Ralph, 20
Sisson, Benjamin, 20
Sizemore, Kenneth, 20
Skaden, Jean, 27
Slinkman, H., 44
Smallwood, Jesse, 1
Smith, Ann, 80
Smith, C., 11
Smith, Capt, 9
Smith, Charles, 83
Smith, Freeda, 11
Smith, Harriet, 77
Smith, Harry, 50
Smith, John, 80
Smith, Margaret, 82
Smith, Mary, 15, 92
Smith, Mercer, 62
Smith, Merhl, 12
Smith, Michael, 116
Smith, Philemon, 80
Smith, Preston, 42
Smith, Rosie, 85
Smith, Walter, 84
Snapp, Margaret, 75

Snapp, Robert, 86
Snooks, Ellen, 45
Snowden, Mary, 84
Snowden, Richard, 69
Snyder, Mark, 64
Snyder, Sarah, 74
Soelkey, Alice, 50
Soelkey, Ann, 50
Soelkey, Chrisitian, 49
Soelkey, Clara, 49
Soelkey, Cora, 49
Soelkey, Fredercik, 46, 49
Soelkey, Margaretta, 49
Soelkey, Maria, 49
Soelkey, Oliver, 49
Soelkey, William, 49
Soper, Blanche, 25
Soper, William, 25
Spann, Marilyn, 62
Sparks, Dwight, 109
Spencer, Gertrude, 117
Spignall, Lillian, 82
"Squirrel Trap", 8
St. Clair, Barbara, 99
St. Clair, Deede, 99
St. Clair, Marylyn, 99
St. Clair, Thomas, 99
St. Clair, Wilbur, 99
Stansfield, Annie, 45
Starr, Mary, 45
Staub, Eunice, 86
Steele, James, 82
Steele, Samuel, 123
Sterbinsky, Anna, 43
Stern, Denia, 99
Stevens, Clara, 50
Stevens, Edward, 50
Stevens, Emma, 50
Stevens, George, 81
Stevens, Marion, 50
Steverns, Samuel, 123
Stevens, William, 46, 50
Stewart, Ann, 12

Stewart, Eleanor, 71, 80
Stiles, Paul, 73
Stiles, Todd, 73
Stockman, Annie, 17
Stocks, Jane, 38
Stone, Patricia, 46
Stottlemyer, Sarah, 43
Strine, George, 48
Strother, Margaret, 43
Stuart, Mary, 61
Stubbs, Catherine, 7
Stubbs, Christopher, 24
Stubbs, Rick, 24
Stupp, Charles, 17
Stupp, Earl, 17
Stupp, Grayson, 18
Stupp, Robert, 18
Suite, John, 1
Summers, Ethel, 47
Switzer, Emma, 49
Syergley, Saide, 44

Tabler, Harriet, 15
Tabler, Irene, 77
Tabler, John, 15
Tabler, Mary, 15
Tabler, Rachel, 15
Tabler, Robert, 15
Tabler, William, 77
Talbert, Doris, 26
Talbot, Samuel, 92
Talbott, U., 89
Tarbell, George, 100
Taylor, May, 22
Tcherkezian, Harold, 64
Tcherkezian, Kathleen, 64
Tcherkezian, Luke, 64
Tcherkezian, Mark, 64
Tcherkezian, Matthew, 64
Tcherkezian, Roland, 64
Terry, Lettie, 109, 110
"Tewksberry", 88
Tewksberry, Sarah, 88

Thatcher, Marie, 85
Theobold, Johann, 31
Thomas, Arnold, 54
Thomas, Elizabeth, 61
Thomas, Franklin, 54
Thomas, Mary, 42
Thompson, A., 82
Thompson, Ara, 26
Thompson, Barbara, 14
Thompson, Catherine, 99
Thompson, Charlotte, 12
Thompson, David, 12, 25
Thompson, Florence, 25
Thompson, Fred, 12
Thompson, Horace, 14
Thompson, Jerome, 12
Thompson, Julia, 12, 15, 25
Thompson, Lester, 44
Thompson, Mary, 9, 12, 13, 14
Thompson, Richard, 12, 13
Thompson, William, 12
Thompson, Zacheus, 14
Thomsone, Jonet, 79
Thurston, 59, 77, 80
Tiers, Clarie, 74
Timmer, Anna, 31
Toms, Mary, 36
Tschiffley, Cecil, 5
Tschiffley, Frederick, 5
Thomas, Elizabeth, 1
Todd, Joshua, 89
Toffemaire, Carl, 43
Tomey, Louis, 39
Tomey, Margaret, 39
Toole, James, 7
Townsend, Grafton, 61
Tranter, Robert, 25
Trembly, Joe, 65
Trembly, Taylor, 65
Tritapoe, Anna, 38
Troost, Franklin, 3

Truax, Inez, 39
Tuckberry, William, 88
Turnball, Margaret, 27
Turner, Catherine, 86
Turner, Isaac, 33
Turner, Mary, 33, 80

Urquhart, Bonnie, 63

Vallone, Thomas, 64
VanSise, Virginia, 116
Vaughn, Aaron, 24
Vaughn, Heather, 24
Vaughn, Rodney, 24
Vaught, Danny, 76
Vaught, Edward, 76
Vaught, Linda, 76
Vinson, Laura, 74

Wade, Mary, 19
Wagner, Louisa, 93
Waggoner, Edmund, 83
Waggoner, Fannie, 83
Wagner, Malcolm, 20
Waite, Joel, 121
Walden, Mary, 112
Walker, Albert, 60
Walker, Alice, 61
Walker, Annie, 66
Walker, Aquilla, 66
Walker, Beverly, 60
Walker, Catherine, 61
Walker, Charles, 61
Walker, Christy, 61
Walker, Edward, 61
Walker, Edwin, 60, 64
Walker, Elizabeth, 61
Walker, Francis, 61
Walker, George, 61, 78
Walker, Helen, 66
Walker, Henry, 61
Walker, Isaac, 61
Walker, James, 61

Walker, Jane, 61
Walker, Joan, 61
Walker, John, 61, 64
Walker, Jonathan, 61
Walker, Karen, 60
Walker, Kristenn, 61
Walker, Laura, 64
Walker, Margaret, 33, 66, 78
Walker, Martha, 61
Walker, Mary, 61
Walker, Nathan, 61
Walker, Oscar, 61
Walker, Richard, 60, 61
Walker, Robert, 60, 61
Walker, Roland, 26
Walker, Samuel, 60, 61
Walker, Scott, 61
Walker, Zachary, 61
Wallace, Robert, 91
Wallach, Bessie, 75
Walls, Cheryl, 85
Walter, Charlene, 20
Walter, Charles, 20
Walters, Margaret, 7
Walton, Joseph, 97
Wand, David, 81
Wand, Donald, 81
Wand, James, 81
Wand, Kenneth, 81
Ward, Charles, 15
Ward, Dorothy, 81
Ward, Ezra, 8
Warfield, Basil, 1
Warfield, Chloe, 3
Warfield, John, 3, 89
Warfield, Mary, 89
"Waring's Lot", 105
Warne, Duane, 72
Warner, Helen, 22
Warner, Sarah, 70
Warren, Fred, 82
Warren, Jessie, 51

Warren, Martha, 124
Warren, Mercy, 123
Washington, George, 105
Waters, Ella, 5
Waters, Julia, 5
Waters, Julian, 5
Waters, Lorraine, 5
Waters, Mary, 5, 12
Waters, Miranda, 89
Waters, Richard, 82
Waters, Somerset, 82
Watkins, Alonzo, 78
Watkins, Arthur, 75
Watkins, Bessie, 75
Watkins, Bradley, 77
Watkins, Clinton, 75
Watkins, Frances, 76
Watkins, Frank, 109
Watkins, Garrott, 75
Watkins, Grace, 76
Watkins, Elizabeth, 75
Watkins, Herbert, 75
Watkins, Howard, 77
Watkins, Irma, 43, 78
Watkins, Iris, 85
Watkins, James, 85, 86
Watkins, Jane, 75
Watkins, Jessie, 85
Watkins, John, 75
Watkins, Josiah, 85
Watkins, June, 86
Watkins, Leah, 75
Watkins, Laura, 57
Watkins, Lillian, 75
Watkins, Marjorie, 77
Watkins, Maurice, 24
Watkins, Mary, 75
Watkins, Nelle, 76
Watkins, Noah, 73, 75
Watkins, Nora, 75
Watkins, Oliver, 75
Watkins, Ollie, 75
Watkins, Raymond, 76

Watkins, Ronald, 75
Watkins, Ruth, 86
Watkins, Virginia, 75
Watkins, William, 75, 86
Wayman, Deborah, 69
Wayman, Edward, 69
Wayman, Leonard, 69
Webb, Catherine, 71
Webster, Daniel, 122
Weddle, J., 11
Weiss, Jane, 62
Welch, Abner, 81
Welch, Jemima, 81
Weller, Lona, 11
Welsh, Rachel, 79
Welsh, Warner, 89
Welty, Grace, 52
Westerman, Heinrich, 31
Westerman, Johann, 31
Westerman, Justina, 31
Wetzel, Glennard, 45
Wetzel, Robert, 45
Whaley, William, 32
Wheatley, Mark, 39
Wheatley, Rudolf, 39
Wheatley, William, 19
White, Barbara, 72
White, Charles, 100
White, Craig, 36
White, Deborah, 36
White, Eleanor, 80
White, Lawrence, 36
White, Marquis, 108
White, Maryanne, 72
White, Pamela, 36
White, Oliver, 3
White, William, 72
Whitmer, George, 99
Whitney, Asa, 121
Whittles, Vincent, 81
Wickers, Brent, 110
Wickers, Claude, 109
Wickers, Dale, 110

Wickers, Linda, 109
"Widow's Purchase", 7
"Wildcatt Springs", 7, 8
Wienecke, Maria, 31
Williams, Arthur, 5
Williams, Eleanor, 5
Williams, Humphrey, 2
Williams, Jane, 85
Williams, John, 5, 8
Williams, Julia, 5
Williams, Nancy, 71
Williams, Mary, 25
Williams, Rachel, 2
"Williams Range", 105
Willson, John, 8, 10
Willson, Priscilla, 8
Willson, William, 8, 10
Wilson, John, 48
Wilson, Mary, 73, 74
"Wilson's Discovery", 15
"Wilson's Lot", 9
Windsor, William, 26
Winemullen, John, 8
Winter, Phil, 85
Wire, Paul, 84
Wiswell, Mary, 123
Wolff, Johannes, 95
Wolfe, Alice, 59, 63
Wolfe, Alisa, 65
Wolfe, Ann, 57
Wolfe, Beulah, 58
Wolfe, Catherine, 56, 57
Wolfe, Cecil, 59, 64
Wolfe, Charles, 59, 64, 65
Wolfe, E. Gertrude, 58
Wolfe, Eli, 10, 57, 58
Wolfe, Elizabeth, 56, 57
Wolfe, Ethel, 59, 60, 115
Wolfe, France, 66
Wolfe, Frances, 65
Wolfe, Garrott, 10, 56, 59, 62

Wolfe, George, 56, 57, 58, 59, 65, 89, 90, 92
Wolfe, Grace, 58
Wolfe, Happy, 23, 62
Wolfe, Jack, 60
Wolfe, Jacob, 56, 65
Wolfe, James, 57, 58, 65
Wolfe, Janie, 59, 60
Wolfe, Jesse, 57
Wolfe, Joann, 65
Wolfe, Joel, 56, 58, 73
Wolfe, John, 57, 59
Wolfe, Johann, 56
Wolfe, Johnannes, 56
Wolfe, John, 22, 56, 59, 60, 62
Wolfe, Jolie, 65
Wolfe, Josiah, 56
Wolfe, Joyce, 60
Wolfe, Kelly, 65
Wolfe, Lavinia, 58
Wolfe, Lillian, 59, 61
Wolfe, Linda, 43
Wolfe, Maggie, 57
Wolfe, Margaret, 56, 65
Wolfe, Mercer, 23
Wolfe, Maria, 56
Wolfe, Mary, 57, 58, 59, 65
Wolfe, Myra, 59, 60, 66
Wolfe, Myrtle, 59, 66
Wolfe, Nettie, 62
Wolfe, Norman, 57
Wolfe, Ollie, 58, 77
Wolfe, Pauline, 59, 63
Wolfe, Ralph, 59, 60
Wolfe, Randall, 65
Wolfe, Richard, 85
Wolfe, Sarah, 56, 57, 84
Wolfe, Susannah, 58
Wolfe, Thomas, 65
Wolfe, William, 58, 77
Wolfe, Zacharieh, 58

Wood, Henry, 79
Wood, Marian, 27
Woodfield, Alethia, 84
Woodfield, Shirley, 86
Woodfield, Tarra, 84
Woodfield, Thomas, 84
"Woodland", 105
Woodward, Sabra, 61
Worman, Margaret, 49
Worthington, Thomas, 8
Wright, Jesse, 91, 92
Wright, Norma, 47
Wright, Owen, 76
Wright, Sarah, 71, 77

Yates, J., 109
Yewell, Angeline, 19
Yewell, Mary, 19
Yewell, Octavia, 19
Yinger, Clarence, 53
Young, Ardella, 4
Young, Arthur, 4
Young, David, 4
Young, Druscilla, 4
Young, Elmer, 4
Young, Helen, 5
Young, Henrietta, 4
Young, Henry, 4
Young, Joshua, 54
Young, Margaret, 4
Young, Mary, 4, 47, 54
Young, Mildord, 4
Young, Mildred, 4
Young, Richard, 73
Young, Samuel, 2
Young, Sarah, 2
Young, William, 4
Youngman, Rhoda, 121
Youtz, Charlotte, 72

Zacharias, Daniel, 32, 42
Ziegler, Clara, 34
Ziegler, William, 34

Zimmerman, Benjamin, 54
Zimmerman, Catherine, 44
Zimmerman, Daniel, 54
Zimmerman, Dorothy, 54
Zimmerman, Francis, 54
Zimmerman, George, 54
Zimmerman, Henry, 48
Zimmerman, Lester, 54
Zimmerman, Lovaletta, 54
Zimmerman, Lucretta, 48
Zimmerman, Margaret, 54
Zimmerman, Rhudelia, 54
Zimmerman, Robert, 48
Zimmerman, Tobias, 54
Zimmerman, Walton, 48
Zorn, Donna, 81
Zorn, Kurt, 81
Zorn, Trent, 81
Zorn, Robert, 81

ABOUT THE AUTHOR

Dona L. Cuttler is a Maryland native who descended from several pre-colonial Maryland family lines. She is a graduate of Takoma Academy, and USC. Her great-grandfather and grandmother started the family interest in genealogy, and local history, and Ms. Cuttler has expanded the project throughout several counties in Maryland.

Other Heritage Books by Dona L. Cuttler:

Montgomery Circuit Records, 1788–1988 [Maryland]

One Man's Family

Paperclips: Selected Clippings from
The Montgomery Sentinel *[Maryland], 1900–1950*

The Cemeteries of Hyattstown [Maryland]

The Genealogical Companion to Rural Montgomery Cemeteries.

The History of Barnesville and Sellman, Maryland
Dona L. Cuttler and Ida Lu Brown

The History of Clarksburg, King's Valley, Purdum, Browningsville and Lewisdale [Maryland]

The History of Dickerson, Mouth of Monocacy, Oakland Mills, and Sugarloaf Mountain [Maryland]

The History of Comus [Maryland]

The History of Hyattstown [Maryland]
Dona L. Cuttler and Michael Dwyer

The History of Poolesville [Maryland]
Dona L. Cuttler and Dorothy J. Elgin

www.ingramcontent.com/pod-product-compliance
Lightning Source LLC
Chambersburg PA
CBHW050639160426
43194CB00010B/1740